Praise for

CONFESSIONS

'A model of its kind. Calmly, bravely written, infused by his
Catholic upbringing, and intriguingly haunted by the posh question.
Confessions is filled with qualities that are the marks of a good life:
candour and courage, deployed with generosity and modesty,
all of them here in spades.'
Adam Nicolson

'*Confessions* is a moving reflection on forty years adventures
in journalism and a lifetime of religious faith (and doubt). It is
refreshingly clear-sighted and unsentimental and above all, energized
by an engaging desire to reach the ever-elusive heart of the matter.'
Lucy Lethbridge

'A book brimming with surprises and insight. Edward Stourton
has led "a Life in Full" – and has the brainpower to analyse
it all with wit and perspective.'
Nicholas Coleridge

'Fascinating. Much more than a series of swashbuckling journalistic
yarns, *Confessions* also describes the "awakening", as Stourton puts it,
of someone born to privilege who has come increasingly to question
the assumptions of his caste. He retains a kind of shaken, chastened
faith, and a moral passion which he has, on the right occasions,
allowed to break through the mask of journalistic impartiality.'
Harry Eyres

'A delightful memoir full of wit and insight, from one of the most
talented broadcast journalists of our time.'
Sarah Helm

'I have worked with many journalists during my sixty years in the trade
and Edward is among the very best. He is untainted by the cynicism that
infects so many of us, deeply thoughtful and committed to telling the
truth. This important book reflects all that. And it's great fun too.'
John Humphrys

CONFESSIONS

LIFE RE-EXAMINED

Edward Stourton

doubleday

TRANSWORLD PUBLISHERS
Penguin Random House, One Embassy Gardens,
8 Viaduct Gardens, London SW11 7BW
www.penguin.co.uk

Transworld is part of the Penguin Random House group of companies
whose addresses can be found at global.penguinrandomhouse.com

First published in Great Britain in 2023 by Doubleday
an imprint of Transworld Publishers

A CIP catalogue record for this book
is available from the British Library.

ISBN 9780857528339

Text design by Couper Street Type Co.
Typeset in 11/16.5pt Palatino LT Pro by Jouve (UK), Milton Keynes
Printed and bound in Great Britain by Clays Ltd, Elcograf S.p.A.

The authorized representative in the EEA is Penguin Random House Ireland,
Morrison Chambers, 32 Nassau Street, Dublin D02 YH68.

Penguin Random House is committed to a sustainable future
for our business, our readers and our planet. This book is made
from Forest Stewardship Council® certified paper.

To my parents

CONTENTS

INTRODUCTION

It is a cliché that, once we can see middle age in the rear-view mirror, we tend to fool ourselves into feeling younger than we look to other people. But it is still a shock to be hit with the evidence. It happened to me when a BBC producer curtseyed on being introduced to me, actually bobbed down briefly at the knees when we began working on a programme together.

At around the same time my cousin and old friend James Stourton, a writer and art historian, told me at the launch of another friend's book that he had been invited to write our host's obituary for a national newspaper. He added that he had offered to write mine too, but was told that I had 'already been done'.

After a beat or two I decided to take this as a kind of compliment rather than an intimation of imminent mortality, but it did raise all sorts of questions that have kept tugging at the corner of my mind. What on earth had the unknown author said about me? Did I mind, given that I would never read it? Did I, indeed, mind whether or not anyone would read it, or how they would react if they did? And did this mean, crucially, that I had, in my early sixties, already done everything of interest I was going to do? Could I still manage something sufficiently exciting to provoke the obituaries editor into the expense of a rewrite?

The obituary episode came hard on the heels of an unwelcome reminder of one of those curve-balls age can throw at you: my oncologist warned me that the impact of the chemotherapy I had had a couple of years earlier was waning, and predicted that at some point in the following six months or so I would probably need more treatment. It is now seven years since I was first diagnosed, and I have got quite good at what he calls 'living with cancer' – which mostly means not thinking about it except when I have to. Now I had to think of it again.

Prostate cancer is, usually, slow-moving, and even when it is incurable – as mine is – it can be managed for a long time. Doctors are, of course, reluctant to be too precise in their prognosis, but the admirable consultant who treats me at London's Royal Marsden Hospital is clear about the treatments currently available: they are all time-limited and, on the basis of what he has said, it only takes a little maths to work out where I am. It seems likely that he will be able to stretch my years to the biblical 'three score and ten', but I shall probably not celebrate my eightieth birthday.

The psychological impact of this knowledge is odd. It is, of course, nothing like being told that you have a very short time to live, a horror that many cancer patients face when they are diagnosed. And it is perfectly possible that the science, which seems to move forward all the time, will always stay a jump or two ahead of whatever stage of the disease I have reached, so it really does not do to be too maudlin. For the most part I plough on, enjoying both work and leisure almost as if the cancer was not there.

But the finishing line is now that bit clearer, and it will probably become more predictable as the disease progresses. That creates a tug, not unlike the one James set off, which is ever more insistent – a tug to reflect on the past, to look for some sort of sense and order in the helter-skelter life that has brought me, on the whole very happily, to this autumn day, which I am enjoying on the crest of an intoxicatingly beautiful hill at our home in south-west France.

The clincher was an encounter outside the loo of a café in Sevenoaks.

The death of the broadcaster Peter Sissons came as a real shock to many of those who had worked with him – and had been inspired by him. Seventy-seven seemed too young for someone with such a great appetite for life, and most of us had no idea he had been ill. I was touched to get an email from his agents with details of his funeral, and at London Bridge station I bumped into another old hand from my days at Independent Television News: Michael Green had worked with Peter as an industrial correspondent in the days when Britain's trade unions dominated the news agenda.

Our train delivered us early for the funeral, and he, his wife and I took refuge from the rain in a cramped little coffee shop down the road from the church of St Nicholas. Gerald Seymour, who had escaped ITN before I arrived there by writing the bestseller *Harry's Game*, pitched up too, and the reminiscing began in earnest.

The loo was on the first floor, and waiting outside was a face that seemed familiar. It looked thinner than I remembered, but the odd combination of innocence and guile struck some long-buried chord. It was not until the owner of the face came downstairs and brushed past us on his way to the door that I placed him as the home news editor during my days as a reporter on *Channel 4 News* in the 1980s.

'Garron,' I greeted him. 'Garron Baines.' Michael had been blessed with matinee-idol looks during his television career and, as he too recognized Garron, his face broke into one of his famously winning smiles; 'Garbled,' he shouted, 'Garbled Brains,' the memorable nickname for this inspired but sometimes bonkers figure of our past springing instantly from his lips. It was like being whooshed backwards in a time-machine: the years simply peeled away and I was, for a moment, in my twenties again. Suddenly it seemed worth expending a little effort remembering – not just worth it, in fact, but an imperative. We shall meet Garbled again later.

St Nicholas's Church, standing solidly in its churchyard on this grey-sky funerary afternoon, is one of those pieces of Old England that have survived the encroachment of suburban modernity without losing a sense of the sacred; it seemed fitting to read in the porch that the poet John Donne had held the living and preached there for fifteen years in the early seventeenth century.

Outside the rain dripped steadily from the yew trees, and inside there were eulogies from the news presenter Angela Rippon, Stewart Purvis, Peter's editor (and mine) in his *Channel 4 News* days, and, very movingly, Peter's daughter Kate. Stewart took over *Channel 4 News* when its ratings were in freefall, and it looked as if it might stumble into oblivion after less than a year on the air; he reminded us of Peter's wry comment that with so few viewers 'it would be cheaper to ring them up and tell them the news individually'.

There were stirring hymns to revive our spirits, although I noticed that some of the senior television executives present could not quite bring themselves to bellow out the words of 'He Who Would Valiant Be', looked a bit queasy during 'Jerusalem' and, confirming their secular stereotyping, fluffed the 'Our Father'.

Moving to the crypt afterwards for tea and sandwiches was like entering Plato's Cave, where prisoners are forced to watch shadows of real objects projected onto a wall by a fire behind them. I followed Peter's career pattern (though always at least two steps behind, and never achieving his dominant position in television news) from the news on ITV to *Channel 4 News* and then the BBC, so my fellow mourners represented every phase of my professional life; they all looked a bit fuzzier at the edges, flickering, imperfect versions of the younger selves I had known.

In the poem 'An Arundel Tomb', Philip Larkin describes an ancient earl and countess lying side by side in stone effigy; he notices they are holding hands, and suggests they prove 'Our

4

almost-instinct almost true:/What will survive of us is love.' Quite a lot of people in the crypt after Peter Sissons's funeral had, to my certain knowledge, hated one another in times long past – the media world is cut-throat. Looking around I also identified a few who had – at least, I strongly suspect this – once enjoyed adulterous affairs, but I do not think that is quite what Larkin had in mind.

The emotions that afternoon were gentler. As the tea urns steamed, the burble of conversation rose pleasantly in volume. Old friendships were rekindled, old jokes retold, old wars – real ones and those fought out in the office or neighbouring wine bars – remembered. On the train home, reflecting on that light-bulb moment in the Sevenoaks coffee shop, I concluded that what ought to survive of us all is simply the fun we had. Journalism is a surprisingly jolly trade, given the daily miseries that are our usual fare. And even though many of the obvious sources of pleasure that once enlivened it – like generous expense accounts and comfortable travel – are long since gone, the young producers I now work with are every bit as cheerful, resilient and idealistic as we ever were.

But as soon as I began thinking about my life I realized there were some ghosts to lay to rest in my pre-professional youth – even though going so very far back feels more like archaeology than personal history. Part of my ambition is to explore the world that made me, privileged and male-dominated as it undoubtedly was. Because my generation is slipping into history.

Quite a number of my friends and contemporaries have done well and, in some cases, become prominent in public life. Many of them are now exes – ex-ministers and MPs, ex-editors, ex-judges, ambassadors and generals, and even those of us who are still in harness have, as one put it, 'slimmed down the portfolio'. As we edge away from the centre of things, we find ourselves caught up in battles we never imagined – about everything from words and statues to our country's place in the world.

That is not to say we do not welcome change: I am startled by the number of old friends who have become steadily more radical as they have got older. But when I bump into sixty-something friends on my dog walks, the conversation often turns to our bewilderment with the world and the world's bewilderment about us. It seems worth reflecting a little on who we are, and why, before we wave goodbye.

A Catholic education forms young minds in a manner it is difficult to escape from, and the old Catholic claim 'Give me a child until he is seven and I will show you the man', attributed to the Jesuit founder St Ignatius Loyola, reflects a reality. I was taught by Benedictines, not Jesuits, but even those school contemporaries who have emphatically rejected their former faith are distinctively Catholic in their atheism.

The natural Catholic model of autobiography is the spiritual journey, books like St Augustine's *Confessions* and St John Henry Newman's *Apologia pro Vita Sua*. These titles seem humble, but the books themselves are monuments to spiritual pride. Newman was not making 'an apology' for his own life (*pro Vita Sua*) in the sense of saying sorry, the word *apologia* in this context means something much closer to 'manifesto'. I also find both these saints very difficult to like: Augustine's treatment of women was shameful (he threw over a mistress to get engaged, took a new one while he waited for his eleven-year-old fiancée to reach puberty, and finally rejected all three when he found God), and Newman was famously described – by a fellow cardinal, no less – as a 'great hater'.

But I cannot quite shake off their model: the idea that life is a journey with a moral destination is part of who I am. So I have decided to focus on what I have learnt from some of the professional passions and personal pleasures – like reporting, broadcasting, history, books and travel – that have made the ride worthwhile. And ticking away beneath the surface – mostly hidden in deference to this secular age – is a search for values.

It is more than likely that I have left out events and people who should really be here, and I apologize to anyone I offend by omission. When the broadcaster Sir John Tusa published his memoirs, I bought a copy thinking I might be mentioned, because we were, for a period, joint presenters of a BBC news programme. When I – somewhat furtively – searched the index I drew a blank: my name did not feature at all. But my wife's did – in relation to an incident of which she had absolutely no recollection.

LEARNING

1 · THE OLDEN DAYS

The news editor of the *Newcastle Journal* saved his curviest curve-ball until the very last moment of the interview. 'I hope you won't mind me saying this' – his tone was all mock apology – 'but your background seems a little cosmopolitan.'

He had me bang to rights: my childhood had included homes in Lagos, Freetown, Accra, Malta, Lausanne and Geneva. In fact, with the sound nosy instincts of a good news hound, he was even more right than he realized. Every member of my immediate family could claim a different birthplace – Mauritius for my father, Hong Kong for my mother, Nigeria for me, Malta for my sister, London for one brother and Switzerland for another – but I do not think I would have mentioned that on my application form. I certainly had not talked about the sophisticated treats – like breakfast in bed in a Venetian palazzo, or peach juice and champagne on the sunny terrace of a Black Forest schloss – that had come my youthful way, thanks to my parents' globe-trotting lives and their great talent for forming friendships.

What threw me was the way the man from the *Journal* sneered 'cosmopolitan' as if it was an insult almost too vile to sully his mouth. I thought of it as a compliment, suggesting sophistication and openness to adventure. The British edition of the American magazine *Cosmopolitan* had been launched a few years earlier, and in the 1970s *Cosmo*, as we all called it, seemed the very acme of glamour. My interviewer clearly thought of the term as the worst kind of abuse.

It was a good job – part of a trainee scheme that should have led eventually to what was still known as Fleet Street – so I buckled to and talked passionately about my affection for the north-east of

11

England (which was real). It must have convinced, as I was offered a place on the scheme (annual salary £2,900, flat share with another trainee to be arranged by the paper and an extra £10 per week on offer for good productivity). A week before I was due to head north to begin work, I was offered a better job in telly (and in London) and bailed out, which no doubt confirmed the news editor's views about cosmopolitans.

The episode should have alerted me to a fundamental mismatch between some aspects of my upbringing and the trade I chose. One of the narratives of my life, I now see, has been a process of working out which of the values I learnt when I was young to keep, and which to judge and reject. You might – in today's terms – call it a process of 'awokening'.

I did not think of this process in any very conscious way until, during my time on the *Today* programme, the *Daily Mail* started referring to me as 'posh Ed'. 'Posh' – like 'cosmopolitan' – was, when I first heard the word, a compliment, not an insult: you might, when I was a child, praise someone's posh new tie or pen. And I think I would have been puzzled to be called posh when I was young: my father had to work for our living, and he did so mostly by running companies owned by the tobacco giant BAT in foreign parts – which was not particularly posh in the sense the word was used then or in the way it is used today.

It is, however, true that I instinctively understood the bogus but colourful etymology that holds the P-word derives from the acronym for Port Out Starboard Home, said to indicate a passenger who was, in the days of empire, rich enough to enjoy a cabin on the shady side of the ship on the passages to and from India. Because I was – and I should make this confession up front and immediately – a colonial child.

My parents met in colonial Nigeria, and what was then known

as the Federation of Nigeria was still under British control when I was born in the Northumbria Nursing Home, Lagos, in 1957. And I can, just, remember life in Malta before it gained independence in 1964; the memories include lots of swimming parties on government launches and swarms of glamorous naval officers in crisp white uniforms, but not many Maltese.

I 'confess' this background not because I feel I must personally apologize for it – how could I, since I did not choose it? But it does fall into the category of what theologians call 'structures of sin' or, to use the preferred term of thinkers on the left, 'structural evil': being part of, and therefore influenced by, a damaging system. Both my grandfathers devoted their careers to Britain's empire, one as a lawyer and judge, the other as a police officer. They were dutiful, able men, hardened by war (my mother's father had been a PoW in the notorious Omori camp in Tokyo, and my father's father lost my grandmother to a German torpedo in 1942), and both were knighted for their services to the Crown and its colonies. I was, of course, brought up to love and admire them.

Because my own parents lived abroad for so much of my childhood, I often spent half-terms and weekends out from boarding school at my paternal grandfather's home. He was not greatly given to reminiscence, but I remember him discussing, with a lunch guest, the period when Ian Smith's white minority regime in what was then Rhodesia – now Zimbabwe – defied Whitehall's efforts to set a timetable for handing over power to the country's Black majority. My grandfather, who was a senior colonial police officer during the crisis, explained that he had told the force in Rhodesia they would not be given any medals unless they promoted more Black officers. To my young mind this clearly put him on the side of the liberal angels; the sheer weirdness of two groups of white people wrestling over the future of a Black country – and using honours from a white monarch in London in their armoury – did not strike me.

My parents, of course, were a generation on from all that, but a colonial flavour lingered in the rhythms of our lives. Instead of holidays, we went 'on leave'; in the summer months, when many people left Britain for the sun (which they often found in the very places where we lived), our family packed up and headed back to the country we were told was really 'home'. Each year we made a pilgrimage through a network of relations scattered around the shires, and our progress always included a spell in Norfolk, thanks to a curious connection formed during my mother's youth.

After the war her father was seconded to Haile Selassie's court in Ethiopia, with a brief to persuade the emperor of the virtues of the British justice system. He and my grandmother judged Addis Ababa too harsh an environment for their young daughter, so my mother was, courtesy of an advertisement in the *Lady* magazine, despatched to share a governess with the daughters of a family she had never met.

During her years of what today we would probably call fostering, she formed a lasting attachment to the household, and our stays at the grand but echoingly dilapidated pile where she had grown up felt more like going home than any other visit on those soggy summer tours. That was partly because it was so big, more like a small village than a house and, like many traditional country homes then, somewhere that could accommodate and welcome all sorts of folk of different estates in life. There was an actual butler in residence, and he would take us on rambling walks around the park, pausing to fish for leaves in the cattle grids on the drive.

For the most part England felt like a foreign country. The past, however, did not.

Looking back with more clarity now, I realize that what marked out my childhood was not being posh or cosmopolitan: it was the belief that the past had, on the whole, been better than the future was likely to be, and that its values should be honoured. One of my father's favourite anecdotes was about an evening when, going to kiss my sister goodnight, he found her in tears in her bed. When he enquired why, she replied, 'Because I'll never know what it was like to live in the olden days.' The instinctive nostalgia this reflected, though never explicitly articulated, permeated every area of life: our understanding of family and relationships at home, religion – which loomed large – and education.

It is not quite as odd an idea as it now seems. Most early Europeans would have thought that way, certainly until the eighteenth-century Enlightenment, and a properly conservative respect for tradition and the value of institutions that have endured remains a powerful political and social force. But it was an odd training for a trade in which, as one of my first editors put it, 'today-ness has impact', and which is driven by fashion. The news is, by definition, new – at least, it should be.

Tradition dictated my schooling. My father had been sent to board at the Catholic prep school Avisford, so I would go too. The names of all new boys were painted in fine lettering on the oak panels of the dining room, so I could see N. J. I. Stourton listed in the roll call for 1939 even as an elderly craftsman in an apron added E. J. I. Stourton in 1966. Around ninety of us, aged between eight and thirteen, inhabited a rambling country house surrounded by Sussex countryside.

Our shared world was a very odd one, and looks ever odder as the years increase its distance. Britain in the 1960s was galloping forward to modernity, shaking off the chill of post-war austerity, while we prep-school boys were being deliberately propelled in the opposite direction, back to a pre-war version of Britishness, which was fading fast outside the school gates.

The transition was brutal. I arrived halfway through a school year, so my companions in the junior dormitory had already become friends. They chatted away merrily after 'lights out' and I did my best to join in. Suddenly the door burst open to reveal the tall and terrifying figure of our dormitory monitor. 'Who was talking?' he demanded.

Having been brought up in a home where telling the truth was good policy, I cheerfully responded, 'I was, and so was everyone else,' thus simultaneously admitting to breaking an iron school rule – no talking after lights out – and the even more sacred code of *omertà*, which made 'sneaking' on your fellow inmates the greatest crime of all.

Being institutionalized made us natural conservatives: we very quickly accepted the rules, both the discipline imposed by the school and the more informal honour codes dreamt up by the boys – and seldom questioned them. 'Blubbing' was frowned upon, so after a few days of misery I gave up crying. As my parents were living abroad at the time, there seemed little prospect of rescue. After about a week, prep-school life came to seem entirely natural and hugely enjoyable.

At least, that is how I now remember it. My letters home, scribbled and sometimes barely legible bulletins, which were, touchingly, filed by my father (preserving personal archives is another aspect of minding about the past), suggest that settling-in was possible partly thanks to a nimble ability to adjust my identity. The early letters are signed 'Love Edward', but the use of first names was discouraged during term time. Quite soon I began to sign my letters home 'Love from E. Stourton', or simply 'E. Stourton'. One ends like this:

> Today there is a first eleven match against Bishop Sutton and Balcombe Place. I hope you are well. Love Stourton.

The terrifying dormitory monitor was known as Jennings 1 – he is now rather better known as Luke Jennings, the author of *Codename Villanelle*, the collection of novellas that gave the BBC its *Killing Eve* series. He was also the headmaster's eldest son, which made him even more terrifying.*

The headmaster, Michael Jennings – or MJ, as he was universally known – took his Catholicism very seriously, and Jennings 1 was the first of eleven children, most of whom went through the school, so at any given time it was likely that a significant proportion of the pupils were members of the headmasterly family. This might have turned them into regimented clones, but it produced quite the opposite effect: Jenningses have continued to drop in and out of my life ever since, and they are the most individualistic breed you can imagine. Their professions have included stone-cutting, ballet dancing, soldiering in the French Foreign Legion, writing history and interpreting at the UN.

Jennings 4, my contemporary, remains a close friend and tells me that being part of this vast Catholic family meant they had to strive to stand out among their siblings. Martin became a distinguished public sculptor, and created the wonderfully wiry and alert bronze George Orwell who stands outside the BBC's New Broadcasting House. It is thanks to him that all BBC bosses must walk past Orwell's great dictum on free speech when they arrive at work each morning: the words 'If liberty means anything at all, it means the right to tell people what they do not want to hear' are chiselled into the wall of the building.

MJ himself was a war hero who had won an MC in the Netherlands in 1944, and he had been horribly burnt trying to rescue his

---

* When I met him in later life he turned out to be anything but that, and proved very good company.

men from a stricken tank. The great wartime plastic surgeon Sir Archibald McIndoe had done his best to rebuild his face, but the narrow nose and permanently discoloured skin were, at first sight – especially to a young boy away from home for the first time – alarming. His hands had been badly damaged too, the fingers permanently retracted against his palms like claws, and he had a habit, especially when in a rage, of beating the palm of his left hand with the back of his right.

This gesture – much imitated by us boys – would often be accompanied by a tirade against some 'little pill' (as in 'pillock'), his favourite term for a tiresome boy. And it would, in extreme circumstances, be followed by 'the swish', a series of swipes delivered to a bent, usually pyjama-clad bottom with a gym shoe or slipper.

If this description makes him sound like a Dickensian monster it is misleading. MJ was indeed eccentric and irascible, but we quite quickly got used to his appearance – just as we accepted so many other unusual facets of prep-school life – and instinctively understood that he minded very much about our welfare, 'little pills' though we may have been. He had a zero-tolerance policy on bullying, and MJ was most emphatically not – it seems necessary now to make this explicit about any prep-school headmaster, especially a Catholic one – a paedophile.

He was, however, ever on the alert for signs that the insidious sixties counterculture might be seeping into the school, and would inspect and censor the books we brought home from the holidays. One of the most intense controversies that exercised him surrounded what he called 'Chelsea boots': some parents began to send their boys back to school with slip-on shoes instead of the brogues we were supposed to wear to mass on Sundays, and MJ seemed to regard this solecism as a step towards decadence akin to the Sack of Rome. At the same time he was extremely indulgent about the more old-fashioned pastimes that little boys enjoy when they are allowed to run wild in their natural habitat.

The land around the house had, like most English country-house parks, been planted out with a magnificent collection of trees, many of which had grown to great heights in their maturity. We were allowed to climb almost all of them without any form of super-vision. One, a deodar, stood a mighty eighty-foot tall just across the lawn from the main building, and its thick canopy of branches made for easy climbing. At the top there was a natural chair, and when you reached the summit you could swing wildly back and forth while gripping the branches that formed the arms around it – bellowing out, if you so wished, 'The British Grenadiers' or one of the other hearty songs we were taught in singing lessons.

My letters home also reported a certain amount of violence. Many of them mention having had 'a super fight', these duels vari-ously taking place in the Bamboo Jungle, the Ha-Ha or what was known as the Icehouse, the ruined remains of an eighteenth-century form of fridge in the grounds.

I wrote a piece in the *Swallow*, the school magazine, describing a pillow fight in the dormitory known as the 'Palace' – it had once been a ballroom – which culminated in multiple injuries when the chandelier was brought crashing down from the ceiling; I had one boy rolling out of bed to escape the impact but 'even as he did so a fragment of glass caught him between the shoulder blades, and he flopped to the floor with a shriek'. This was, of course, imaginary, but there is enough relish in the reportage to suggest the riotous pillow fight had at least some basis in reality.

In the anti-utilitarian manner characteristic of most private schools at the time, bright boys at Avisford were made to give up geography at the age of ten to give them time to learn Ancient Greek as well as Latin. The classics master, Mr Cornwall, was a

Mr Chips-like character, eternally sporting baggy grey flannels, and varying his jacket according to the seasons – heavy tweed in winter, fawn linen, much darned, in the summer.

How much of his eccentricity was affected I cannot now be sure. He made a great show of taking pleasure in conversations with the cows that were grazed in the fields on the way to the cricket pitches, and had a stock of truly dreadful donnish jokes. 'Have you heard the one about the bishop who posed the theological conundrum "What does the Devil do if he loses his tail?",' he would chuckle, 'and shocked his Oxford audience by suggesting Satan would go to the pub. Why? "Because pubs are where noxious spirits are *retailed*."'

His rigour in Latin and Greek was utterly unforgiving. He taught us (another hallmark of an English private education then) to be snobbish about minutiae that would have meant nothing at all to the vast bulk of humanity – and belonged, indeed, to fields of knowledge that had, for most of the world, long since slipped over the rim of history.

In 'Golden Latin', for example, the sort written by Cicero and Co., 'it is impossible' was rendered as *'fieri non potest'*, literally 'this cannot be'. To use the more obvious translation of *'impossibile est'* is the sort of thing a medieval Latinist might have done, and would be – according to the Cornwallian ethic – the grammatical and stylistic equivalent of a mortal sin. This I learnt sometime around 1968, when students not so very much older than me were tearing cobblestones off the streets of Paris, going to Woodstock and protesting against the Vietnam War.

The fastidious academic standards expected by Mr Cornwall and his colleagues co-existed with some very boisterous reading habits. The favourite forms of entertainment – there being no television or radio – were comics, like *Beano* and the *Dandy*, and what were known as 'trash mags', adventure picture books that told

heroic Second World War stories. The latter were traded like a bar-
ter currency, sometimes swapped for prize conkers.

Many of them were part of a series called War Picture Library,
which cleverly set fictional military adventures against the backdrop of real Second World War episodes, and they relied heavily on
national stereotyping: trash mags were full of square-jawed Ger-
mans shouting 'Die, Britisher Pig Dogs' as they hurled grenades at
the British lines, this usually followed, a page or two later, with
curses of *'Donner und Blitzen'* as the brave Brits fought back.

One senior Conservative of my generation admitted to me over
lunch that his view of the Brexit debate was coloured by his early
trash-mag addiction. It seems inconceivable that young boys would
be allowed to read this kind of material today, but we, after all, had
a headmaster who had nearly lost his life fighting the Nazis, and
the mags themselves were often written and illustrated by people
who had served in action during the Second World War.

And the war, which was only a little over two decades in the
past, loomed very large in our imaginations. The list of films
screened in the gym by way of Sunday-afternoon entertainment
consisted largely of classics like *Reach for the Sky* (the story of the
ace fighter pilot Douglas Bader) and *The Great Escape.* There were
lectures with titles like 'Operation Chariot: the raid on St Nazaire',
and one boy, James 2, enjoyed a certain status because his father
had escaped from a German prisoner-of-war camp disguised as a
Bulgarian naval officer called Lieutenant Ivan Bagerov – which, he
told us to our wicked delight, was pronounced 'bugger-off'.

There was a brief eruption of glamour into school life with the
arrival of an assistant master called Robert Nairac. He swept up the
gravel drive in front of MJ's office in an open-topped 1930s Austin
7, painted British Racing Green, and on the front seat next to him
was a cage containing a kestrel. This he attached to a long leash

21

pinioned to the front lawn, and on those long Sussex summer evenings he would allow us to join him when his raptor took him hunting.

He was dark-haired, strikingly good-looking and stylishly dressed in well-cut tweeds, and was soon observed stealing a kiss from Miss Burt, the senior matron with creamy English-rose looks, over the toaster at the staff breakfast table. Mr Nairac was in his gap year before Oxford, so he can only have been eighteen or nineteen, but he seemed to us to belong to a different order of being.

He was a keen boxer (at Oxford he would revive the sport), and he trained us in the gym that had been kitted out in the old stable block at the back of the school. One afternoon he instructed me to hit him as hard as I could on his chin, jutting it towards me to goad me on. I was an obedient boy, large and strong for my age, so I knocked him out cold. There was a beat or two while the boxing class wondered what to do – school regulations covered most eventualities, but not decking one of the masters on his own instruction – before Nairac bounced off the canvas and congratulated me.

Robert Nairac became famous by association as the owner of the star of the Ken Loach film *Kes* – the bird, that is, not the young actor David Bradley – which he kept in his Oxford rooms. He later acquired an altogether grimmer celebrity when, while serving as an intelligence officer in Northern Ireland in 1977, he was abducted from a pub, brutally interrogated by the IRA in a field and killed. His body was never recovered.

Nairac was perhaps the most extreme example of Cavalier romanticism we encountered, but there was a powerful cult of eccentricity in this strange world, and it was often tangled up with the ideal of military service. MJ's father, CJ, or Old Major Jennings, who had been my father's headmaster in the 1930s, had survived the Western Front during the First World War and run the local Home

Guard in the Second. Of a great age by the time I arrived at the school but remarkably fit – he took pride in touching his toes – he made a late-life hobby of behaving badly. We were awestruck with admiration when word went round that at the age of ninety-five he had, on some whim, answered an ad for a doctor's receptionist's job in Harley Street, faked some references and turned up for interview.

The cult of martyrdom was strong too. Most of the dormitories were named after men who had died horrible deaths for their faith in Tudor Britain – I slept in More (after Sir Thomas, who was beheaded), Campion (Father Edmund, who was racked in the Tower of London, then hanged, drawn and quartered at Tyburn), and Fisher (for Bishop John, beheaded in his late sixties). Only much later, when I saw posters of suicide bombers hailed as martyrs in the Palestinian cause in the streets of Gaza and the West Bank, did I realize how dangerous a death-addiction could be.

2 · ENVELOPED IN MIST

If Avisford took its pupils back to a pre-war Britain, Ampleforth – to which I was next despatched, again in obedience to tradition, again following in my father's footsteps – was an altogether more epic reverse time-journey. The basic rhythms of community life went right back to the sixth century, when St Benedict wrote his monastic rule amid the dying embers of the Roman Empire. The 1957 prospectus – parents were expected to put down their boys for a place at birth, and I assume that is why there is a copy of this in my father's files – made great play of the institution's roots in history.

'The school,' it stated, 'may fairly claim a heritage as old as any in the country, for it traces its origins to St Edward the Confessor.' This somewhat tenuous connection was based on the fact that after Henry VIII's dissolution of the monasteries, the last surviving monk of Westminster, one Sigbert Buckley, passed on the 'corporate succession of the Royal Abbey' to a new Benedictine community, which was founded in France in 1608. 'Expelled from France at the time of the Revolution,' the document continued grandiloquently, 'the community after some years of wandering settled at Ampleforth in 1802. Thus the present school inherits through Westminster and Dieulouard an ancient English tradition, and the ideal of Christian education in the liberal arts, which had been fostered and preserved by the monasteries, still inspires its work.'

This claim that the school was not some Johnny-come-lately Victorian foundation was partly rooted in snobbery – a two-fingered salute to Eton – but it was also a shot in what today we would call History Wars: the Catholic establishment of the late

24

twentieth century fought hard to have its version of British history remembered, just as Black Britons do today. And the way the school was sold was clearly bringing in the punters: the prospectus ends with the instruction that a registration fee of three guineas would be payable when a boy's name was moved from the 'Provisional Waiting List' to the 'Waiting List'.

I quite quickly discovered that my own family had a dog in this fight.

The list of former heads of school displayed in the Big Passage, an echoing thoroughfare at the heart of the main complex of Victorian buildings, included one 'Hon. Edward Plantagenet Joseph Corbally Stourton', and there was a Stourton shield among the armorial bearings that adorned the library.

One of the most surreal moments in my broadcasting career came when the Labour grandee John Prescott whipped round and, in the middle of a *Today* interview about social class with my colleague Evan Davis, attacked me, live on air, with the words 'He's descended from nineteen barons' – a fact he can only have picked up from my Wiki page. Lots of us are descended from barons, and it would have taken a nuclear-holocaust-scale elimination of my relations for me to become one.

The fact that the Wiki contributor had thought this worth a mention reflected one of the oddities of English Catholic culture: families that remained true to the old faith at the Reformation – 'recusants', as they were known, because they refused to accept the penal religious laws imposed by the Tudors – huddled together for mutual support. Men and women with the same surnames kept marrying each other for centuries, so even those who, like us, were only distantly related to the real grandees – 'collateral branches' of the family tree, as genealogists like to say – were kept within a tribal 'cousinage'.

This nurtured the strange idea that holiness and heraldic quarterings go hand in hand. It was very obviously untrue but, like the martyrdom cult, it had real imaginative power. In the year I arrived at Ampleforth, Pope Paul VI canonized a Tudor-era group known as the 'Forty Martyrs', which meant that I could count a saint or two among my ancestors.

The cousinage was well represented among the boys, and when one member, a little older than me, was busted for being drunk, I reported in my diary that he had been found 'wandering around the galleries [the sixth form floors] firing an imaginary submachine gun and reciting the Stourton family tree'. The miscreant (not, I should add for friendship's sake, the sober and scholarly James Stourton) was on duty as a server at High Mass the following day, in charge of the incense. Halfway through the service he was discovered slumped over the altar in a side chapel, his thurible gently puffing out clouds of perfumed smoke beside him, which compounded his disgrace.

Ampleforth's setting is surpassingly beautiful. The barrack-like buildings of the school and monastery – dominated by the bulk of the abbey church – lie along the edge of a gentle valley, which is dotted with games pitches and pavilions and surrounded by woods and lakes. An area known as the Monks' Wood, where members of the monastery are buried, rises just above it, divided from the main buildings by a narrow lane; the bridge that spans it was built with exaggeratedly high sides in the days when Catholic clergy could not be seen on public highways in their religious dress. And immediately above the Monks' Wood, the North Yorkshire moors begin.

So, the weather conditions are sometimes extreme. In one of my letters home I reported, 'There is really nothing to say in this letter, I am afraid. The Valley is, as usual, enveloped in mist and nothing of any interest has happened – nor is it likely to for some time.' And escape was difficult; another letter towards the end of term included a request for '35p for my bus fare to York Station'.

The isolation of our valley made it possible for the monks to control us, without undue effort, in a kind of religious and educational Petri dish, uncontaminated by the modern world to a surprising degree. The backwash of 1960s rebellion was still churning in the early 1970s, and we were teenagers, but few of us tried to smash the religious foundations on which our lives were built.

The most serious outbreak of doctrinal revolt I can recall occurred in a religious-instruction class when we challenged our teacher, Dom Henry Wansborough,* about the Resurrection of the Body. In the glorious pomp of our youth we were unsettled by the idea we could be forever saddled with the sort of paunchy, balding body we might have at our deaths. What, we demanded, if we lost a leg along the way? Would we spend eternity hopping around Heaven? Father Henry (who became a very grand theologian and edited the New Jerusalem Bible) assured us that a disability becomes part of a person's nature, and was not something to be ashamed of.

The monks lived their Benedictine life alongside us, and we absorbed their world view rather than feeling it forced upon us. In the evenings we were allowed to skip the half-hour set aside for catching up on homework if we wanted to attend Vespers in the abbey church, and High Mass on Sundays always included a choir of young boys with beautiful voices. Religion, dressed up like this, seemed strangely seductive. The monks, to their credit, encouraged us to be questioning, but there was almost no open atheism.

---

* The Dom title is used for all Benedictine monks, an acronym for *Domine Optime Maxime*, 'To our Lord the Best and Greatest', and not, as we joked, for Dirty Old Man.

The gentle character of our indoctrination owed a good deal to the leadership style of the abbot, the future cardinal Dom Basil Hume. Abbots, though elected, have traditionally enjoyed near dictatorial powers over their communities, but Father Basil seemed a wise rather than autocratic figure. He had no formal position in school life – although he gave away school prizes, and we had to kneel and kiss his ring when we received them – but he was a quiet, constant presence.

A keen squash player and Newcastle United fan, he always turned out for the big school rugby matches. On summer afternoons he would potter down to the playing fields with his walking stick and offer tips on high-jump technique, ticking me off for practising the then new-fangled 'Fosbury Flop', rather than the 'Western Roll', which had been popular during his own high-jumping days in the 1930s.

For the most part we admired the monks as clever men who had made big sacrifices to lead the life they had chosen. Their vow of celibacy, we were taught, was perhaps the greatest sacrifice of all. The occasional public lapse – my youngest brother's housemaster abandoned the monastery for his matron – was seen as reassuring evidence that the monks had healthy, natural sexual appetites. The prior left to marry the mother of boys who had given him no end of grief when he had been their housemaster, and it made the papers. Some wag noted that Father Prior had always been keen on Dante, and could thus be marked down as a dangerous romantic.

Only much later, when the Independent Inquiry into Child Sexual Abuse investigated Ampleforth, did we discover that some of the monks had had appetites that were anything but healthy. We will come to that.

Just behind the high altar in the abbey church there was a small shrine, protected by iron bars and covered with an embroidered silk cloth, containing a piece of charred flesh that was said to have belonged to St Lawrence, our patron saint. Lawrence was barbecued alive in Rome in the middle of the third century, and has one of the best last-words lines of all time: *'Assum est. Versa et manduca,'* he is reported to have said. 'I am well done on this side. Turn me over and tuck in.' He is the patron saint of cooks and comedians, and the grisly manner of his despatch on a gridiron was reflected in the school magazine, which was called the *Grid*.

The 1974 editions, when I was part of the editorial team, included an attack on the Vatican's birth-control teaching – 'Viewing the Pope's refusal to allow Catholics to use any form of artificial birth control from a purely practical angle, it seems short-sighted and dangerous' – a thoughtful piece by a teacher in one of the new comprehensive schools and an essay in praise of Darwin. The fare was an accurate reflection of Ampleforth's intellectual climate: loyally Catholic but with freedom to dissent.

The liberal spirit was enlivened by bracingly conservative sallies from some of the boys. The letters pages included the view that 'It must surely be obvious to the clear-sighted that the principal cause for the post-war moral decline in the West is due primarily to a lack of objectivity, a refusal to see matters in their proper perspective, with a clear sense of priorities based on a well-defined moral order.' Strong stuff from a 1970s teenager. Similarly thundering self-confidence coloured a piece I wrote on pornography, a subject about which I was almost entirely ignorant.

It is striking above all for the complete absence of any references to women. 'The second area in which the anti-porn squad's case falls down is their gross over-estimation of the moral damage caused by sexually explicit books, films or posters,' my fifteen-year-old self opined. 'They apparently feel that a man may go into a pornographic film with a soul as pure as driven snow, and

29

burst through the cinema doors at its end a depraved and twisted monster, ready to swoop on the innocent and unsuspecting man in the street.' The valley was a very male environment.

The monks used Latin a good deal in their liturgy, and since we were, at a minimum, required to attend mass in the abbey church on Sundays, it was not quite such a dead language to us as it would have been to most of our contemporaries living a more normal educational life, but even so the resources the school devoted to the teaching of classics seem, in retrospect, extravagant. The classical staff was huge, brilliant and, in keeping with the customs of the day, eccentric. It included 'Two-fingers' Lenten, who got me through Greek O level – I never discovered how he had lost the other three fingers on one of his hands – gentle Bernard Vazquez, who taught himself Chinese in his spare time, and offered a Mandarin O level as a sideline, and Father Barnabas, who looked like a Roman senator and referred to Marcus Tullius Cicero as 'Tully', as if he were a mate.

Presiding over them all was the magnificently other-worldly figure of Walter Shewring, for whom the idea that the past was better than the future was much more than a background assumption: it was, in fact, the driving passion of his life.

Most masters moved between classrooms as the timetable dictated, but Mr Shewring, the head of classics, had his very own Classics Room, a book-lined sanctuary at the top of a turret. Shewring had been a friend of the sculptor Eric Gill – whose letters he edited – and many of his ideas were rooted in the thinking of the Guild of St Joseph and St Dominic, the Roman Catholic community Gill established at Ditchling in Sussex. This was, of course, long before the revelations about Eric Gill's sexual abuse (of his daughters and even, apparently, his dog) did catastrophic damage to his standing.

Followers of the Ditchling school looked back to the Middle Ages as their source of example and inspiration, and Shewring was profoundly sceptical about the eighteenth-century Enlightenment and everything that flowed from it. He refused to use telephones, watches or, strangely, umbrellas – on the basis that they were products of the corrupt modern world – and regarded most classical music as decadent and effete. He once remarked, when the tinkling of a piano up the turret staircase became especially insistent, 'I do wish that boy would stop practising a piece which is so very, very vulgar, even by Mozart's standards.' Mr Shewring had his own modest vice: an inordinate fondness for Green Chartreuse, a bottle of which could always be found nestling behind the Odes of Horace on the Classics Room shelves, available for an emergency tipple.

Like most classics teachers, he had a taste for obscure donnish humour. The film-maker Jamie Muir, another Shewring alumnus, revealed to me during a dog-walk in Brockwell Park many years later that he had preserved a list of the great man's one-liners, including 'Returning to my original thought – though thought is perhaps rather strong in relation to Pliny . . .' Decades of intellectual striving and the exercise of a high critical faculty lay behind that sally, but it was made in an age when almost no one cared what he meant.

Mr Shewring took the fastidious style Fascism I had learnt at prep school to new heights. As a young scholar he had published – in 1930 – a monograph on 'Prose rhythms and the comparative method', and he taught us to write Latin prose with the rhythms Cicero developed to lend gravitas to his orations. This involved a set mix of long and short vowels at the end of each sentence, or 'period', as we called them – not easy to nail on top of the usual Latin carry-on of making sure nouns and adjectives agree with one another and worrying about gerunds, subjunctives and the

31

pluperfect. By the time we reached our A levels we had, I suspect, outstripped most of the examiners in our ability to write like a Roman statesman from the first century BC.

That fluency has long since gone, but the prose rhythms taught me to listen to language as well as reading it, and I blessed Mr Shewring's memory when, many decades later, I began writing for radio.

Sport, rugby especially, was taken almost as seriously as religion and classics, and its undisputed high priest was the rugby coach, John Willcox, who had played full-back for England in the early 1960s. He too became a focus for myth-making. Such was his passion for the game that it was rumoured – unjustly, I am sure – that he tied his infant daughter's right leg to her crib so that she would grow up able to kick with both feet. He had a taste for anachronistic slang: when explaining a defensive strategy, he would offer the view that it made the other side's chances of scoring 'all Lombard Street to a China Orange', which meant very unlikely – or at least had meant that early in the nineteenth century.

'Johnny Will' introduced us to the more sophisticated side of the game, encouraging me – as scrum leader – to be imaginative about my coded instructions to our pack. I would shout commands like 'Recitative' and 'Lohengrin', or 'Rimbaud' and 'Lamartine' as I shoved my head between the meaty thighs of the front row. The idea was to confuse the opposition into wondering whether our codes were based on opera or nineteenth-century French poets; by the time the boys from Sedbergh or Stonyhurst realized that any word beginning with an R simply meant 'wheel the scrum right' and any word beginning with an L meant the opposite, they were usually several tries down.

My year group included an unusually talented collection of schoolboy rugby players, and forty years after our triumphantly successful first-fifteen season, we gathered in dinner jackets in a London club to celebrate the memory. My neighbour, now Father Jock Hamilton-Dalrymple, a parish priest in Edinburgh, was still just about recognizable as the speedy winger who topped the list of try scorers, but most of us were not wearing our years so well.

At the end of dinner our former coach, still sprightly in his eighties, rose to his feet and told us he had had difficulty recognizing some of us. 'Frankly,' he declared, 'you're fat.' The old gents gathered around the table – as well as the Edinburgh priest they included a shrink from LA, a gynaecologist from the West Country and the usual sprinkling of portly lawyers and City men – looked aghast. Was Willcox about to demand fifty press-ups on the spot? The Legend Lived.

Most of my contemporaries enjoy our shared memories of the mix of eccentricity and brilliance that marked so many of our teachers, but I now see how close the cult of eccentricity came to an entitled sense that the normal rules did not apply to us.

In my final year my friend Nicholas Mostyn and I battled our way through to the national finals of the Observer Mace, a public-speaking competition run by the English Speaking Union and the *Observer* newspaper. We were accompanied to London by one of the monks, Dom Alberic Stacpoole, who ran the Debating Society. Arriving at York station he got muddled between trains, leapt the ticket-barrier and yelled to us to follow him in an attempt to board a moving train. We were hauled up by an irate railway official, who pointed out that it was heading for Bristol.

Corrected, we reached King's Cross on time, won the competition, and returned to school bearing the enormous silver mace – modelled on the one in the House of Commons – which was our prize. (Nick became a successful barrister and is now a High Court judge, so we both went on to make a living by talking in public.) But the following week the police turned up to discuss the unfortunate episode at York station.

We were placed under caution, and to explain why such matters were treated seriously the sergeant cited a recent fatality involving an elderly lady who had fallen onto the track. 'That would never have happened to us,' Father Alberic explained suavely. 'Mr Mostyn is captain of swimming, Mr Stourton is captain of athletics and I'm a former paratrooper.'

He was similarly disdainful of the rules of the road. In our last term Nick and I managed to arrange – I cannot now think how – a double date in a Yorkshire country house and, as a reward for our debating success, Alberic agreed to drive us there in one of the monastic Land Rovers. He had won a Military Cross in the Korean War and was a dashing soldier before joining the monastery (my parents had known him in Nigeria). Halfway across the moors he threw his hands into the air and began to steer with his knees, shouting, 'This is how we used to do it in the army.' We ordered a taxi to get us back to school after dinner.

My housemaster, Dom Benedict Webb – also known as Pod, for his girth – took an equally relaxed view of the laws of the land. After three boys were arrested while trying to buy dope in York, he gave us a lecture I summarized in my diary. The censorious tone suggests that – with a teenager's conviction that I had right on my side – I thoroughly disapproved of his pragmatic approach: 'Webb drew the "moral" lessons and spouted about them to the house: don't go to a pub stuffed with plain-clothes men, don't make a statement, it stops your solicitor lying your way out, and watch out for opium in your reefers.'

Pod, who had been a naval surgeon before joining the monastery, was, however, an enthusiastic policer of the school's own rules and regulations, hiding in the matron's drying room in the evenings in the hope of frustrating illicit socializing (or worse) after lights out. One evening he spotted that one of the house's regular troublemakers was missing at an event. 'Halfway through the concert (the Baroque Yorkshire Ensemble, with a very powerful soprano),' I reported to my diary, 'Webb leapt across to me and said, "Meet you on the square in five mins. I'll get a car and we'll go and bust him in the pub."'

The missing boy turned up while he was collecting the car, but that did not dampen Pod's ardour. 'We roared away to the Malt Shovel for a quick raid. I felt rather sheepish rushing in looking important and finding only a few locals at the bar.' Monitorial status had its consolations, however: I took the opportunity to enjoy a 'swift half' myself.

Pod's naval days had left him with a robust view of sex. He held that everything was best talked about openly, and would offer us very frank advice – including the suggestion that if tempted to masturbate we should wrap a rosary around our hand. To demonstrate that 'we are all the same' he would, from time to time, join us naked in the showers, which today might be thought, to put the proposition at its mildest, unwise. And even then we understood that this was rum behaviour – no other housemaster behaved like this. There was a shared understanding that if everyone bolted for the door on Pod's arrival it was likely to provoke a housemasterly lecture on the theme of 'healthy minds in healthy bodies', but we all slipped off as soon as it was decently possible.

Even more sinister than the burnt-flesh shrine in the abbey church was the copy of a Renaissance triptych of the Virgin and Child that hung in the school Monitors' Room. The names of all the boys who had been beaten by past head monitors were recorded on the back, along with dates (back to the early 1920s) and the number of strokes.

Beating had been abolished by the time I became head of school, and I found my powers were in fact very limited. The Tom

Brown-like paraphernalia of office – according to the mythology I had the right to grow a moustache and get married – co-existed with a very liberal post-1960s disciplinary regime.

Smoking was allowed in the sixth form (after 4 p.m.), as were visits to the pub at weekends and on Holidays of Obligation (religious festivals like the Assumption and All Saints Day, when the entire school shut down). With very few serious punishments available to me, I took up a pipe in the hope of terrifying miscreants by summoning them to my study and staring at them silently, as if contemplating some ferocious fate, while I puffed away.

I think this may have been an unconscious nod to the influence of the headmaster, Dom Patrick Barry, who, though of modest stature, had a theatrical ability to impose his will. He had developed a knack of lowering his voice so that everyone in his audience strained to hear him, and when he addressed the school a great stillness spread over several hundred boisterous boys.

He also had an unnerving manner of walking, propelling himself along in complete silence – so the risk of being surprised by him in the corridors was ever present – and without any apparent evidence that his legs were moving beneath his monk's habit. Someone compared this surreal motion to a flow of black molasses, and his nickname of 'the Black Mole' stuck for ever.

Father Patrick's *Times* obituary noted that 'Although a modernizer he was a monk, accustomed to a Spartan lifestyle . . . heating was frugal; in cold weather boys found the towels at the end of their bed semi-frozen', but the chilliness of the school was as nothing to the chill of his anger. I can still hear him delivering a searing lecture on self-pity, which he compared to 'a sponge, which soaks everything up and gives nothing back'.

The obituary includes a little gem of memory, which will ring true to anyone who knew him: 'Painfully shy, Barry was inscrutable: one boy expecting a punishment was asked to fetch *The Times*, read aloud the crossword clues and enter Barry's answers. Within the allotted timespan – fifteen minutes – Barry had completed it.' The paper adds, 'His scholarship was renowned, as was his stone-cutting. He was a master calligrapher and promoted the art among the brethren.'

School mythology made Father Patrick the hero of an almost certainly apocryphal story about a public-schools meeting: when the headmaster of Eton declared, 'We prepare our boys for life,' his Benedictine counterpart is said to have replied, 'At Ampleforth we prepare our boys for death.'

There was a widespread belief in the Catholic world of the inter-war years that England could be 'reconverted' to Catholicism 'from the top down'. Under Dom Paul Nevill, who became head-master in 1924, Ampleforth (along with other Catholic public schools, like Downside and Stonyhurst) had expanded rapidly to meet the demands of this great project: the monks recognized that training the leaders of the future meant extending the reach of a Catholic education beyond the narrow circle of the cousinage.

Father Patrick, inspired by Father Paul's example, made academic excellence the heart of his mission as headmaster. He recruited an unusually clever group of lay masters (no mistresses, of course) to teach alongside the monks, and Oxbridge entrance became a priority. The policy created a fiercely intellectual culture.

In my school diaries the passion for ideas and learning comes through again and again, despite all the drinking, the occasional brutality and the sports worship. Quite often I broke into ancient Greek and even classical Mandarin.* These diary passages are now well beyond my comprehension, which is probably just as well.

---

* Mr Vazquez insisted we slip the study of Mencius – a Chinese philosopher of the Warring States period – into our O-level work.

Awkward adolescent emotions usually tipped me into French: *'J'ai reçu une lettre d'Hélène'*, I confided to the diary pages one morning, *'pour m'encourager, j'espère'* – sadly I have no recollection of Helen, and the hope that she wanted to encourage me must have been vain, as she disappears from the diary quite soon afterwards. One dull Sunday morning I declared that *'Je me sentais accablé d'une lassitude profonde.'* Feeling myself 'overwhelmed by a deep languor' – I suspect it was a quote from some decadent nineteenth-century poet we had been studying – seems an excessively dignified way of describing what was no doubt run-of-the mill teenage boredom and sloth.

I do not think I was alone in this unembarrassed celebration of the life of the mind and, however pretentious it was, it still seems attractive. Of course, it sometimes slid into arrogance. I remember my home life as very happy during these years, and the diary supports that memory, but I did privately take my father to task for his intellectual diet: when he became a regular reader of the *Daily Telegraph*, I condemned this as 'the ultimate form of bourgeois degradation'.

Father Patrick's shyness could be difficult to negotiate. One of my duties was a weekly meeting, which, so the management theory ran, would allow me to pass on any concerns about school life that had been raised among the boys. Quite often I came empty-handed: the school seemed generally to run smoothly, and his surprisingly liberal regime had removed any obvious sources of revolutionary discontent. Since the nature of our relationship did not encourage small-talk – which, anyway, he was not naturally given to – we sat in agonizing silence for ten or fifteen minutes before he dismissed me.

In the autumn of 1975 Father Patrick became chairman of the Headmasters' Conference, the public schools' lobbying body, the first monk to occupy what was then regarded as a prestigious position. The way *The Times* reported his appointment reflected the highly charged ideological atmosphere of the day. It published a piece by its education correspondent under the headline 'The monk standing up to battle for public schools'. It quoted the new chairman's opening address to the organization, in which he accused Harold Wilson's Labour government of 'taking every opportunity they can to knock us'.

The idea of abolishing private education had much more currency in the Labour Party then than it does today. The Conservative education spokesman, Norman St John Stevas, who was himself a Catholic, liked to compare Labour's policies to Henry VIII's dissolution of the monasteries, and Father Patrick stated explicitly that he regarded the survival of a school like ours as a matter of religious freedom.

So, being a public-school boy in the mid-1970s felt pretty good: we were not just privileged, we were warriors for freedom. The great ideological divide of those days – between, as many of us crudely saw it, Communism and the forces of the left on one side, freedom and democracy on the other – made us all the more righteous.

Being an English Catholic felt pretty good then too, especially when, in my last year at Ampleforth, our abbot, Basil Hume, became the Archbishop of Westminster (and soon thereafter a cardinal). Hume had a French mother, but he was, with his courtesy, his understatement and his love of football and fly fishing, a quintessentially English figure.

On the night of his consecration in Westminster Cathedral, the monks of Ampleforth sang Vespers in Westminster Abbey, the first Benedictine service there since the Reformation. Hume very quickly established himself as a voice of moral authority in the life of the nation, and the kind of Catholics I had been at school with began to feel they were part of the Establishment again. We were on a roll.

During my last summer at the school, a master called Ian Davie drove my sculptor friend Martin Jennings and me to dine at a pub high on the moors. It was one of those rare but radiantly beautiful Yorkshire moments when late, slanting sunlight turns the bleak landscape gold, and over a long dinner and too much wine, he lamented the loss of the more mystical Catholicism he had known in his youth (he converted not long after the war).

Mr Davie, a well-reviewed poet as well as our teacher, was universally known as Dirt Davie: with his camp gait, heavy paunch and rich laugh, he fitted a certain stereotype of the predatory schoolmaster, though I never heard anyone complain that he had actually predated upon them. Towards the end of dinner he regretted the passing of the days when, as he put it, 'the whole Valley [where Ampleforth lay] was throbbing with male love'.

My very vivid memory of this suggests that it was an unusually frank admission of the sexual currents that flowed through the school and monastery. But I don't recall being especially shocked by it. The contours of our attitudes to sex are only really apparent viewed from the distance of many decades. I think we understood that it was inevitable – though not necessarily desirable – that there would be same-sex attraction among boys locked up in a remote location while their hormones boiled away, but at the same time we judged homosexuality to be profoundly unnatural. It now seems the oddest and most shocking of all the attitudes we absorbed. The revolution in attitudes to sexuality has been the social change of my lifetime.

Years later the Independent Inquiry into Child Sex Abuse would record a chilling history of abuse at Ampleforth. If you had told those of us who left in 1975 that we had been part of an institution marked by systemic abuse we would have found the idea quite mad. Perhaps we should have been more open to the warning signs: it was commonly known, and much joked about, that the only book that could never be found on the shelves of the school bookshop was *Monk Dawson*, Piers Paul Read's best-selling novel about abuse at a school that was clearly based on our own.

The shock of the truth – which I shall return to – was all the more violent for being long delayed, and when it came it cast a dark retrospective shadow over what, the mist notwithstanding, I remember as a largely sunny youth.

3 · AS MANY STRINGS AS ARE LEFT TO PULL

I put my bad behaviour at Cambridge down to being drunk on people. By bad behaviour I do not mean the sort of rowdy partying in silly clothes that is so often associated with the Oxbridge scene – though there was certainly plenty of that. I mean the pretentiousness and arrogance I often find when I encounter reminders of my much younger self.

Until then my social life had been largely limited to school friends, relations, and a small group of teenagers who met at the Tesano Sports Club in Accra, Ghana, where my family were then living. Most of the Tesano crowd were, like me, white expatriates, and although life in Ghana greatly appealed to my lotus-eating tendencies, Tesano teenager was much more interested in water-skiing, sunbathing and clubbing than in intellectual debate. The thrill of finding myself suddenly afloat in a sea of clever contemporaries with similar interests turned me socially tipsy.

On my first day at Trinity in 1976 Sebastian Davey, an Ampleforth friend who had arrived a year earlier, brought a Girton undergraduate called Sarah Helm to welcome me to my rooms in Angel Court. The 'set' – a bedroom with a small washbasin and a generous sitting room looking down on Trinity Street – was the first space I could really call my own. I made them tea, put a Haydn symphony on the gramophone (I remember this detail because it was the only record I had) and we chatted away the afternoon.

Sebastian liked to drink with Alastair Campbell, the future Downing Street media maestro, and Sarah later married Jonathan Powell, who served as Tony Blair's chief of staff. She and I hunted foreign office ministers as a pack when we were both diplomatic editors (she had the job at the *Independent* when I was dip ed at ITN), and we swapped contacts when we were both writing books about the Second World War.

The Cambridge friendships I made were very real and often very deep – and many have endured ever since. But were we also building a contacts book of friends for the future? Of course we were. It was not quite such a knowingly cynical process as that sounds – it was more that it felt good to know people who were likely to achieve. But if we had been accused of constructing a Cambridge Mafia back then we would have found the accusation odd – that was part of the point of being at Cambridge.

Networking came naturally – indeed, it was part of the culture, even if the term itself did not become widely used until the following decade. Frederic Raphael's *The Glittering Prizes* – which followed a group of Cambridge students from first friendship to middle age – had been broadcast on BBC Two that spring, and everyone seemed to be reading Anthony Powell's novel sequence *A Dance to the Music of Time*, which is built around the conceit of a group of characters who flow in and out of one another's lives from school and university onwards. So popular was *Dance* that when I went to buy the last of the twelve-volume series in Heffers, the university bookshop, the assistant sighed, 'Oh, bad luck, you're reaching the end,' as he rang up the bill.

I was introduced to *Dance* by Nick Coleridge, whom I had met at a grand teenage party in Chelsea during our gap year (it is worth stating for the record that he had been invited, I had gate-crashed), and who then turned up again as one of my neighbours in Trinity's Angel Court. Cambridge colleges organize their rooms by 'courts' – the equivalent of a 'quad' at Oxford – and 'staircases'. B staircase, Angel Court seemed to be entirely populated by

Etonians and Harrovians, plus a son of the Singaporean prime minister Lee Kuan Yew.

Although this world was thrillingly new to me, I cannot claim it was what you might call diverse. There were no women in Trinity until my last year there, and very few Black faces among either the students or the dons.

Kwame Anthony Appiah, the brilliant cultural commentator and philosopher, was at Clare College not far away, and was a familiar figure on the Trinity social scene – it was widely rumoured that he was a member of the Apostles, the secretive intellectual society that had nurtured the Trinity men among the Cambridge spies. He was descended from the Labour Chancellor Sir Stafford Cripps on his mother's side and a long line of Ashanti nobles on his father's, so he could out-blue-blood all of us.

Wesley Kerr, who remains a friend and was, I think, the only Black undergraduate in my year at Trinity, had travelled a longer journey than most of us – after being fostered by a remarkable Hampshire philanthropist, he had won a scholarship to Winchester from his grammar school, and from there his Cambridge scholarship – but had picked up plenty of Wykehamist graces along the way.

A reminiscence he later wrote of his Trinity time opened with a truly world-class piece of name-dropping: 'Mother Teresa smiled seraphically. The Duke of Edinburgh guffawed. "Why on earth would you want to do that?" Rab Butler had just informed them that, having graduated that day, I now hoped to be Prime Minister of Jamaica.' Mother Teresa was given an honorary degree that day, Prince Philip was the university chancellor, and R. A. Butler was the college master, so I am sure it is all true, but it takes a special talent to get a saint, the Queen's consort and a legendary politician into a single paragraph.

During our brief encounter in Chelsea, Nick and I had established that we both wanted to start a Cambridge magazine. *Rampage*, which we put together with a group of friends (my cousin James Stourton, whom we have already met, and two more of those ubiquitous Etonians, Nick Allan and Harry Eyres), appeared in our second term, and bore marks of the flair that would take Nick to the top of his profession.

Part of his brilliance was his determined attention to detail. I had an ornamental silver knife I had inherited from some great-aunts – it was distinctive because they had buried it with the rest of the silver in their Sussex garden during the war, and most of the shiny thread that once adorned the handle had eroded away. During an evening of 'pasting up' the magazine's pages on the floor of my rooms it slipped off a table and pierced the back of Nick's hand. It was a deep cut and he went very pale so we despatched him to bed with a bandage. Ten minutes later he reappeared, clearly in great pain, to make a minute adjustment to the placing of a cartoon.

If you go in for this kind of archaeological digging in your past you are bound to turn up some nasty finds that would have better been left to rot. I have discovered an old copy of *Rampage*'s first number, and honesty compels me to admit that my contribution was an article called 'Let's talk about me', dedicated to 'the art of elegant and subtle self-advertisement'.

New technology made printing cheap and Cambridge advertisers were keen to reach the undergraduate market, so student magazines sprang up like mushrooms. By far the cleverest was *Definite Article*, edited by two Trinity luminaries, the future *Telegraph* grandee and Thatcher biographer Charles Moore and the future Tory minister Oliver Letwin; the edition I have found in a box of Cambridge papers includes pieces by Oliver (on late medieval monasticism), Dominic Lawson (on chess and paranoia) and the commentator Daniel Johnson (on conservation and politics). Elsewhere a certain Montagu Don could be found, in the pages of *Moment*, breaking into poetry (an elegy for a lost love).

Rampage aimed to be funny, glossy and clever. Nick, who had a formidable contacts book even then, gave it a plug in a *Harpers & Queen* article on student journalism, and this in turn led to the *Rampage* editorial team being given the run of the then-popular magazine *Punch* for a week. Nick summed up the zeitgeist in his leader column:

> The Angry Young Menopause of the 50s and 60s has given way – perhaps owing, in part, to the recession – to a tepid acceptance of the status quo, and the energy that was formerly directed towards a Fair Deal for the Third World has been tempered with a certain anxiousness about a Fair Deal for oneself in the 'Outside World'. Suddenly it's OK to pull as many strings as there are left to pull – and Ambition, especially at Oxford and Cambridge, is no longer an (especially) dirty word.

Belief in ambition underpinned one of the few features of *Rampage* that remain genuinely funny today, mostly because real life has caught up with it. We asked a group of prominent undergraduates to imagine their worst and best future entries in *Who's Who*. The offering from the future Tory minister Andrew Mitchell was especially instructive. His 'best' version of his future career culminated in 'European Minister of Defence 1992; Prime Minister, United States of Europe, 1997; President of the World, 2002 (Resigned: lack of job satisfaction)', and his list of putative publications included *Controlled Megalomania, an Autobiography* and *The Way Ahead; a selection of Lord Mitchell's speeches*.

I came to know Andrew through the Cambridge Union, the

university debating club, which, like its Oxford counterpart, was regarded as a training ground for future MPs and ministers. He was a year ahead of me, asked me to join his electoral slate (in the hope that I could deliver him votes from Trinity, which is the biggest of the colleges), and we climbed the greasy pole of union office in tandem. We were both involved in an episode that, more than any other, underlined how very un-PC our generation was.

I served as the union's secretary during Andrew's presidency, and he turned to me for advice on his pet project. All presidents in those days wanted to attract a member of the royal family to a debate, as this was a sure way to fill the chamber. Andrew managed to attract Princess Anne by staging a charity event in support of Save the Children, of which she was then a relatively new president. The princess agreed to attend – not, of course, to participate, simply to watch. Andrew decided that, to avoid any risk of involving a member of the royal family in political controversy, the event should be a so-called 'funny' debate. He chose for a motion – even now I gulp a bit as I write this – 'This House believes that a woman's place is in the harem.'

Did I, he asked, know of anyone who could design a debate poster that would play up this provocative theme? As it happened, I had just the man: Kit Hunter Gordon, an old school friend now reading law at Trinity Hall, did a very good line indeed in pictures of curvy women, several of which had graced the covers of *Rampage*. Kit did Andrew proud. I am afraid we all agreed that his scantily clad houri was as full of eastern promise as Fry's Turkish Delight, and she was soon plastered all over Cambridge. The image was a perfect expression of the sexism reflected in the motion.

The union committee included several aspiring politicians, so it seems especially odd that none of us was ready for the reaction Andrew's motion (and Kit's poster) would provoke from

Cambridge's feminists. It did not help that there were no women among the union's officers that term. The organization had in fact already elected three women presidents (including Arianna Huffington* of *Huff Post* fame) but progress towards a less male-dominated institution was jolting along at an uneven pace.

And it was perhaps a sign of the times that neither Princess Anne nor her office raised any concerns about the motion (I do not imagine that she or they had seen the poster). The line-up of guest speakers, although mostly male (Derek Nimmo, Robert Morley and Stirling Moss), included the actor Felicity Kendal.

Because of the presence of royalty among us, cars had been provided for the short journey from dinner in Andrew's college, Jesus, to the debate, and as we pulled up at the union, resplendent in black tie, we were greeted by what the *Daily Mirror* described as 'an angry mob of screaming demonstrators', who tried to 'kick and punch' the princess. The union building is set back from the road, and it very quickly became apparent that the royal protection officers would need some help in getting their charge to safety.

I found myself next to Robert Harris, the future – and hugely successful – novelist and political commentator, who had already notched up the chairmanship of the Fabian Society and editorship of *Stop Press*, the university newspaper, as his glittering prizes, and was now heading up the union hierarchy to the presidency. For just a beat a shadow ran across his face as if he were deciding which side of the barricades he should be on, and then he linked dinner-jacketed arms with the rest of us to form a protective cordon. Amid the mayhem I made a mental note that Robert joined the Establishment that night.

The debate was packed and, inside the chamber, felt like a

---

*   Then Arianna Stassinopoulos.

rollicking success, although the muffled shouts of demonstrators could still be heard outside, and the fire-doors bulged alarmingly as the more militant among them tried to break into the chamber. Kit's picture had its place in the sun in the subsequent press coverage: 'Pin-up started Anne demo' ran one of the headlines. The princess herself showed no sign of being perturbed by the mayhem of the demonstration. Andrew recalled casting an anxious glance in her direction from the president's chair when one of the undergraduate speakers used the F-word, and was relieved to find her laughing as much as everyone else.

Though less famous than its Oxford counterpart as a training ground for prime ministers, the Cambridge Union has a better debating chamber, and its squarer shape encourages aspiring public speakers to work an audience more directly. Your listeners sit all around you and, for a big debate, on the floor in the aisles and in the gallery above you too. There are no microphones, and the members rowdily make it known if they cannot hear you, so you have to establish a relationship with every part of the room.

The Oxbridge debating style encourages a heavy reliance on one-liners, which can give you a roar of approval and command of the chamber. Accusing an opponent of being 'about as much use as an ashtray on a motorbike' always went down well in those smoky days, as did the bigotry and stereotyping of 'Mr Y comes from Wales [or Yorkshire, or Scotland, or anywhere vaguely rural] where the men are men' . . . PAUSE A BEAT OR TWO FOR EFFECT . . . 'and the sheep are frightened.' When, during the Covid crisis, Boris Johnson accused the lawyer Sir Keir Starmer of having 'more briefs than Calvin Klein', it came straight from the union playbook.

Speaking could be an intimidating experience. After opposing Germaine Greer in a debate about abortion – one area where the monks had drilled us thoroughly in Catholic teaching – I recorded

49

in my diary that 'I found my spirit slightly cowed by the packed chamber and the eerie way in which one's words refused to resound and simply sank into the thick-pile carpet of humanity.' Germaine Greer gave a coruscating, stellar performance, and I ended the evening with my certainties shaken.

In the course of my speech I made some flip comment to the effect that the fate of young white girls who were raped during their gap year in India or Africa was a distraction from the main moral issue, and the following day a very good friend turned up in my rooms in tears and told me exactly that had happened to her. I was mortified by the realization that I had unwittingly caused her pain, and it was a searing lesson in how dangerous thoughtless words can be. Today, when I have to find the right language to broadcast about a sensitive subject, I often think back to that conversation – still with a remembered wince.

I failed in my first attempt to become union president, partly because, in the judgement of Adair Turner, who had a well-deserved reputation as the cleverest man at Cambridge, I was completely lacking in political commitment. 'Stourton had other things on his mind,' he wrote in his column. 'One morning in his bath last term he realized he was a Liberal, and by the time he found out he wasn't again he was already on the Liberal Club Committee.' This was cheeky – since, in the incestuous Cambridge way, I was an editor of the magazine in which the column appeared – but entirely fair.

When I did finally become president, I learnt another lesson: I did not particularly enjoy running things. The presidency came with the right to have a telephone in one's rooms – an unbelievably valuable privilege in the pre-digital world – and I was diligent about chairing committees and keeping things running smoothly, but that was mostly a case of being pleasant to the permanent staff (experienced, much older men who were, for the duration, technically my employees). But I did not get the kind of thrill from executive powers that the aspiring politicians plainly did.

Being president of the union is, in terms of what's required in the chamber, much less hard work than the speeches you need to make to get the job. You sit comfortably on your raised dais in a grand chair, stirring to your feet from time to time to introduce a new speaker or rule on a point of order.

Just occasionally a speaker runs amok. One former president – now an extremely distinguished figure in the arts and television worlds – turned up almost catatonically drunk and refused all my efforts to bring his incoherent outpourings to a close. He used words that, taken individually, had meaning, but he had long since lost the capacity to organize them into sentences that could be parsed. By the time he sat down almost everyone in the audience had retired for their bedtime cocoa, and the chamber was nearly empty.

But for the most part speakers stuck to the rules and their allotted times, and I spent debate nights weighing up everyone's arguments without being required to pronounce judgements. After a term of this I realized that my lack of political commitment was no accident: I was much better at being sceptical about other people's views than arguing a position of my own.

Immediately after leaving Cambridge I had a brief flirtation with the newly formed SDP, but I think I grasped even then that I would never believe any political creed with the passion you need to campaign for it. The union saw the end of my efforts to get elected to things.

4 · ONE BLACK BALL SHALL EXCLUDE

Ampleforth mixed faith with snobbery and a love of tradition. The Cambridge cocktail then was much the same, with academic endeavour replacing faith in the shaker.

The most baroque reflection of the old-fashioned Cambridge class system was an institution called the Pitt Club, owner of a fine but diminutive neo-classical building on Jesus Lane, which looks a little like a Legoland version of the grand gentlemen's clubs of St James's and Pall Mall. Founded in the 1830s in honour of the great prime minister William Pitt the Younger, who had spent happy years at Cambridge before entering politics, the club had given up its political character by the mid-nineteenth century and become a purely social organization, with election decided entirely by which school you had been to and who your friends were.

The club rules had not changed very much over the previous century. The names of candidates for membership were written in a book displayed in the club room with 'the name of his College, and of the place of his former education' (women were, astonishingly, not admitted as members until 2017), and existing members were invited to sign the nomination page to show their support. Success or failure was decided by a vote of the committee, and the sinister Establishment system of 'blackballing' held sway: 'No Member shall be elected unless he receives at least two votes,' the Rules laid down. 'Two black balls at each ballot shall exclude, but when only Three Members vote, one black ball in each ballot shall exclude.'

Many of the rules seemed arcane even then. Rule XXII gave

special protection to the stationery: 'No member of the Club shall take away from the Club Rooms, on any pretence whatever, any Writing Paper, Envelopes or other property of the Club.' And there was an even more mysterious prohibition related to communication with the outside world in Rule XXVIII: 'No Member shall send a Club servant out of the Club premise on any pretext whatever. If he wishes to despatch a note, or send a message, he must give it to the manager.' It is striking that while Members, the Club and even the Writing Paper were accorded the dignity of capital letters, the Club servants were not. Dick, the elderly barman, was, however, generally held to be the master of the Bloody Mary.

'Ladies' were allowed in on Fridays and Saturdays after six in the evening, and there was a long and complicated code designed to restrict the number of outsiders who could be entertained. You could bring a guest to lunch or dinner, but not the same guest more than three times in any one term, and you faced a fine of 'half-a-Guinea' if you invited a 'Townsman' into the club without following the rules – 'A Townsman being, for these purposes, anyone resident within 25 miles of Great St Mary's Church'. Fraternization with those who actually lived in Cambridge, rather than studying there, was clearly not to be encouraged.

There was an absolute ban on dogs – 'No dogs shall be allowed in the Club Rooms or entrance.' In most university societies that would surely be redundant – students not generally being big dog owners – but many Pitt Club members enjoyed killing pheasants and were enthusiastic followers of the Trinity Foot Beagles, which chased hares and rabbits across the Cambridgeshire countryside at the weekends.

The Pitt Club still exists, but it has been appropriately humiliated by history: its dodgy finances – like the union, it was run by undergraduates, and Pitt committee members were often drawn from the heavy-drinking set – forced it to lease the grand ground-floor club rooms to Pizza Express, and the small band of remaining members retreated to the attic space. Even those of us who joined in the 1970s – most of us, anyway – realized there was something ridiculous about behaving like portly old gents ('gammons', as we might now call them) when we were around twenty years old. But we were an oddly traditional generation of students. The sixties had happened in Cambridge (the Garden House* riot, the only serious outbreak of civil disorder, in fact took place in 1970) but, like many generations, we reacted against the one immediately before us.

We wore our tweed with pride, and we enjoyed the deeply old-fashioned traditions of Cambridge life. We liked using college slang expressions, like 'sporting your oak' (rooms in the old college courts had two doors, and the outer one could be 'sported' or closed if you did not want to be disturbed), and wearing gowns for meals in 'Hall'. I drew the line at beagling, but I did go Scottish dancing once a week at the Muckle Flugga, a reeling club named for a small island in the Shetlands.

Many of the dons and, even more markedly, the 'college servants' (as they were still called) were even more conservative than we were, and colluded with this enthusiastic pursuit of anachronism. The college porters – with their bowler hats – had a role in maintaining discipline among the undergraduates, but were, at the same time, expected to treat us with the respect due to young gentlemen. My friend Nick Allan recalls trying to climb out of Christ's College after an all-night poker session just as the head porter

---

* A student protest against the Colonels' regime in Greece. The Garden House Hotel became a target because it was participating in a Greek Week organized by the Greek Tourist Board, and the protest turned violent.

unlocked for the day. He was greeted with the words 'Good morning, sir' as the porter swung open the gate beneath him.

The 'bedders', who kept our rooms tidy, had a similarly ambiguous role – part cleaning lady, part intelligence agent and, sometimes, motherly matron to undergraduates in distress. They liked to be tipped at the end of the academic year, and these college jobs were often handed down from one generation to the next of the same family.

Tradition was especially marked in my own college, Trinity, which was (and is) by far and away the richest, and – in its own estimation at least – the grandest. Trinity porters kept their bowlers long after most colleges had given them up, and the bedders were so tribal that those who worked to the west of Trinity Street (in Great Court, Neville's Court and New Court) would not speak to those who worked in the nineteenth- and twentieth-century courts on the other side of the road. For the annual staff outing to Yarmouth, they took separate coaches.

The maleness of the place was still a very prominent part of the mix. Members of Cambridge colleges were not allowed to marry until the second half of the nineteenth century, and even when I arrived in the 1970s a number of old-fashioned bachelor dons made their homes in their college rooms, and lived alongside the undergraduates.

The absence of women and the antiquity of the premises encouraged what we might, in a less gracious setting, call a locker-room culture. It was not uncommon, for example, to see half-naked men, young and old, wandering across one of the college's courts with a towel and a bottle of shampoo, in the direction of the few bathrooms that had been shoehorned into these venerable buildings.

I became a member of an informal male fraternity, thanks to an attack of academic zeal. To keep some kind of hold on my work, I took a vow that, however late I partied in the evenings, I would always be up in time for breakfast 'in Hall'. The few of us who made it usually appeared looking rather smart – Hall always had a formal feel. Most brought along a morning paper – the local newsagent delivered to rooms in college.

And there we solemnly sat each weekday morning, in the soaring Tudor splendour of Hall, like a gathering of trainee clubmen, wearing our blue gowns with their black facings and digesting *The Times* or the *Daily Telegraph*. The breakfast was traditionally English, conversation was acceptable but not required, and the spirit was always one of good fellowship. Some of my breakfast companions remain friends now, and we still meet for all-male meals; long years in single-sex establishments encourage a particular form of friendship.

Did those years also distort the way we interacted with women? They probably delayed mature male–female friendships – as opposed to romantic relationships – and certainly made us less aware of the kind of sensitivities thrown up by the Harem Debate episode. But I think we were saved from enduring chauvinism because we were a transitional generation. Women undergraduates were a minority in the university as a whole when I arrived (most of them in what were then all-women colleges like Girton and Newnham) but the late seventies saw college after college voting to abandon their single-sex status. In 1978 the first women undergraduates joined Trinity and, of course, enjoyed breakfasting rights with the rest of us.

Trinity stands out, even by Cambridge standards, for its beauty; much of it, including the library by the river Cam, was built by Christopher Wren. During my last year I had rooms on M Staircase in Great Court; I awoke each morning to the sound of its huge central fountain, and when I drew the curtains I looked out on a view that had not changed much since the early seventeenth century. Tradition at Trinity, like Catholicism at Ampleforth, was seductive. The fact that my Great Court staircase had once been home to the notorious Cambridge spy Guy Burgess only added to the mystique.

The Conservative grandee R. A. Butler, one of the architects of the post-war political settlement and, in the view of many of his supporters, a contender for the title of 'the greatest prime minister we never had', was the master of the college for most of my time there. Rab was much quoted as taking the view that there were 'only three jobs worth having: prime minister, Viceroy of India and Master of Trinity', and he made the most of the one he got, entertaining groups of undergraduates in the Master's Lodge with thrillingly indiscreet comments about Margaret Thatcher, who had just been elected as the leader of his party, and snide remarks about Harold Macmillan, whom he blamed for scuppering his chances of moving into Number 10.

A favourite Butler boast – often repeated at his dinners – was that Trinity had won more Nobel Prizes than the whole of France. When, many years later, I was invited by my former tutor John Lonsdale to edit a book about Trinity, I included this 'Rab-ism' in a circular we sent out to alumni and alumnae asking for memories of college life. Back came a note from a distinguished mathematician pointing out that this was not only statistically highly unlikely, but demonstrably untrue. The error caused a great flapping of gowns in the Senior Combination Room, and a letter of apology was despatched to the French embassy.

The fact that Trinity thought the French government would mind about the episode is revealing about the college's sense of its own importance. Rab's original claim underlines an even stranger truth: all the stuffy conventions and class-bound traditions coexisted with an extraordinarily adventurous intellectual culture. As long as you wore a gown in Hall and submitted to the Latin graces, you could be as radical as you liked in your thinking.

The oddness of this combination came home to me when I went back to speak at a Commemoration Feast. I sat at High Table, just below the great Holbein portrait of the college founder, Henry VIII, and next to the master, Amartya Sen. Professor Sen, a Nobel Prize-winning economist, first became famous for his theories on the politics of famine; he has written widely and controversially about, among many other things, development and gender inequality, and would be on anyone's list of radical thinkers.

At the end of dinner an elderly retainer emerged from the kitchens bearing an enormous silver pitcher and bowl, which he placed in front of my neighbour. The college choir, lit by candles in the minstrels' gallery, then sang an elaborate Latin grace, and when it ended the elderly retainer reappeared and removed the pitcher. I asked Professor Sen for the meaning of this ritual. 'They do it every night,' he replied, 'and I have absolutely no idea why.'

The Cambridge academic culture allowed undergraduates great freedom, and encouraged us to think for ourselves. Lectures were optional – certainly for arts students – and we usually went for entertainment rather than anything else. There were some academic stars with a flair for the dramatic, like Christopher Ricks, who played Bob Dylan records at his lectures on Shakespeare. Most of the real work was done in libraries or one's own room, preparing for supervisions, the one-on-one meetings with dons that are at the heart of the Oxbridge teaching tradition.

Sometimes these were very rare indeed. For my first dissertation subject I chose Thomas De Quincey, the author of *Confessions of an English Opium-Eater*. As supervisor I was assigned a hairy young PhD student who, at our first meeting, asked me whether 'your interest in De Quincey springs from your own hallucinogenic experiences'. When I said no, in rather shocked tones (I was more partial to Dick's Bloody Marys than hard drugs), he seemed a bit disappointed and thereafter left me largely to my own devices.

I wrote my second dissertation almost without seeing my supervisor at all. I think this was his fault as much as mine – he never showed much interest in my progress – but in my penultimate term I was summoned by my tutor to explain myself: Cambridge tutors are responsible for moral and disciplinary matters rather than purely academic ones. 'Your supervisor says the two of you have only met once. Should I worry?' he asked. I reassured him that it was all coming along swimmingly, and Dr Lonsdale cheerfully dismissed me without further enquiry. 'Pound as a Translator – from Cathay to the Homage to Sextus Propertius' secured me the highest mark of any of my Cambridge papers; I later found it in a box during a house move and could not understand a word of it.

The Cambridge degree system is known as the Tripos, which, in the habitually confusing manner favoured by ancient English institutions, has two parts (the name is said to have been derived from the three-legged stool students once sat on for a *viva voce*, or oral examination). After my Part I results the director of studies, Adrian Poole, took me for a walk in Trinity's Fellows' Garden, a beautifully maintained and secluded spread of lawns, shrubberies and flowerbeds reached by an avenue that led from the river Cam to Queens Road and the playing fields beyond.

'If you work absolutely flat out for the next two years,' he told me, with bracing frankness, 'you could get a first. But your commitment would have to be total, and even then I couldn't guarantee that you wouldn't drop down to a two:one.' Here, in a very Cambridge moment, he paused to admire a peony in the full blush of its summer colours. 'So clever of Keats,' he continued, 'that image in the "Ode on Melancholy": "then glut thy sorrow on a morning rose, or on the rainbow of the salt sand-wave, or [a cupping gesture with the hand at this point] on the wealth of globed peonies".'

We ambled further along the sinuous path towards the rose garden and its sundial. The pep talk continued: 'The alternative would be to keep going with your student journalism, your speeches at the union and so on, and maintain a steady but not overly onerous rate of work in the way you are doing at the moment, and you will almost certainly get a two:one anyway.' It was not a difficult choice. Wise and generous advice like that is almost unimaginable today, because every college, even Trinity, has to be mindful of its place in the degree league table.

I rather wish I had not kept a Cambridge diary. After writing some books of history and biography I have learnt how valuable contemporary accounts can be – they are almost always infinitely more accurate than memory – so I have forced myself to read it for this chapter. It is written on Florentine paper bound in marbled covers, and the level of pretentiousness is well off the dial.

Lay in late to recover from a 5 a.m. paste-up [of *Rampage*] and traumatic *Pearl* essay [*Pearl* is an extremely challenging late fourteenth-century allegorical poem]. A beautiful day, with spring in the air, and people on the streets. I feel dangerously free. Breakfast in the Whim with Adam Mars-Jones [later a novelist and film critic] and his boyfriend the Vietnam War veteran.

Lunch in the Pitt and a little pipe-talk with Nicholas Shakespeare [a near contemporary who went on to write very good novels and some brilliant Second World War history].

Interesting discussion with John Fowles [author of *The French Lieutenant's Woman*] at the English Soc on Wednesday. A dangerously psychological approach to art: putting the emphasis on creator rather than created.

The John Fowles reference brings back a memory of what actually happened, which causes such a cringe it's almost painful. He was
at that time one of the most successful literary authors writing in
English, and I can recall being absurdly patronizing in my judgement
on his books – to the general embarrassment of the other members
of the English Soc, who were very pleased to have lured him to Cambridge for a talk. What a repulsive little toad I must have been.

I cannot quite believe that right back then, at the age of twenty,
I was arrogant enough to think that someone would one day want
to read this burbling, but the tone makes it impossible to escape the
conclusion that the diary was written to be read by a wider audience. My only excuse is a pathology born of all those university
magazines in which everyone wrote about everyone else – a sneaking suspicion that if my life was not being written about somewhere
I was not really living it.

Just occasionally this agonizingly self-conscious twaddle is
redeemed by its innocence, a sense of the delight in being young
and healthy in a beautiful place that represents the best of the
Oxbridge experience. Here's how I spent a bracingly cold Sunday
in January 1979:

> I was tussling with Aristotle when Oliver [Letwin] rang and sug-
> gested a walk to Grantchester. I resisted for a while, but eventually
> joined a party of Harry [Eyres], Oliver and a Russian girl whose
> name I can't pronounce. Sunlit snow and snowball fights all the
> way. Skaters on the ponds.

After a pub lunch – near the church clock that stands at ten to
three in Rupert Brooke's famous Grantchester poem* – we dropped

---

* 'The Old Vicarage, Grantchester'.

in unannounced on an artist friend who had a cottage in the village, and found another lunch party in full swing. 'They were as amazed to see us as we had hoped,' and Harry entertained us all 'sitting at the harmonium in his bobble hat and Scrooge coat and playing piano music'. There was another stop on the walk back for tea, and the entry ends, 'Now sleepily to mass. It all sounds a little silly. But it wasn't, it was wonderful.'

That mass I went to so sleepily would have been said in Fisher House, a rabbit-warren of half-timbered buildings just behind the market square, which had served as an inn before it became the Catholic chaplaincy in the nineteenth century. It was presided over by an extravagantly named member of the cousinage, Father (later Archbishop) Maurice Couve de Murville, who had a passion for good cigars and firmly traditional views on the Faith. He liked to share both the cigars and the views ('The Resurrection was a fact of history; if they dug up a grave in Jerusalem and found the bones of Jesus I would leave the Church immediately') during candle-lit soirées amid the oak panelling and family portraits.

Fisher House was still haunted by the memory – and sometimes even by the real presence – of one of Maurice's predecessors, an even more eccentrically conservative figure, Monsignor Alfred Gilbey.

Gilbey became university chaplain in 1932 – having been at Trinity as an undergraduate just after the First World War – and immediately set about converting, with some success, aristocratic young men. The efficacy of this tactic in the campaign to 'convert England from the top down' was slightly undermined by his habit of encouraging them to go and fight in the Spanish Civil War, where they were liable to be killed or wounded. And unlike Orwell or the brilliant Trinity poet John Cornford, Gilbey's acolytes did not go to fight and die for freedom, democracy and the Spanish Republic, they went to fight for Franco, Fascism and the Holy Mother Church.

Gilbey remained the Catholic chaplain of Cambridge University for more than thirty years, finally resigning in 1965, when he was forced to accept women into the chaplaincy. Armed with a private income from the family gin business, he then took up permanent residence at the Travellers, the gentlemen's club in Pall Mall, where he continued his war of attrition against any female attempts on male prerogatives, passing his days as a kind of informal chaplain to the English upper classes. He remained a frequent visitor to Cambridge during my time there.

He was an unmistakable figure: on being made a monsignor – an honorific granted to priests who were held to have performed some special service – he secured a papal dispensation allowing him to wear the traditional gear that went with the title. His shovel hat and knee-length frock coat could sometimes be spotted in the Pitt Club, of which he was a life member.

Many years later I bumped into him in the Travellers Club morning room while waiting to have lunch with a friend. 'We don't see you here very often,' he said accusingly.

'No,' I replied. 'I'm married with children now.'

'Marriage,' declared the elderly celibate, 'is a great destroyer of club life.'

Did he, perhaps just a little, get the joke about himself? The monsignor is a good yardstick for measuring the way Catholic opinion has changed. When I was young we tolerated his misogyny and allowed a benign view of his odd habits because the grown-ups took him seriously – no grand Catholic wedding was complete without Monsignor Gilbey 'vested and in the sanctuary' – and because he was said to be holy. I now think of his particular addiction to 'the olden days' as slightly sinister.

Religion was still a prominent force in college life in the 1970s, and Trinity's chapel culture was, in contrast to Fisher House,

extremely liberal. The dean, Bishop John Robinson, was famous –
indeed notorious – for a book called *Honest to God*, in which he
questioned traditional ideas about the deity as a 'cosmic supremo'.
His critics saw him as the first in a long line of Church of England
prelates arguing that it was perfectly possible to be a good Anglican without actually believing that God existed.

The college chaplain, the clubbable Bob Reiss, was of a similar
cast of mind; he later became canon theologian of Westminster
Abbey, and wrote his own iconoclastic tome, *Sceptical Christianity*,
on his retirement. His argument, as I understood it, was that it is
still rational, just about, to believe in God, but that the idea of an
afterlife is completely implausible. He asked me for a back-cover
quote when the book came out, and in our correspondence regretted that his radical views had become so mainstream they no longer
provoked the outrage that might have bumped up sales.

The expansive culture fostered by the Robinson–Reiss duo had
the paradoxical impact of making Trinity's chapel – a beautiful
building opposite my rooms on Great Court – something of a no-go
area to the man who was destined to become the most prominent
religious leader of our generation. Justin Welby, a year ahead of me
at Trinity, was a member of CICCU, the Cambridge Inter-Collegiate
Christian Union, which was generally known as the God Squad.

This Bible-addicted evangelical organization had a reputation
for fiercely traditional teaching and was, in the popular undergraduate mind at least, associated with practices like glossolalia, or
speaking in tongues. Its members exhibited a slightly cultish aversion to mixing with the rest of us, which may help explain why
absolutely none of my Trinity friends has any memory of Justin
Welby at all. When he became Archbishop of Canterbury, only the
dates in his Wikipedia entry told us he had been a contemporary.

As well as a future leader of the Church of England, my

near-contemporaries at Trinity included a future cabinet minister (Oliver Letwin), a future national newspaper editor (Charles Moore), a future publishing magnate (Nick Coleridge), a future deputy governor of the Bank of England (Sir Paul Tucker), several future writers and broadcasters and all manner of successful lawyers, business people, scientists and academics in the making. Covering Rajiv Gandhi's funeral for ITN in 1991 (the young leader of the Congress Party, who had already served as prime minister, was blown up by a Tamil Tiger suicide bomber), I reflected that two of the guests of honour – Prince Charles and Douglas Hurd, then foreign secretary – were Trinity Men, as was the corpse. Institutions like Trinity have traditionally taken pride in connections like these. It now seems bad taste to boast about them.

My Trinity contemporaries would have been very happy to hear themselves described as 'an elite'. 'Elitism' – like 'posh' and 'cosmopolitan' – is one of those terms that has lost favour within my lifetime. Britain in the 1970s was full of elites, and even those that look rather silly in retrospect took pride in the label. No one really now defends a hereditary House of Lords, for example, but 'This House believes in the hereditary principle' was a favourite Cambridge Union motion, and it usually passed. So we felt no embarrassment about claiming an 'elite' status for our education.

After I had left Trinity my wise director of studies, Adrian Poole, became the college's head of admissions, and I went back to hear a talk he gave on the college's efforts to broaden its social reach. The programme he outlined for attracting candidates who might not have applied in the past was impressive and energetic, but he ended the talk with an unapologetic flourish: 'In the end we are who we are,' he declared, with a sly reference to Jane Austen's *Emma*, 'Trinity: handsome, clever and rich.'

Could you make that joke today? I am not sure. The concept of elitism is now deeply compromised. Yet everything about our systems of education and professions encourages aspirations towards what would once have been called elitist achievement.

It would be silly to pretend I did not enjoy my time at Cambridge – however painfully puffed-up my younger self now seems. On my last day I sat on a bench on the Backs and gazed at the sun falling across Christopher Wren's library just across the Cam. It was the end of the party season known as May Week (which, in the silly way of these things, is actually the first week of June), so I had probably been drinking. I wept with the thought that nothing else would be quite like it.

Real life had, when it very occasionally intruded into the Cambridge idyll, provided a warning or two about the world of work to come. As Cambridge students we were judged to have good financial prospects, so all the banks competed for our custom, offering generous overdraft facilities. Some bright spark studying economics persuaded me that in an age when inflation was higher than interest rates (these were the Callaghan* years) it paid to borrow as much money as possible, as the value of what you owed was always shrinking in real terms. As a result of this very unsound piece of advice I soon had overdrafts at four different Cambridge banks.

My problematic finances were not helped by the fact that Trinity operated a credit system that allowed undergraduates to sign for bottles from the college's legendary wine cellar. When my 'Buttery Bill' arrived with a thump at the end of my first year I realized that the summer vacation was going to mean work, not play.

Leaving behind the May Balls and dining clubs, I went to work on a Henry Boot building site near my parents' house in North

---

* Jim Callaghan became prime minister on Harold Wilson's resignation in the spring of 1976.

Yorkshire, helping to construct a new water-treatment plant. Most of my co-workers were bussed up from Leeds, spending the working week on site and returning home on Fridays for a weekend that began, I was informed by one, with 'a shit, shave, leg-over and then me tea'.

I learnt how to handle jack-hammers on concrete and how to start the air-compressor pumps that drove them. Observing my feeble efforts with the starting mechanism, my gang-leader told me, 'You're not swearing it proper,' then yanked it into life as a torrent of abuse poured from his mouth. And I very nearly killed a man.

One of the compressor pipes sprang a leak, and I was sent scrambling over the scaffolding to change it. I was working above one of the huge water tanks we were building, and as I attached a new tube the old, damaged one slipped off the length of scaffolding where I had draped it. I watched in silent horror as it described a perfect arc towards the bottom of the tank, and, with what seemed like planned precision, the heavy metal coupling on the end struck the head of a man working at the bottom, sending blood all over the freshly poured concrete he was finishing. I managed to apologize before he left for hospital; he manfully blamed himself for not wearing a helmet, and seemed most concerned that the nurses might complain about his dirty underwear.

On my last day my gang-leader told me to hide my gum boots under the hedge by the roadside so I could come back later and pinch them; this modest act of larceny was regarded as a legitimate perk, part of the 1970s gravy-train culture that encouraged journalists to fiddle their expenses.

MASTERING A CRAFT

5 · FIND AN ESCAPED PRISONER

Learning to be a reporter has been my great redemptive experience. All my school and university journalism had been introspective and opinionated, but reporting made me think about other people, and search for evidence.

Getting a foothold on the journalistic ladder was not easy – in fact, I was seriously knocked back for the first time in my life. I made my first assault on the profession while I was still at Cambridge, through one of the 'contacts' that were supposed to work such magic. My relationship with the contact in question was complicated (he was my girlfriend's stepfather's secretary's son) but he succeeded in securing me an interview with John Birt, who was then running current affairs at London Weekend Television.

My first mistake was wearing a suit: John Birt greeted me in his office high above the Thames in an open-neck shirt and fashionably baggy cords. 'So,' he kicked off, 'what do you think of Carter's chances of re-election?' I was just about aware that an American presidential campaign was due the following year, but that was as far as it went. Some twenty minutes later the great man rose from his chrome and leather sofa with the words 'I could write you a polite note saying we don't have any vacancies, but frankly it would be a waste of the postage stamp.'

My traineeship with Independent Television News, ITN, came my way courtesy of luck and good old-fashioned snobbery – plus a very modest ingredient of extra effort on my part. After the John Birt debacle I took myself along to the careers office at Cambridge, and the adviser told me that to be successful in journalism I would need to enjoy being woken in the middle of the night and told to jump on a plane to somewhere dangerous. This sounded deeply unappealing – it would almost certainly mean missing parties, to which I was addicted. But by then I had made up my mind about my future. More conventional and lucrative careers, like the law or the City, held no appeal. So I learnt at least to sound 'hungry' in interviews.

The luck lay in ITN's lackadaisical administrative habits, which meant that they did not get round to interviewing candidates in the university 'milk round' until long after all the good prospects had been snapped up for other courses, like the prestigious BBC News Trainee Scheme. The snobbery – which was decisive – I only learnt about later: the managing editor's secretary became a friend, and she confided that she had been instructed to go through the applications and throw away any from candidates who had not been to Oxford or Cambridge. Luck and snobbery whittled the list of serious contenders to a handful.

When the ITN offer came through I was doing a touch-typing course with a classful of debutantes at a secretarial school in Mayfair, in preparation for heading north and the *Newcastle Journal*. Suddenly the job offers proliferated.

A letter dropped on the doormat from something called the 'Foreign and Commonwealth Office Co-ordinating Committee'. The writer – his signature was illegible and there was no typed name below it – informed me that 'It has been suggested to me that you might be interested to have a discussion with us about appointments in government service in the field of foreign affairs, which occasionally arise in addition to those covered by the usual Diplomatic Service Grade 2 and 8 Competition.'

There had long been rumours at Trinity that some of the dons were MI6 talent spotters, and years later an officer of the Secret

Service confirmed some of the names to me (in the best le Carré tradition, we were shooting pheasants at the time). But I knew I would have made a rotten spy – I enjoyed gossip too much. So I joined the two others who had come through the haphazard ITN recruitment process.

Michael Crick arrived in January 1980, having stayed an extra term at Oxford to serve as president of the Oxford Union. Mark Damazer, who, much later, was to become my boss on Radio 4, was a little older than Michael and me, and late onto the jobs market because he had spent a year at Harvard after Cambridge. We had friends in common who warned me of his intimidating intelligence. He claimed to have been intimidated by my pee, having, before we even met, encountered what he felt was an unreasonably impressive quantity in a specimen jar with my name on it when he went for his medical with the company doctor in Harley Street.

Mark and I met on what should have been the first day of our working lives in August 1979. In fact, we spent most of that day at the Green Man pub in Fitzrovia and found we had walked straight into two social conflicts at once.

The first was the epic ITV strike of that year, a truly extraordinary moment in the history of industrial relations. That summer, with Margaret Thatcher newly installed in Downing Street, the ITV companies had decided to play hardball with their unions: they offered a pay rise of a mere 9 per cent to their technical staff – it says a lot about the climate of the times that the figure was considered little short of insulting. The ensuing strike took what was then the only commercial television channel off the air for ten weeks. The ratings system weirdly registered a 'discernible number' of viewers who continued to tune in to the test card, which perhaps reflected what a social trauma this was.

The National Union of Journalists – which Mark and I had

both joined more or less automatically when we became graduate trainees – had cleverly negotiated that journalists would be paid as long as we made ourselves available for duty, but would not be required to cross picket lines. Giles Smith, the father of our NUJ chapel (the quaint linguistic trappings of the past had, like the rituals at Trinity High Table, survived into modernity), was ITN's senior industrial correspondent in his day job, so he knew his negotiating onions, and once a week he would brief us on strike developments in the pub just behind ITN's offices in Wells Street. Thus it was that our first day of work turned out to mean a day of, in a much-used phrase of those days, 'beer and sandwiches' in the Green Man.

The dispute was finally settled by a staggering 45 per cent pay rise. The technical staff finally trooped back in late October, when *Coronation Street* and *News at Ten* returned to the nation's screens. After this bruising encounter the bosses were in no mood for another dispute with the NUJ, and when the strike ended, we got an even bigger rise than our technical colleagues. Commercial television really was a licence to print money then.

The other conflict was an internal culture war at ITN, which reflected the wider social divisions of the day. Mark and I were both carrying a copy of the *Guardian* on that first day at the Green Man – I was more of a *Times* reader, but the *Thunderer*'s printers were on strike too. A lean, bearded man – whose accent and leather jacket would certainly have earned him a black ball at the Pitt Club – yelled at us across the lounge bar, 'Oi, you trainees, I see you read the *Guardian*. I suppose you think the 5.45 news is too down-market?'

Those were the first words I heard from my new colleagues. ITN, in those days, was an odd mixture of glamorous foreign correspondents, who might have stepped out of the pages of Evelyn

Waugh's *Scoop*, brainy Oxbridge graduates and hard-nosed, middle-aged men (mostly), who had come up via the school of hard knocks and papers like the *Mail* and the *Mirror*. As I was to discover, the hard-knocks brigade liked to get their retaliation in early.

The phrase 'trainee scheme' was something of a misnomer. We were looked after by a very kind and gentle senior journalist called Frank Miles, whose greatest pleasure was reminiscing about past glory days, and who sometimes rambled on about things that had nothing whatever to do with journalism.

In my diary – more sporadically kept now – I recorded after one training session that Frank was 'full of curious information: I didn't know that Mozart lived in Pimlico. Or that a river flowed from the Serpentine to the Thames over Sloane Square tube station.' Frank also told us about going back to see the bedsit in Chelsea where he lost his virginity; the building was being re-developed and he showed us a picture of himself standing mournfully amid the ruins. This surprised us; it was not the sort of supervision you got from Cambridge dons.

One memorable training session took place in the small cinema where, in television's cleft-stick days, when the arrival of a report from some far-off location was still a big event, editors would gather to watch the material as it came out of the developing baths – this was well before the days of digital recording, and even news footage was shot on film. Frank showed us greatest hits, like the exclusive ITN pictures of three planes being blown up on Dawson's Field airstrip in Jordan after a multiple hijacking in 1970. Work seemed like fun.

The biggest treat at the session – and it fired my appetite for a reporter's future – was footage of Michael Nicholson greeting a Turkish paratrooper during the invasion of Cyprus in 1974.

Michael's car ran out of petrol on the way to a facility with the rest of the resident press corps, and by pure good fortune he found himself with a ringside seat as the first wave of Turkish troops was dropped. He strode over to one of them as the soldier, in full battle dress, unbuckled his parachute: 'Michael Nicholson, ITN,' he announced, holding out his hand. 'Welcome to Cyprus.'

The episode was characteristic of the buccaneering, free-wheeling *esprit* that animated ITN and – this belief was shared by all the ITN tribes – gave the organization an edge over the more flat-footed BBC.

ITN's first editor was Aidan Crawley, a first-class cricketer who flew night patrols over the Channel in 1940, spied on German forces in the Balkans, and, after being shot down over Tobruk, spent much of the war trying to escape from various *stalags*. Chris Chataway, an Olympic middle-distance runner and future Tory MP, was one of the first newscasters, broadcasting alongside the abrasive and bow-tied Robin Day. You could be grand and clever if you wanted, we learnt, but stuffiness was a mortal sin.

The real training was 'on the job', and here members of the hard-knocks tendency had the run of us. It was a little like arriving at one of those parody public schools where – as a popular 1970s myth had it – new boys were sent to warm the lavatory seats for sixth-formers. Late duty on Saturday nights, for example, was routinely assigned to us. This meant staying on in the newsroom until the entire ITV network had come off the air, just in case some dramatic story forced you to take control of the airwaves and put out a newsflash.

It never happened – just as well, since no one actually told us what we should do if such circumstances arose. Most of the network closed down around midnight in those days, but Grampian Television always broadcast an old black-and-white movie in the

Highlands, which finished around 3 a.m., so we were stuck at our desks long after the screens in London had gone blank. Now, of course, there is no moment of the day or night without some form of television available to view.

The news editors delighted in sending us on the wildest of wild-goose chases. Working under the direction of an old-school tabloid man called Don Horobin – who called everyone, irrespective of status or gender, 'sport' or 'old cock' – and with apparently limitless budgets, they loved taking a punt, and whenever they had a particularly off-the-wall assignment the finger fell on us.

One morning I arrived in the office to be greeted with a shout of 'Oi, you . . . yes, you, trainee . . . Go to Brixton and find an escaped prisoner.' One of the red-tops had run a piece claiming that prison inmates were slipping over the wall in the evenings for a pint or two, and it was my job to stand up the story.

I still had not shaken my suit habit, so I was resplendent in pinstripe. I dutifully spent long hours sidling up to burly men in Brixton's pubs muttering, 'Can I buy you a pint, er . . . mate . . . and . . . you wouldn't happen to be an escaped prisoner, would you?'

Not long afterwards the late Tory MP Winston Churchill (grandson of the great war leader) was caught in an affair with Soraya Khashoggi, the ex-wife of a Saudi arms dealer. The allegation that he had driven at a hundred miles an hour down an American freeway with Mrs Khashoggi telling him, 'The faster you go the more I take off,' made the story irresistible to the news desk, and I was sent with a camera crew to ambush the erring MP outside the House of Commons. Unfortunately, I was spotted by an Ampleforth contemporary who was working as a parliamentary researcher: he berated me for going along with this salacious assignment, and I slunk away in shame.

It was disillusioning, dirty stuff, but it made me appreciate the value of telling a good story. One of the great battle cries of the age, popularized especially by the prominent left-wing MP Tony Benn, was that politics should be about what, with his trademark lisp, he called 'ishoos' and not 'personalities', but most of the millions of viewers who tuned into ITN's programmes every day cared much more about personalities.

These forays also taught me some of the tradecraft needed for life on the road. When the art historian Anthony Blunt was unmasked as a former Soviet spy in November 1979, the news desk threw everything they could at it. It was an absolutely pitch-perfect match to ITN's news values: spying was box office in those Cold War days, the way Blunt's activities had been covered up reeked of Establishment corruption, and his homosexuality – legal by then, but still widely regarded as a perversion – added prurient piquancy.

After a morning huddle on the news desk – part of the ITN culture was that no one took formal meetings seriously – reporters and crews were despatched to absolutely everywhere the disgraced art historian might be hiding. The huddle took the view that the least promising place to look was his home in a block of mansion flats in Marylebone, as he would surely have gone to ground somewhere else. But just in case . . . I was despatched with a cameraman, but no sound recordist, so we could not have interviewed him even if we'd caught him. The assignment was 'belt and braces'.

The cameraman, Sebastian Rich, was immensely self-confident (he became a distinguished war cameraman), so I assumed he knew what we should do. He was fooled by my suit habit, and made the same assumption about me.

The suit got me into the lobby, but the uniformed porter threw me out as soon as I explained what I was about. I poked around the dustbins at the back of the building for a while, assuming this was suitably sleuthish news hound form. When I found a phone box (this was, of course, long before mobile phones) to report back to the news desk I was told to 'stake out' the building.

Seb took charge. 'Go to an off-licence and buy half a bottle of whisky,' he instructed me, 'and put it down on your expenses as coffees. We'll sit under this porch to get out of the rain while we drink it, and every so often you can ring in and tell them nothing's happening.' I did as I was told.

Half an hour later a car swept past us and a face looked out of the back window with a huge grin; the owner of the face – who, I later discovered, was Blunt's art-historian friend Brian Sewell – was waggling his hands either side of his ears in a classic yah-boo gesture. 'Blunt seen at London flat' screamed the *Times* headline when the paper dropped on the doormat the following morning. 'We whisked him away beneath the noses of two astonished journalists,' Sewell told the paper. Fortunately, I was rota-ed off that day, and since no one in the newsroom really knew who I was – 'You, trainee' was the nearest we came to being given individual identities – I got away with it.

The most valuable – though challenging – training stint was an attachment to the *News at 5.45,* a brilliant piece of tabloid journalism that went out at that time in the afternoon. A script for the whole half-hour of *News at Ten* would, we were told, fit into a single column of the old broadsheet *Times;* the *5.45* was a mere fifteen minutes long, so brevity was at an even greater premium.

The reporter 'packages' were generally allowed to run for no more than a minute and fifteen seconds. The newscaster 'cues', which introduced them, were limited to ten or fifteen seconds, which meant summing up even the most complex of stories in a maximum of forty-five words – three words per second being the speed at which it was estimated most newscasters delivered their lines.

As well as explaining what the story was about – accurately and without breaking any laws – these tiny nibs also had to be written in a way that would hold the viewers' attention, telling them why the story mattered. The writing skills were rather different from those required to turn out ten thousand words on 'Pound as a Translator – from Cathay to the Homage to Sextus Propertius'. In fact, I had to take pretty much everything I had ever learnt about writing and turn it on its head.

The 5.45 was run by a man called Derek Dowsett, who could not have been more unlike the stereotype of a tabloid editor. He was so laconic he would have made a Trappist monk seem chatty, he was kind and thoughtful, and he never swore or drank to excess – rare qualities in journalism then. His deputy, Phil Moger, was a more extrovert figure, and was the man who had challenged our newspaper tastes on that first day in the Green Man.

Phil's title was chief sub film, which meant that he was responsible for all visual, as opposed to spoken, material. The role did not exist at the BBC, and it reflected the ITN view that in television pictures mattered as much as, if not more than, words. Phil revelled in his tabloid persona, and sometimes allowed one to glimpse that he was much cleverer than the persona allowed. When the former German chancellor Willy Brandt produced his seminal report on the north–south divide in 1980, Phil yelled across the newsroom to the correspondent assigned to the story: 'This report on the future of the world – minute fifteen do you?'

Our target audience was defined as 'Mum in Wigan' – it was pointed out to us that she had 'tea', not supper or dinner, so the programme was scheduled to allow her and her family to catch up on the day as they sat down to eat. Even complex political or foreign stories had to pass her acid tests: would Mum in Wigan understand, and would she care? There was a test for me too: how could I write for Mum in Wigan when I had never really met her, and had spent my early years in company where the main evening meal was most definitely supper or, on more formal occasions, dinner?

The answer was provided by those bonkers assignments we were sent on by the news desks. They very often involved vox pops, the street interviews that were, and remain, such a staple of broadcast news programmes. Television in those days had more of an aura of glamour than it does now, and almost everyone would talk to you in the hope of 'being on the telly'. Finding people inter-esting is an essential element in the reporter toolkit, and I discovered I had the gene.

And, in an odd way, the respect for good manners bequeathed by my conventional upbringing helped with the learning curve. At the beginning of the 1984 miners' strike I was sent to a pit-head in South Wales with one of the rougher cameramen. There was acute tension between the miners and the media throughout the strike, and I was again wearing the wretched pinstripe suit that featured in so many of my early misadventures.

'How dare you come down from London and report on us,' one of the pickets yelled, 'when you earn twice what we do?'

'Twice?' taunted the cameraman. 'Twice? More like four times.'

This seemed like bad manners to me. It was also dangerous, and we only narrowly escaped being pushed into the pit.

The disparate ITN tribes were united in their faith in one over-riding principle: accuracy mattered more than anything. The hard-knocks types enjoyed ramming this message home to the Oxbridge trainees by assigning us to type out the football results for newscasters to read on *News at Ten*. It was explained to us – in case we had missed it while locked away in our ivory towers – that viewers minded very much about their football teams.

This was the heyday of the football pools, when millions of

Britons sent in their coupons predicting the results of each week's games; the first pools prize of over £750,000 was scooped up in the year I joined ITN, and by the mid-1980s a hospital syndicate in Wiltshire had taken the record over the million mark, so there was big money at stake.

Getting the football results wrong was regarded as one of the very few offences you could be sacked for. And the clincher was this: 'If you make little mistakes in a subject the viewers know about,' the subs told us, 'they'll never trust you when it comes to the big things they don't know about.'

It was the closest those grizzled pros came to an abstract state-ment, and it was profoundly wise. They would have fought shy of loose talk about journalism as a vocation, a search for truth, but for the first time in this alien world I heard an echo of the monks preaching the primacy of moral principles. No media organization can survive without the trust of its viewers, listeners or readers.

I knew nothing about football, but Mark Damazer did. So did Alastair Burnet, the senior newscaster (as a former editor of both *The Economist* and the *Daily Express* he represented all ITN's tribes in his august person), and the two of them crossed swords, in the way that experts often do. There was never any doubt about who was going to win, and Mark left for TV-am, moving crabwise via the World Service to BBC News. Michael Crick and I stayed on for the great adventure of founding a new news programme when Channel 4 went on the air in 1982.

6 · THEY ARE ONLY PLAYING

Channel 4 News, produced by ITN, was born in an institutional climate of fear and loathing. ITN was part of the television establishment, precisely the culture the new channel had, in the view of the senior team there, been set up to challenge. ITN's bosses were equally sceptical about the idea of doing news in a new way, not least because they felt it was a rebuke to how they had done it in the past. *News at Ten*, the country's first half-hour news programme, had been revolutionary when it was launched in 1967; the organization behind it, run by young rebels turned middle-aged conservatives, did not believe another revolution was needed.

But the finances of running a television news operation forced ITN and Channel 4 into an uncomfortable arranged marriage. Television news was – and remains – hugely expensive, and there was no other organization around with the financial muscle to get a new programme on the air. And for a generation of young idealists the chance to expand into an hour-long programme was a dream come true.

We set ourselves what we called 'the Chad Test'. That vast, landlocked north-central African republic was caught in the coils of an apparently unending civil war, which had begun in 1965. Its rebels were constantly splitting and fighting among themselves, the country's ethnic make-up was bewilderingly complex (Wikipedia lists more than twenty different ethnic groups), there were periodic invasions (by the French and the Libyans), and its people were, unsurprisingly, mired in deep poverty.

The story bubbled up from time to time in the foreign pages of the broadsheets – the *Telegraph* was very strong on foreign news then – and the challenge we set ourselves was to turn it into television. Could we make Mum in Wigan understand Chad?

We tried it in a pilot programme, persuading Trevor McDonald, our main front man for foreign stories, to sit in front of an electronic map covered with towns no one had heard of, an alphabet soup of acronyms denoting the various factions, and arrows that zoomed in all directions to show the ebb and flow of the fighting. We failed spectacularly.

But the Chad spirit animated *Channel 4 News* for its first months nonetheless.

The editor, Derek Mercer, was a lean and hungry newspaper journalist from the *Sunday Times*, with a passion for serious news and matters of, to use one of his favourite words, the 'intellect'. But he had never made a television programme before joining, and it showed. It was during this period that Peter Sissons made his bitter joke about ringing the viewers one by one to tell them the day's news. Channel 4 could not even sell all the advertising in the programme's breaks, and the screen was sometimes filled with a card saying that the news would be back soon.

Those early days of *Channel 4 News* sometimes felt like being in a comic novel rather than real life. In the summer of 1983, I was asked to work as a producer with Trevor McDonald in Lebanon, and since this was a somewhat hazardous assignment, Derek called us in for a pep talk.

We found him more interested in the in-fighting at home than he was in Beirut's factions. He told us, 'I want you both to know that David Nicholas [ITN's editor-in-chief] has expressed complete confidence in me.'

'My God, I had no idea things were that bad,' Trevor said to me as we closed the door and, sure enough, we got a telexed message in Beirut a week later to say that Derek had gone.

The programme really took off when Stewart Purvis took over as editor, bringing with him a reputation for populism of a most un-Channel 4-ish kind, and a brutal determination to drag up standards. Each evening after the show there was a post-mortem, and he would light on one item and tear it apart in front of the entire programme team. He was almost always right in his critique. We all soon realized what a sharp journalist he was, and how well he understood the grammar of television. I worked through every day driven by the ambition to make sure I was not that evening's victim.

The mix of old-fashioned ITN tabloid flair and brainy Channel 4 ambition turned out to be a good one and, though I do not think we ever actually covered Chad, we did develop a new reporting form. We relied on the main ITN news desk to supply basic cover-age of the main events of the day, and focused our energies and resources on context and consequence, adding 'Why?' and 'What next?' to the traditional journalistic questions, 'Who, what, where, when?'

The information that came in from news agencies had just been transferred to a computer system, so the wheezing, thumping machines that used to churn out paper copy had been retired. But every other form of research and information-gathering was man-ual. Instead of the internet there was a cuttings library, kept up-to-date by a team of librarians, who chopped up each day's newspapers and filed the stories under sometimes idiosyncratic headings, and there was the telephone – landlines only, of course.

We kept our notes in green A4 books with red bindings, cover-ing the pages in a spider's web of telephone numbers and jottings, many of them impenetrable because of the private shorthand we developed. Everything we learnt had to be cross-checked with another source. During the Libyan civil war in 2011 I interviewed a long-standing anti-Gaddafi dissident, who had sought asylum in Britain and settled in Manchester. 'You won't remember this,' he said, 'but you rang me after the killing of WPC Yvonne Fletcher [who was murdered outside the Libyan embassy in London in 1984] to double-source a story line.' I was well into my fifties but, reminded of the long-ago rigour of my younger self, I swelled with pride.

Working on *Channel 4 News* allowed us to float above the social and political divisions that were such a feature of British life in the early 1980s. The programme had a vaguely radical and anti-Establishment reputation, so we were welcome on the left and in union circles. But television was glamorous – or at least looked that way to outsiders – so we still went to all the good parties.

In party conference season, we packed our dinner jackets and ball gowns to attend the Tory dances by the seaside, and my memory of the day the IRA tried to kill Mrs Thatcher is indelibly marked by the impression of being at an enormous cocktail party. I had been to the *Spectator* lunch, where my neighbour, Marigold Johnson (wife of the writer Paul), snapped pictures of the attending grandees for her album. In the small hours of the following morning I found her snapping away again, now on the seafront in the bright lights of the fire brigade as they tried to dig Norman Tebbit out of the rubble. There was Keith Joseph sitting firmly on his red despatch box in his silk dressing-gown. There, to chat to, was my Trinity friend Oliver Letwin, looking up at what should have been his bedroom.

The *Channel 4 News* team was, mostly, very young, and because it was small we had extraordinary reporting opportunities early in our careers. That assignment to Lebanon took me to my first war, and because it went well, I became, in my mid-twenties, the programme's regular Middle East reporter.

Today anyone heading off somewhere dangerous will be given

elaborate training and preparation. Not so then: I was simply told, 'Go to Stores and find out what they've got,' by way of protective equipment. In the basement below ITN's studios near Oxford Circus, the Stores manager dug around a bit and finally produced what looked to me like a thick vest. 'I used to have a list of what this thing would stop,' he said cheerfully. 'It'll be just my luck if whatever hits you isn't on my list.'

I went ahead of Trevor to organize interviews and work out where to film, and when I arrived in Beirut, I sought the advice of an experienced local correspondent. She suggested dinner in a restaurant by the Mediterranean, and the evening proved so startling I recorded it in my notebook.

The Spaghetteria is on the Corniche just south of the old town and the Green Line [which divided Muslim West Beirut from the Christian East]. It has a large three-sided glass window giving out onto the sea. Halfway through an excellent dinner – large langoustine and Ksara wine – Amal [a Shia militia] set up a large gun of some sort – I am too inexperienced to know what – and started blazing away. I did my best not to flinch, but my companion noticed my discomfort and said, 'Don't worry, they're only playing.'

The gun was being fired in the street just a few yards from our table, and when the Christians started firing back a Lebanese family moved away from the window. We remained firmly in our sea-view spot. This, I was soon to learn, was daily life as it was lived in the middle of a civil war.

The Commodore, where I stayed, was one of the world's great war hotels, and it was in its heyday in the 1980s, complete with its living myths. There was a parrot, kept in a cage by the plate-glass picture window looking out on the swimming-pool, which could imitate the first few bars of Beethoven's fifth symphony and the sound of incoming shells. The neat bullet hole in the glass next to its cage was said to have been made by an enraged journalist, driven mad by constantly taking cover behind the furniture, only to discover that the bird was performing its favourite party trick.

During one of my stays there the cameraman found a bullet lying in the middle of his bed when he checked in. He suggested to Reception that he might move rooms. 'It's stray bullets on your side of the hotel,' he was advised, 'and car bombs on the other.' He stayed where he was.

I had come all the way to Lebanon and I felt I was still in a satirical novel. But, in truth, I had made a very long journey from the Pitt Club.

Because of the cataclysmic conflicts of the first half of the twentieth century, most men of my parents' generation grew up with the expectation of being warriors. My father was just too young to fight in the Second World War, but after his National Service he joined the SAS as a Territorial volunteer, and spent most of his youthful weekends yomping over Welsh mountains. His maroon beret (the headgear of airborne troops) hung amid the coats and walking sticks in the hall at home in Yorkshire.

Towards the very end of his life he sometimes became confused, but the soldiering instinct was always there. The day before he died (in 2021, at the age of ninety-one) he rang to say that he had received his army call-up papers, and worried that 'I won't be much good to them now.' Rather than challenge him directly I gently reassured him that Britain was at peace, so it was almost certainly an administrative mix-up.

I, in contrast, absolutely loathed the military training in the 'Corps', which was still compulsory when I arrived at Ampleforth, and escaped all that spit-and-polish attention to boots and 'blanco-ing' of belts as soon as I could. By nature and conviction, I was as unmilitary as it was possible to be. Yet here I was in the middle of a war – and working in Beirut in the 1980s meant a quick study in the misery war can inflict.

The Green Line, originally designed to be a temporary truce line, had settled into a permanent scar dividing the city, not unlike one of those resolutely immobile First World War lines of trenches. It ran right through the heart of the old city and the lovely French colonial villas and apartment blocks that had once been so fashion-able in this rich Mediterranean playground.

The line had been fought over for a decade by the time I was reporting from Beirut, and I jotted in my notebook that 'The build-ings are, without exception, pockmarked with bullet holes – so much so that it appears sometimes like a form of adornment, a lace-like tracery that matches the Ottoman scrolls above the doorways and the Gothic windows of the souks and restaurants of the nine-teenth century.'

I went down to the Line one day with my camera crew in search of an ordinary-people-living-through-war story, and this is what we found:

The curious half-life that continues here has developed its own logic and order. Telephone lines run through the rubble, hooked up by a friendly engineer to the main network . . . The 'Green Liners' – the civilians, not militiamen – are half mad, half mercan-tile. Some make a living by collecting spent rounds and selling them to the few remaining visitors in the safer parts of the city.

One child has been driven completely simple, and spends his days climbing up and down a ladder that he moves from one wrecked building to another. He moves his ladder right up to the

89

firing line in which sniper duels are being fought, but no one bothers to shoot him.

We found a Kurdish woman living with twelve children in an enormous but empty flat. She had been driven from the east side by the Christians when the civil war began, and moved into the flat, which was abandoned because of the fighting. Two years ago her husband was hit by a sniper as he left for work. She said she couldn't move because she had nowhere else to go.

I cannot remember whether any of this found its way on screen – I suspect probably not. But reading back my notebook brings some of the images vividly to mind, especially the vast, echoing apartment where that Kurdish woman was squatting with all of her children. It still had the mantel mirrors and double-doors that recalled its opulent past, but it was utterly desolate.

I would not have been able to articulate this back then, but I realize now I was beginning to learn another 'awokening' lesson. Reporting teaches compassion.

7 · TALENT ONLY

I really should have grown out of it by now, but live broadcasting is addictive, and it still gives me an adrenalin rush. It is a little like the thrill I get from skiing. I was lucky enough to learn as a child, and I can push myself beyond my comfort zone while remaining confident that I have just enough skill to claw back control when I need to.

Sometimes, of course, this confidence is misplaced, and I have had my share of wipe-outs, on the slopes and on the air. I came perilously close in the course of a *Sunday* programme item marking the second anniversary of the Grenfell Fire.

One of our guests was the Methodist vicar who took in people who had escaped from the blaze, and comforted families of the victims. I noticed from my briefing notes that he had only just moved to his parish at the time of the tragedy, and began a question with 'This must have been a real baptism of . . .' I managed to stop myself uttering the word 'fire' when I realized where I was heading, but it was too late to turn the sentence into anything coherent.

The fire left an especially bitter legacy because many of the families involved felt their suffering had not been given due weight by the Establishment – the then prime minister, Theresa May, later apologized for visiting the site without meeting any survivors – so any hint of levity on the BBC would have been doubly offensive. I was saved by our guest who – with true Christian charity – threw me a lifeline by picking up smoothly and keeping the tone sober and respectful. My colleagues on the production team were kind enough not to mention it, but *Private Eye* noticed – and ran a gleeful little nib.

The wartime French leader Charles de Gaulle – who built his

political future almost entirely on his wartime BBC broadcasts – wrote vividly in his memoirs about the sense of danger that comes with live broadcasting, describing the way his life was changed as 'the irrevocable words flew on their way'. That jeopardy is always there: once those words are out of your mouth you cannot get them back.

At the same time, you must never allow the audience to be unsettled by any sense that you are nervous or unsure about what you are saying. In deference to the conversational nature of radio, I generally try to avoid the impression that I am thinking too hard about my questions. The discipline required to sound relaxed while remaining utterly focused brings with it – when everything comes together – an exhilarating clarity of thought.

I originally planned to write about my love of reporting and my love of broadcasting together, but they are very different disciplines. It is quite possible to be a brilliant reporter and a rotten broadcaster, and vice versa. One of my first jobs on *Channel 4 News* was to produce the programme's inspirational political correspondent (later editor), Elinor Goodman. No one could match her ability to truffle out the truth of what was happening behind the scenes at Westminster, but her mastery of the technology and techniques of broadcasting was woefully lacking; most of my energies were consumed in really basic lessons like reminding her to wind her stopwatch before timing her scripts.

Both radio and television – television especially – are theatrical media, and performance really matters. So, too, does mastery of the technology, which can be wonderful at its best, but is a beast offering beguiling temptations, and must be handled with care. And while good reporting relies on being attentive to others, their views and their stories, good broadcasting is rooted in egotism. It is, above all, like a gambler's addiction, fed by the thrill of risk.

It has taken time to enjoy broadcasting enough to indulge my addiction freely. I have ended some of my efforts along the way painfully, like a teenager who is determined to become a nicotine addict but keeps being interrupted by coughing fits.

In January 1981, just a few months after I had joined ITN, the United States and Iran signed an agreement for the release of the fifty-two remaining American embassy staff, who had been held as hostages in Tehran for over a year following Ayatollah Khomeini's Islamic revolution. It was a huge story – America, the 'Great Satan', had been humiliated as never before, and Jimmy Carter had lost the White House as a consequence – and ITN planned a live special programme for the handover of the hostages, which was to take place in Algiers.

I was sent out to help our reporter, Sam Hall, purely on the basis that I could speak French. This enabled me to secure a room in the basement of Algerian Television, with a live feed of the pictures from the airport, where the hostages were due to touch down before they were formally discharged into the care of the United States secretary of state.

After some slightly more complex technical negotiations, I managed to arrange a 'four-wire' – a *quatre fils*, as I was told by a helpful producer at ABC News – which allowed Sam to commentate in broadcast quality. He duly picked up smoothly as the plane touched down and, using a pre-prepared pile of notes, talked fluently over the pictures until the hostages took off again on their way to a refuelling stop in Ireland. The programme was deemed a triumph and the office was delighted.

Afterwards I fear I exploited my language skills dishonestly. We were both ravenous, and Sam wanted a steak, but I fancied an Algerian meal (having heard that France's colonial influence still lingered in the cooking) and directed our taxi driver accordingly. We ate delicious plates of couscous and lamb, sprawled on cushions by a low table, the nearest we got to 'local colour'. We caught the first plane home the following morning.

And here was food for thought. We had been in Algiers for roughly thirty-six hours, and Sam had spent almost all of that time stuck underground beneath the television station, several miles from the scene of the action. Since he could not speak the language he had not bothered with the government's briefing – despatching me instead – and almost all the information he included in his commentary had been gathered in London before we left. But he was fluent on air and, through the alchemy of television, appeared to the viewers to be delivering vivid on-the-spot reportage.

The lesson was not lost: you can get away with quite a lot on telly. Six months later I was doing my first reports for ITN's *News at One,* and I kept one of those early scripts. The introduction was read by Peter Sissons: 'Commodity brokers in the City of London – who normally deal in raw materials such as copper or coffee – can now take bids for potatoes. A futures market for the humble spud has been set up in the hope that it will stabilize prices in the British potato trade – which is finding it difficult to cope with European imports. The organizers say the first day's trading was encouraging. This from Edward Stourton.'

'The European Commission still hasn't finalized the sort of common policy on potatoes which guarantees farmers a price for other products like milk,' I informed a no-doubt grateful nation. I knew nothing very much about potatoes, still less about commodities. But I had learnt enough technique to get away with it. I did, however, pay a modest personal cost: my colleagues called me 'Spud Stourton' until the joke ran out of puff.

Television technology was a little more Heath Robinson in those days. Things often went wrong, and when they did the results could be very funny. One evening there was some late-breaking news about a terrible crime (I think involving a back-packer) in Darwin, the capital of Australia's Northern Territory. The *News at Ten* studio director shouted her instruction to the graphics department on the squawk box: 'I want a map of Australia with Darwin marked.' When it came up on screen the viewers were treated to the familiar outline of Australia, with the image of a bearded Victorian scientist in one corner.

Today the technology seldom goes awry, almost everything on rolling news channels is live (it is cheaper) and the audience is likely to be small. *News at Ten*, back in the seventies and eighties, routinely made it onto the list of the most-watched programmes of the week, and almost everyone in the control room and studio (often including newscasters) had been drinking. Each evening's broadcast was fraught with peril, and therefore exciting.

One of the duties of the junior writers – for some complicated reason to do with the unions we could not be called producers – was to give live cues to the newscasters. You would supervise the editing of some pictures into what was known as 'underlay' – because they ran under the newscaster's voice – and if they included some crucial sound, an interview perhaps, you wrote a script with appropriate pauses, the timings dictated, as ever, by that iron rule of three words a second.

As the item went out you would squat on the control-room floor next to the director's chair with your stopwatch, and shout, 'Cue,' when it told you the newscaster should start speaking again. It sounds a relatively simple operation, and it was, but when it worked – when it all sang, when the words enhanced the pictures and the pictures enhanced the words – it carried an electric charge. I knew that millions of people would see this small miracle – without, of course, having any idea of how it was done – and it felt like writing poetry, an act of pure creation.

With reporting duties came the even more alarming performance challenge of live voice-overs. One of the cultural differences between BBC News and ITN has always been that BBC reporters lay their words down first, and an editor paints in pictures afterwards, while the ITN teams did things the other way round. The ITN practice was designed to ensure that even short reports were edited like mini-films, giving pictures their proper priority over words, but it also meant we quite often ran out of time to record our commentary.

This meant dashing down several flights of stairs, script in hand, and squeezing into the stuffy little box at the back of the main control room. When the red light flashed you started reading, with one eye on the pictures rolling in a tiny screen set into the desk. Reports on *Channel 4 News* could be as much as eight minutes long, and if you got into a tangle at the beginning – by, for example, turning over two pages of script at once – you never really recovered.

I learnt to relax by reminding myself that the worst that could happen was looking like a prat. It was not, after all, like being a doctor doing heart surgery, or even a city trader managing millions of other people's money.

Going live from anywhere outside the studios was almost impossible in my early television days, and filing reports from around Britain was almost always done from regional television stations. News editors liked to believe that the laws of physics did not apply to television journalists, and routinely set us schedules that could only be achieved by breaking the law. Garbled Brains, the ghost-like presence I met outside the loo before Peter Sissons's funeral, was a serial offender, and it is surprising that more of us were not killed or maimed in the hair-raising journeys we made around the nation's motorways as we struggled to meet the deadlines he set us.

But America was, of course, well ahead of us technologically, and when I arrived in Washington as a correspondent in the mid-eighties the possibilities seemed dizzying: there were live points all over the city, and my crew simply had to plug in a cable to send my picture and voice all the way to London from, say, the White House lawn or the steps of Congress. Because I was *Channel 4 News*'s first bureau-based correspondent, the programme's editors treated me as a new toy, despatching me to broadcast via one of these new miracle-working gizmos whenever they could.

The technology distorted news values. The programme had a long-term contract for a half-hour of satellite time between Washington and London every day, so it cost nothing to bring back one of my reports. Satellite time from most other parts of the world was extremely expensive and, of course, in large areas of the developing world there were no satellite facilities at all.

As a result, our foreign-news coverage was heavily skewed towards the United States, and I found myself broadcasting about all sorts of places – Asia and Latin America, for example – simply on the basis that I was very slightly closer to them than London was.

The constant demand for live 'two-ways' was, at first, a strain. For several months I suffered from a pull, a little like the vertigo that draws you to the edge of the train platform when a fast train is approaching, to commit career-suicide by doing something outrageous in front of the camera. Usually this took the form of a temptation, hovering just behind my eyes throughout the broadcast, to whip my trousers down while shouting, 'But who cares about the arms-control talks with Gorbachev . . .'

I resisted, and learnt to look the camera steadily in the eye. And then I began to enjoy it. On-air broadcasters in the States are referred to as 'the talent'. At a big George Bush (senior) rally during the 1988 presidential election campaign I had a live spot booked through a local television station, and found it cordoned off with a rope that carried the sign 'Talent Only'. What a sugar-rush it was to unhook it and walk through.

8 · GOING UP TO LONDON TO DO IT

Looking back over my notes and diaries, I am startled by how much of my time I have spent trying to avoid being shafted by my colleagues. This anguished note was scribbled in a notebook in late August 1991, just after the Russian leader Boris Yeltsin had helped frustrate a coup against Mikhail Gorbachev, the last general secretary of the Soviet Communist Party. I was ITN's senior reporter on foreign affairs at the time; I have disguised my rival as 'X' as she remains a friend.

> Humiliated in front of the prime minister yesterday.
>
> 6 p.m., instructed to go to Downing Street for interview. Told there was a dispute with *Channel 4 News* [about who should do it] but the decision was me. All the way down beeped with messages from Stewart [Purvis, my boss] on questions. Met X in Downing Street – she appeared to accept decision.
>
> Taken through to the back room of Number 10. Major offers champagne to toast the failure of the coup. Yeltsin comes through on the phone.
>
> Then I get called out by X to talk to Stewart on the phone; the reason, he's changed his mind. Downing Street people clearly think we are barking mad – this is only reinforced by Stewart calling Haslam [the press secretary] to explain. Stewart's justification: the BBC are trying to poach X, so she must have what she wants.

X duly bagged the prize of that day's big interview. I was far too excited about drinking champagne in Downing Street while the prime minister took a call from the man who had saved Russia to worry about office politics, and I never really got my head around this kind of carry-on. But friendly fire is a fact of life in broadcasting.

And it is something of a commonplace among the broadcasting bosses I have worked for that presenters and reporters are 'monsters'. Some of these bosses have used the word with bitter envy, mostly, I think, because they would have liked to do our job themselves – indeed, one or two have confessed this to me (they cannot quite bear the way the waters close so quickly over their heads when they step down). But the monster conceit is tinged with reluctant admiration too – a recognition that to be a good live broadcaster you need an unusually large dose of self-belief.

Plenty of monsterishness is required to be a convincing correspondent or on-air editor, even more to be a presenter. Most presenters would, if pressed, acknowledge that 'ego' is a suitable collective noun for us. Eddie Mair, of *PM* and now LBC fame, prefers a 'C—t of presenters'. And in television during the 1980s and 1990s, presenting was an even bigger career goal than it is today.

The cult of the news 'anchor' – the old pro who had knocked about a bit before settling into studio life and was trusted by the nation – had been established in the United States by figures like Walter Cronkite and, like so many cultural trends then, crossed the Atlantic. There were only three television channels when I joined ITN in 1979, so if you watched the news – television was trusted much more than the written press – you quickly became familiar with the faces who fronted their news programmes. The multiplication of television channels and the digitally driven fracturing of traditional broadcasting habits have eroded the anchor's role, but it still amazes me that when I mention, say, Sir Alastair Burnet, many millennials have no idea who I am talking about. He seemed a god to those of us starting out back then.

The job offered fame and money – as, indeed, it still does – and, most importantly for trainee monsters, presenting a programme meant no one could drop your story at the last minute (a constant anxiety for reporters). In the early 1990s, after switching between ITN and the BBC in a flibbertigibbet-like manner, I scrambled far enough up the career pole to secure one of these coveted jobs on the BBC's *One O'Clock News*.

I had, by my mid-thirties, managed to acquire much of the necessary skill set.

Mastery of the technology is essential. Unlike radio, live television studios use 'open talkback', which means that the presenter can hear absolutely everything that is being said in the gallery. It is necessary, partly because television presenting involves all sorts of instructions – like which camera you should be looking at – and partly because it gives the presenter advance warning of any sudden shuffling around of the stories. The *One O'Clock News* is especially challenging in this regard because so much is happening in the middle of the day: reports come in late and stories change while the programme is on the air, so it is much more fluid than the evening programmes.

I found it oddly easy to listen to the babble from the gallery while simultaneously speaking to camera. The metaphor of a swan is often and accurately used for newscasting: you paddle furiously beneath the water while gliding with apparently unruffled calm along the surface. One of the more alarming conversations conveyed down my discreet earpiece reached a climax with the director shouting to the editor, 'Amanda, if you do not make up your mind now about what to do we shall fall off the air.' I did not even quiver an eyebrow or twitch a lip.

I had also shown that I could be a fluent ad-libber when occasion demanded. Very soon after being formally appointed to

full-time reporting on *Channel 4 News*, I was sent down to Gatwick
to commentate on the return of a group of hostages who had been
held in Libya by Colonel Gaddafi; their plane touched down with
perfect timing as the programme went on the air, but there was a
delay before the newly freed men emerged onto the stairs (later
gossip suggested they might, quite understandably, have enjoyed a
drink or two after months in a dry Libyan gaol), and I had to talk
for more than half an hour over a single wobbly shot of a plane
parked on a wet runway – without any idea at all of what was
going on.

I had had the presence of mind to bag a set of research notes
about the airport, which had been compiled when Pope John Paul
II arrived there on his 1982 tour of Britain, and I think at one point
I went into a long riff about the model of the plane. The senior programme editor who had been sent down to produce me could do
very little more than hope I would keep talking, but I made it. As
we rattled back to London on the airport train, he told me I had
done my career a lot of good.

And I had become – so I thought, at least – better at playing the
monster game.

In the aftermath of the BBC's now notorious interview with
Diana, Princess of Wales, I opened the *Mail on Sunday* one weekend to read that Martin Bashir was about to be given my job as the
presenter of the lunchtime news on BBC One. It looked a well-
sourced story, and was entirely credible: the *Panorama* reporter had
given the BBC bosses such a scoop that he could have asked for
pretty much anything he wanted.

But leaking to the press can be a dangerous tactic: you cannot
always control the consequences. I have no idea who gave the *MoS*
their tip-off, but if they hoped to nudge Martin Bashir's appointment into reality they miscalculated. The report allowed me to call

my immediate boss. I was quite sure the piece was a fantasy, I told him, but since it was now in the public domain, could he perhaps put out an official statement denying it, just to put matters beyond any doubt?

In the circumstances he did not really have any option, and the note that went out to the Press Association secured my job. I subsequently received a handwritten note from Martin Bashir expressing the hope that the episode would not damage our relationship; this surprised me, as we had not, as far as I was aware, ever met.

But there is another, more nebulous talent in the toolbox you need if you are to become a really successful telly presenter: the trick of conveying who you are in a way that commends you to the viewers. They, of course, need to feel they are in safe hands – there is nothing more unsettling than watching a nervous presenter – and I was reasonably sure-footed in the studio. But beyond that, viewers need to feel that they like the person telling them the day's news, that he or she is someone who shares their values. And here I fell short: when the BBC conducted a survey on public attitudes to its newscasters, I attracted some extremely unflattering reviews.

And I do now wonder whether that reflected a failure to reconcile the social attitudes of my youth with the demands of a mass medium. Elitism and exclusiveness simply do not play very well if you are trying to reach a BBC One audience – in fact, 'broadcasting' must, by its nature, fight shy of elitism. I was good at constructing a neutral BBC persona to hide behind, but my newscasting style was just a little chilly.

I have discovered a devastating example of what was wrong floating around the internet. We broadcast an item about a proposal to allow gay people to serve in the military (it finally became law in 2000), and booked an interview with an especially crusty old general, who we knew could be relied upon to take a thoroughly reactionary view. When we discussed questions, one of the produc-ers suggested challenging him with the example of Lawrence of Arabia, a famously daring soldier who was also gay.

Crusty old general surpassed himself. 'Well,' he puffed, 'at least he went up to London to do it.' I froze. Some odd instinct stopped me reacting with the outrage or laughter that his answer demanded, and the clip shows me thanking him and moving on to the next item as if nothing untoward had occurred.

During my time as a BBC newscaster, Mark Damazer, who had by then become head of television news, told me some of his senior colleagues had remarked that I was unusually 'un-monsterish' – the Bashir incident notwithstanding. I thought it was a compliment, but it was a warning. My newscasting career began early and, after seven years in the hot seat, ended early too.

The job of delivering this news fell to Richard Clemmow, who had become a friend when we had worked together on the road during the 1988 American presidential election, and had then risen to great heights in the BBC hierarchy. He did it very well, encour-aging me to keep reporting for television, but propelling me as a presenter in the direction of radio – where I eventually learnt how to make the audience like me.

ABROAD

9 · I GUESS WE DIDN'T GET TO ENGLAND YET

The call from the foreign desk came through in the small hours of a snow-dumped Manhattan morning in January 1986. 'There's been a coup in Haiti. Fly down to Florida, buy some tropical gear and get yourself to Port-au-Prince pronto.' I climbed into my elderly British Warm overcoat, hailed a cab to take me through the freezing New York dawn to LaGuardia, and emerged blinking into the Miami sunshine a few hours later.

I was greeted with the disappointing news that Haiti's airport was closed to regular passenger traffic. This was unsurprising in the middle of a full-blown revolution – when we eventually got there we found members of the Tonton Macoute, Baby Doc's* feared secret police, being stoned to death in the streets. But the foreign editor did not miss a beat. 'Charter a Learjet,' he instructed, 'and put it on your company Amex card so the accounts department don't notice for a while.' What a thrill it was to set off for my first coup in the comfort of a deep leather seat on an executive jet, gin and tonic in hand as I watched the Florida Keys slide by in the sparkling sea below.

Expenses stories from that era – which are legion – are guaranteed to turn today's journalists green. Television, especially commercial television, was simply awash with money in the 1980s, swimming in great gouts of the stuff. The overwhelming imperative was to spend it – or, in the view of some practitioners of my

---

* Jean-Claude Duvalier, who ruled Haiti from 1971 to 1986, inherited the presidency from his father, François Duvalier, aka Papa Doc.

trade, simply to steal it – and worry about accounting for it later. No one even pretended this was not happening, and when I was first appointed a reporter one of my bosses reassured me that 'Your salary may not be quite what you expect, but you can make it up on your expenses.'

Some of the corruption the culture encouraged was comic-opera grade. For any trip that involved a few days in a decent hotel, some members of the team could be relied on to turn up brandishing bulging laundry bags. Hilton staff from Hong Kong to Hanoi, Honduras and beyond found themselves laying out mountains of newly pressed designer polo shirts, smart chinos and multi-pocketed bush jackets that had been languishing for weeks in Home Counties washing baskets.

Most of this clothing technically belonged to the company, having been bought on the company card as 'emergency' supplies after last-minute deployments. But more mundane household items – children's football socks, rugby jockstraps, ballet tutus and the like – often crept into the mix, and were starched into shape a long way from their natural habitat, the laundry bill to be settled, of course, by the long-suffering accounts department.

There was big money involved too.

War zones have always worked on cash. Flying to Amman on my way to Baghdad during the first Gulf War,* I spent an awkward half-hour at Heathrow explaining why it really was necessary to carry the $30,000 in used notes that had shown up in my briefcase at security.

And cash economies in a country like wartime Iraq created limitless opportunities for playing the black market. If you changed your dollars for dinars on the street you got a very good rate indeed,

_____

* January–February 1991.

much better than the official rate you were supposed to claim on your expenses form.

Arriving in Baghdad on that trip I found that the Iraqi authorities had imposed what was described as a 'garden tax', a payment for the privilege of broadcasting by satellite from our hotel garden. If you bought your dinars on the black market this could be settled for just over $200 a week. Those who claimed it back from their employers at the official exchange rate trousered a weekly profit of no less than $21,000. The ITN team – for the record – stayed clean in the face of this provocative temptation.

In foreign bureaus, the gravy-train rules were semi-institutionalized. During my time as BBC Paris correspondent, part of my job was to sign the camera crew's expenses, and I queried modest but regular claims for an item described on their forms as 'humps'; it was explained to me that these represented 'notional porterage', the tips the crew would have paid someone to carry their gear had they not done it themselves, and could be claimed for every location where we filmed.

ITN's Washington Bureau operated a similarly creative system for its correspondents known as the gardening allowance. One of our predecessors had pointed out to the finance department that the company's lease on his house required him to keep the garden in good order, and that since he was always on the road reporting he could not be expected to do this himself. The gardening allowance was therefore incorporated into the system to cover the cost of employing someone to cut his grass and trim his shrubs, and all future correspondents, whether they actually employed gardeners or not – or, indeed, whether they had a garden – were able to claim it.

That kind of thing sometimes troubled my Catholic conscience, but this was the 1980s, and such practices were routine. The money certainly took the edge off the privations of life as a foreign correspondent. The Haiti incident took place at the end of a house-hunting tour when I secured that job as resident Washington correspondent for *Channel 4 News*. It was one of the best gigs of my career, and not just because it was so rewarding professionally: it changed me personally in a way that only a close encounter with another culture can do.

Washington in the Cold War era of Ronald Reagan and Margaret Thatcher felt like Rome to London's Athens, both in the physical grandeur of its architecture and in its self-confidence. The London I had left behind still had some of its exhausted post-war shabbiness; it was only a few years since the so-called Winter of Discontent, the strike-bound season when Leicester Square was converted into a gigantic rubbish tip, the bin bags piled high around its deserted restaurants and cinemas. This great city on the Potomac, with its vast neo-classical public buildings, was a bright and brilliant contrast to London's scruffy streets, its mists and its muddy river.

Like anyone who had knocked about the Palace of Westminster a little, I had become familiar with the dingy, cramped and often shared offices where British MPs conducted their business in those days; American senators, by contrast, presided over vast suites of rooms in the Dirksen, Russell and Hart buildings on Constitution Avenue. And they were looked after by a flock of press secretaries, administrative officers, policy advisers and sundry other 'staffers' that would have been the envy of most British cabinet ministers.

Everything about the place projected a sense of power, and it really did feel like the capital of the Free World. But for all that, the city's daily rhythms still reflected those of the sleepy southern town it once was.

It was – and remains – a very segregated city, so most of those who exercised all that power lived in the relatively small area of NW – the white middle-class north-west quadrant. Anyone with an

NW address felt an oddly intimate relationship with those who were running the world; the grocery store in Georgetown was known as the Social Safeway because if you shopped there you were almost bound to spot a senator or a secretary of this or that.

One lunchtime I bumped into a White House and Pentagon foreign-policy wonk called Robert Hunter at the swimming club just across from the office; he had been extremely generous to us with his time and had given us numerous trenchant interviews on the state of Cold War relations, but once I had seen him full-frontal naked in the changing room of the 16th Street YMCA I found it quite impossible to look him in the eye (I definitely blame boarding school for that).

My first wife and I married and had children when we were both quite young, so we arrived in Washington as a fully formed family. We lived in Chevy Chase, a smart Maryland suburb just across the District line from NW, and at Halloween my wife and I would sneak out trick or treating with the children, hoping to spot some of the Reagan White House grandees who were our neighbours. Richard Perle, fabled at the Pentagon as a ferocious Cold Warrior, lived just up the road, and we speculated that his Halloween costume might match his political reputation as the Prince of Darkness. Sadly there were no candle-carrying pumpkins outside his front door.

My White House pass gave me access to the heart of power, allowing me to pop into the press room in the West Wing whenever I wanted. It is a much smaller area than it appears on television in that familiar shot of the spokesperson of the day declaiming in front of the presidential seal – the room was built over the Kennedys' swimming-pool – and the atmosphere at the daily briefings was gossipy and collegiate. On 4 July my pass allowed me to take the children down to picnic on the White House lawn as we watched the Independence Day fireworks along the Mall.

The children acquired a slight southern drawl, and learnt to pledge allegiance to the Stars and Stripes at school. They made American friends, and so did my wife and I. Our younger son was born in Georgetown University Hospital. During the summers we rented a house on stilts on the Outer Banks, a sliver of land off the coast of North Carolina, and the children fished for crabs by dangling pieces of raw chicken in the shallow waters of the sound that divided us from the mainland.

We became, in fact, part of the society I was reporting on.

Towards the end of *English Journey*, J. B. Priestley's account of his exploration of working communities across England in the 1930s, the novelist and left-wing polemicist tries to square his love of country with his internationalist instincts, and reports a revealing family exchange: 'One of my small daughters, bewildered, once said to us: "But French people aren't *true*, are they?" I knew exactly how she felt. It is incredible that all this foreign-ness should be true. I am probably busting with blatant patriotism. It does not prevent me from behaving to foreigners as if they felt perfectly real to themselves, as I suspect they do, just like us.'

Being a resident foreign correspondent is exactly that: an exercise in finding out that your hosts are indeed 'true' and, in the case of America in the 1980s, not just the fantasy collection of stereotypes made familiar by the movies.

Work meant I travelled widely across the continental United States. I was ever eager to see more of its variety, and each journey began with a cigarette on the front porch, or stoop, of our double-fronted 'colonial'-style home, a pause to enjoy the tender promise of the morning before the Chevy Chase Cab Company ferried me to the airport. Some of those journeys turned the identity tables, bringing home to me that in the eyes of many Americans I was not 'true' at all.

On a trip to rural Tennessee, I recorded that

As my camera crew and I drove deeper into the ever-thicker pine forests I was reminded that rural America really is remote from modern urban life in a way you simply no longer find in Britain. The trees closed around us and the homesteads – many of them flying the Confederate flag – grew smaller and scruffier. I had a sense of entering an older, unreformed America of hillbillies and dark, secret deeds.

We had come to investigate one of those strange religious stories that make Europeans shake their heads at the sheer weirdness of some aspects of America. A group of fundamentalist Christian parents were suing their local school board because they believed their children were being corrupted by the texts they were using in reading classes. *Goldilocks and the Three Bears* was, for example, faulted because the heroine escapes unpunished despite her wickedness in breaking and entering, then stealing porridge.

One of the schools involved had agreed to allow us to film there, and a teacher explained to her class of ten-year-olds that 'This camera crew are from England.' This was greeted with mute incomprehension, so she added, 'Oh, I guess we didn't get to England yet.'

I had a similarly disorienting conversation with a Midwest farmer I asked for directions while covering the Iowa caucuses during the 1988 presidential election campaign. He listened very carefully to my request, and made me repeat the address I was looking for a couple of times. He then pronounced, with a sense of triumph as he unravelled the mystery of my accent, 'Y'all must be from out of town.'

It is true that we all sounded odder and even more strangulated then; I have some old recordings of my broadcasting in the 1980s, and everyone, including me, speaks like the Queen, only posher. But what kind of a world was this where even the Englishness of my voice was not recognized?

At Cambridge – barely a decade in the past then – I had absorbed a culture in which the way someone spoke told you everything you needed to know about them; not just whether they had been to a private or a state school, but, if the former, which one. Most of us, like sommeliers identifying the very south-facing hillside where a good wine had been grown, could distinguish a Wykehamist from an Etonian by the length of his vowels.

The whole carapace of class-ridden identity that had formed around me during a traditional English education cracked open and quickly fell away.

No one out here on the plains of Middle America knew anything about those small gradations of snobbery that attached to British institutions and ran through every limb of British society, much less did they care. Some of our neighbours in Washington were Anglophiles, with a taste for British flummery, but everything had to be explained. Try rehearsing why Eton celebrates the Fourth of June, but not always on that actual date, why May Week does not happen in May, why the autumn term at Cambridge is called Michaelmas, and why the Michael in that word sounds more like 'nickel' as in 'nickels and dimes': you quickly realize how dull and inconsequential it all sounds.

As for the cousinage, neither the history nor family names nor the armorial quarterings meant anything to anyone. It has been said that Vita Sackville-West's ancestors 'emerged from the mists of the Middle Ages wearing coronets on their heads'; in Washington I waved goodbye to mine as they marched off into the mists of irrelevance. It felt like liberation. During that tour in Washington, I learnt that putting down roots somewhere new can be a deeply enriching experience.

My travelling passion was probably inevitable. I began very early.

BOAC, or the British Overseas Airways Corporation – the state-owned carrier that succeeded Imperial Airways before the war and was eventually absorbed into what is now BA – used to run a kind of early air-miles scheme called the Junior Jet Club. Each journey you made as a member was logged in a gold-embossed book and signed by the captain (the club did not offer any actual financial benefits, recording the glamour of the journey being considered reward enough in itself).

My logbook – the back pages carry black-and-white photos of planes like the Argonaut, the Viscount and the Comet IV – records that I made my first air journey in early March 1958, when I was just over three months old. I flew – presumably with my parents in tow – from Lagos to Kano in northern Nigeria, from Kano to Barcelona and from Barcelona to London. The journey took two days, we covered 3,400 miles, and we flew the last leg in a Stratocruiser, a great beast of a plane developed from America's wartime Superfortress bomber and, with its pioneering double-decker passenger accommodation, famously luxurious.

Luxury and glamour play a big part in the way I look back on my early foreign ventures. They are painted in bold colours: the brilliant blue of the Mediterranean outside my bedroom window in Malta, and the honey-coloured stone of our villa, with its burntumber terraces rising up the hillside behind, a perfect home for the household's pair of tortoises; the vitreous green of the mountain lakes where we picnicked in summertime during the Swiss chapter in our childhood; and, of course, the gleam of sun on snow during the Alpine winters.

The few netsuke-like nuggets of actual memory from those early days are polished by time but still seem precise in their details.

In the 1960s Lausanne was notorious as a retreat for exiled royalty; my mother reported after a party that her dinner neighbour had complained, 'My knees creak every time I curtsey.' Describing another high-society evening, she brought home a grown-up joke from a UN official involved in the prolonged arms control negotiations then under way in Geneva. It went well over my head, but stuck in my mind because it seemed clever and sophisticated: 'Disarmament is like love,' he had declared. 'The slower the better.'

Winter sports were still very much the preserve of the jet set – a term that then meant something. We smuggled ourselves into the club by climbing up the gentle hill just opposite our Lausanne flat, and sliding down – on second-hand wooden skis with cable bindings – until we got the knack. I had lace-up leather boots, which froze my fingers at the end of every day.

When we moved to Geneva, we could see the slopes of Mont Blanc from the verandas of the chalet-style villa where we made our home, and the brilliant snow tempted us into the mountains almost every winter weekend. My mother would make a sandwich for my lunch, which delivered a powerful calorific punch – a slab of bitter cooking chocolate thrust into a fresh baguette – and because I was faster than the adults they simply released me onto the mountainside.

All day I was foot-loose and – of course, in the 1960s – phoneless in this foreign world with its foreign tongue, trusted to find my way back to the car when dusk began to fall and the bars began to fill. I was ten years old. Can you imagine how free that felt?

10 · RED SEA RIG

I keep revisiting the years when Accra, the capital of the West African state of Ghana, was our home, endlessly revising the meaning of our time there in my mind. It has become a palimpsest, the original raw experience now overlaid with memories of later African journeys and, above all, with twenty-first-century debates about Britain's colonial past and the way we remember history.

Ghana came into being in 1957, the year of my birth, the first West African country to gain independence from Britain, so by the time we arrived in the early seventies the modern state was only some fifteen years old. It had been created by uniting four British colonies (Gold Coast, Ashanti, Northern Territories and Trans-Volta Togoland), and had a turbulent history of slaving, gold mining and colonial conflict, notably the Ashanti Wars against the British in the nineteenth century. The Portuguese, Dutch, Danes, Swedes and French as well as the British had all, over the centuries, come through looking for precious metal and, as the traders saw it, productive human flesh to buy and sell.

The country's early years as an independent nation state were not easy: periods of civilian rule were regularly interrupted by coups. General Acheampong, the military dictator when we arrived, was himself ousted and executed by the young Flight Lieutenant Jerry Rawlings towards the end of our time there. My father was briefly detained during the Rawlings coup.

But European lifestyles sailed on largely undisturbed by the procession of coups, elections and counter-coups. 'This place is quite unreal,' I wrote, when I arrived. 'The heat, the palm trees, the servants, it's like a corny film . . .'

We had lived in Munstead, the woodland area near Godal-ming which is best known as the home of the gardener Gertrude Jekyll, while my father was between foreign postings. Africa came as an explosion of sensuality after dank Surrey home life and chilly Yorkshire term times.

And I revelled in it. 'This place is beautiful for the body. I have not felt so healthy for a long time,' I enthused in my diary, adding, 'The greatest, truly Epicurean pleasure here is lying in the evening breeze, physically mellow and mentally vacuous.' I was, despite my apparent social self-confidence, a rather anxious teenager in some ways, and much given to making tallies of tasks that needed to be accomplished. A list I drew up during that first visit to Ghana includes, alongside various set texts to be read during the school holidays, the instruction to 'become golden' during my weeks in the sun.

Old Place, our home, was an airy, spacious bungalow with wide verandas, set well back from the road amid its lawns and trees. I was assigned to the guesthouse, a separate bungalow just beyond the swimming-pool. As for all those servants, 'Godwill, the steward, is an excellent fellow,' I assured my diary, adding smugly, 'I get treated with extraordinary deference as the oldest son.'

Our domestic arrangements were based on those of an English country house sometime in the 1930s. Godwill presided, like the old-fashioned butlers made familiar by *Downton Abbey* or *Upstairs, Downstairs*, directing the rest of the staff but always in attendance when it was time for tea, drinks or meals. Dressed in an immacu-lately pressed white tunic with shiny buttons, he served everything with ritualistic solemnity. The silver, the tea cups and the glassware always shone.

I had grown up with my parents' stories of colonial childhoods, and terms like 'syce' (a groom originally in India), 'amah' (my mother remembered her Chinese nanny in Hong Kong with great affection), and 'house boy' (a demeaning term, I now realize, since it was used of adult male domestic servants in Africa), were familiar to me. But the reality of colonial-style living with servants still required some adjustment.

Godwill, the cook, the maid and the gardener were all housed in the staff quarters behind our house, largely screened from the grounds. I did – at least I think I remember this accurately – feel a twinge of social guilt the first time I saw these modest little buildings around their concrete compound. It was neat and well-swept, but it looked like a miniature version of the kind of African settlement you might see in a film, and the contrast with our comfortable elegance next door could not have been greater.

Godwill and the cook, Kweku, had left their families behind in their villages, and seldom saw their wives and children. This disruption to home lives was the norm, and entirely consequent on the domestic demands of European society. Their lives were so closely intertwined with ours that they became almost part of our own family, but that somehow made the inequities between us stand out more starkly. And a small bit of me – the querulous teenager rather than anything nobler, I'm afraid – reacted against this archaic set-up. 'Having servants hanging around all the time does keep up the standard of behaviour,' I confided, somewhat ambiguously, to my diary.

At weekends we escaped to a beach house on the lagoon formed where the river Volta meets the Atlantic Ocean; the pleasures here were very European – water-skiing, sailing, fishing for barracuda – but the hot, un-airconditioned nights by the water and the blazing days on the sand at least felt African. Social life in Accra was designed to seem as un-African as possible – indeed much of it was based around imitations of the English summer season.

My father's company sponsored a race day at the Accra Turf Club: the Old Place Handicap was named for our house, and the company's best-selling brand of cigarettes was promoted in the big race of the day, the State Express Challenge. Formal dress was required: I think I must have been teasing myself when I recorded that 'Elegantly garbed in a grey-flannel suit, Wedgwood blue shirt and [school athletics] colours tie, and carrying a shooting stick, I descended from the Presidential box to greet various friends in the Members' Enclosure.'

For formal events in the evenings, we opted for a dress code known as Red Sea Rig, which was first popularized by nineteenth-century British naval officers suffering from the heat in their elaborate uniforms; it consisted of dress trousers and shirt, a bow tie and, to make up for the abandonment of a dinner jacket, a showy cummerbund. I had inherited a magnificent maroon number from my grandfather, part of the dress uniform, he assured me, of the Madagascar police. My brothers had new ones made from Kente cloth, the golden silk and cotton mix that was traditionally worn by Ashanti royalty.

There was plenty of casual racism among the European expatriates, who enjoyed this recherché lifestyle. Some of my parents' friends made racist jokes, and I took to noting them in my diary. I think that keeping a record like this was a way of processing the awkward reality that people we saw socially had prejudices I knew to be wrong.

It is clear from the way I wrote about this topic that racism was not considered acceptable, far less funny, within my own family. And while my teenage friends and I tended to keep company with the other white teenagers who had flown out from England for the school holidays, my parents made Ghanaian friends and enjoyed mixing cultures in the way they entertained. Describing a large party we gave in the Old Place garden, for example, I recorded that it began with a Ghanaian ritual: 'Mr Justice Sowah poured libations with strange Ga incantations, and then we all ate and drank to the sound of the [Mozart] Flute and Harp concerto.'

My parents were also omnivorously curious travellers, and took every opportunity they could to explore the country and its neighbours. My father's job required him to make frequent 'tours', staying in company guesthouses in far-flung corners of Ghana to inspect tobacco farms and cigarette factories, and he would take the family with him whenever he could. We visited the ancient mosque of Larabanga, a jumble of beehive-like structures squatting in the barren landscape of the northern desert; we were received in an audience with the Bolga Naba of Bolgatanga in his round mud-and-wattle palace; and we attended – I still have the formal invitation from the King of the Ashanti, the Ashantihene – a durbar at which magnificently accoutred princesses were carried on palanquins in honour of a visit from Prince Charles.

It was in the course of one of these trips that I made my first visit to the slaving forts of Elmina and Cape Coast, on the Atlantic shore west of the capital. These were the embarkation points for slaves on their journey to the Caribbean and the Americas, and the first thing that strikes you as you approach them is the extraordinary beauty of the stretch of coastline on which they lie. If you visit the forts as a casual tourist, it is perfectly possible to be overwhelmed by the majesty of the views: the walls of Cape Coast Castle look out on miles of beach and rolling Atlantic breakers.

But as soon as you engage with the history of these places you realize that all of this sun-drenched gorgeousness was very much part of the numberless individual tragedies that were lived out here. At Cape Coast there is a tunnel leading from the cells, where slaves were held, to the beach where the longboats waited to row them to the slaving ships, and as you step out of the darkness through the

121

Door of No Return, as it is known, you see nothing but palm trees, white sand, sea and sky. This was their last look at home.

My work as a journalist has involved visiting a number of places where evil was done – I accompanied, for example, an Auschwitz survivor back to the camp to mark the fiftieth anniversary of its liberation – and there is always a danger that assignments like that are voyeuristic. I try instead to use them as a means for bringing home the reality of what happened in these places, to give concrete form to a piece of history that my audience may, until then, have understood only in the abstract.

Those who now run Cape Coast Castle have done that to great effect by the simple device of a cut in the floor of one of the dungeons where slaves awaited transportation. There was, of course, no sanitation for the people who were kept – sometimes for weeks in the tropical heat – in these pits. Their faeces gradually formed a crust, which, over time, raised the floor level. When someone died, and many did, the slave traders did not generally trouble to remove the corpse, so the mix was enriched by human remains. To bring home what this meant, the Ghanaian tourist authorities hacked through the encrustation to the original floor, leaving an exposed face on view. It is several inches deep.

I made a note of this in my teenage diary, but my main impression at the time appears to have been 'Rather disturbing to find that half of the castle is being used as a prison: one could look over the wall and watch a scene which is strikingly reminiscent of conditions at the height of the slave trade' – a not entirely unsympathetic comment, but surely, now I reflect on the observation for a moment or two, a grotesque exaggeration. I do not think I really understood the weight these places carry until I went back there some thirty years later, by which time the history of slavery was much better understood, more widely written and talked about.

I was making a Radio 4 documentary about the spread of Christianity in Africa, and while recording on this later trip I noted a piece of hypocrisy that should make any white Christian wince: at Cape Coast there is a neat little whitewashed chapel perched in the centre of the courtyard – just above the main entrance to the slave cells.

Thinking deeply about the slave trade at the time of my teenage visit to the forts would, I suspect, have been extremely unsettling. Of course, the way we lived in Ghana did not involve slavery or anything remotely like it, but we were still white people enjoying great privilege in a Black country, our needs taken care of by Black servants. There was continuity between the past and the present, which did not bear too much scrutiny.

The fundamental unhealthiness at the heart of European households in Africa then was brought home by an incident just before the family left Ghana for good. During a skiing holiday in the Italian Alps my sister had a bad fall and broke both legs, leading to a spell in a wheelchair while she recovered.

My father imparted this news to Godwill on his return to Accra, and our faithful steward fell to his knees and began beating his head against a doorpost, keening the while, to demonstrate his grief. This kind of devotion seemed beyond reason. Why, I wondered uncomfortably, should he have been so moved by a misfortune in a family who were, in the end, just visitors?

It is possible that Godwill's response was a ritual one, that he was expressing himself in the way he imagined we expected. I cannot, of course, judge how genuine his feelings were, especially not now, at the distance of all these years. But I was by then a few years older than the teenager who had been so seduced by tropical sensuality when he first arrived in Accra, and more questioning. It was evident to me that his extreme reaction reflected a relationship with roots in the colonial past.

On that later working trip to Ghana, I sought out our former home at Old Place, and found it looking shabbier, the boundary wall not quite so well whitewashed, and the lawns a little less well trimmed. But Accra as a whole was buzzing, and looked infinitely more prosperous than the city I remembered. I am glad I let Ghana seduce me when I was young – all the best relationships begin that way, and my teenage years there introduced me to a new kind of pleasure. But I am also very glad I went back: returning to a place you have loved is like rereading a favourite book – you will always find something new there, not least because you yourself have changed.

Can you take pleasure, especially sensual pleasure, from visiting a place with a grim history that is partly your own history? I think you can, but the Ghana chapter of my life taught me travelling lessons we Brits – especially we white Brits – should never forget: there is almost no corner of the globe where we have not, for better or for worse, left our mark, and if you are British you are likely to stumble on bits of your history wherever you go. That means travelling with a degree of humility, always ready to learn more about your own past as well as the place you are visiting.

11 · BOSPHORIZING

The natural British attitude to 'the abroad' in the 1970s was still coloured by imperialism and class privilege. The introduction of the
Interrail Pass in 1972 was a huge step towards democratizing foreign travel, but most of the scruffy teenagers I bumped into on train
journeys round Europe during my gap year still seemed to be the
products of private schools and comfortable homes. My diaries
recorded convoluted conversations with other Interrailers at Italian
stations and on Greek beaches as we played the who-do-you-know
games so beloved of the English upper-middle classes.

In that summer before Cambridge my Ampleforth friend Kit
Hunter Gordon and I drove a battered Mini through the Balkans all
the way to Istanbul, and before setting out we arranged a rendezvous with a group of Kit's friends at Cape Sounion, some fifty miles
south of Athens. Amazingly, as this was long before mobile phones
or email, we all turned up on the appointed day at the right time,
and spent happy hours picnicking and swimming together.

The cape is a magnificent setting for a fifth-century BC Temple of Poseidon, which stands starkly on a bluff above the
Mediterranean – a numinous spot, if ever there was one, for Byronic
dreams of ancient Athens and its civilization. But that was not what
we had come for. We chatted away about mutual friends and university plans as if we were meeting at a London pub, cheerfully
exporting the cocktail-party culture of Sloane Square to that remote
headland in Attica.

This kind of travelling – in which you colonize a foreign space
and make it an extension of the world you have left behind – is

almost inevitable when you are on the road for broadcast news. Convenience and good communications are everything, and the way big broadcasting networks can take over and transform a hotel in foreign parts is simply awe-inspiring. I have seen suites of rooms from Amman to Afghanistan metamorphosed overnight into mini versions of BBC New Broadcasting House in London or CBS News Headquarters on Manhattan's West 57th Street.

The great war hotels – the Commodore in Beirut, or the Holiday Inn in Sarajevo – have flourished because they have learnt how to keep this trick easy. Even when suicide bombers and snipers were creating their mayhem, these havens kept the beer flowing and the phone lines humming, allowing us all to work as if we were back on home turf. And at the end of a long day you could always be sure of a good steak as comfort food. The problem with all this European convenience is that you do not really 'travel' at all – however many thousands of air-miles you rack up.

During my time as ITN's diplomatic editor, which coincided with the aftermath of the fall of the Berlin Wall, I spent most of my time checking into one colonized hotel lobby after another.

The end of the Cold War was managed by an alphabet soup of acronym-named institutions. As well as the familiar NATO, UN, G7 and EU (or EC as it was then), lesser-known bodies such as the OSCE (Organization for Security and Cooperation in Europe) suddenly became prominent, and new ones, like the Two-plus-Four (the four foreign powers who carved up Berlin at the end of the Second World War and the two halves of the divided Germany), sprang into being.

All of them made their diplomatic démarches and held their summits and councils, and for months we hacks followed the continent-trotting diplomats from one European capital to another, confined for much of the time in the concrete car parks beneath conference centres where we built our villages of Portakabins and put together our reports. It became commonplace to visit a great European city without seeing it at all during the hours of daylight before the caravanserai moved on, and one centre of European culture merged with another in a whirligig of briefings, live-spots, and late-night unwinding in anonymous hotel bars. Even my drinking companions were likely to be the same wherever I went.

As I shimmied between summits, took in the odd war (the Balkans, Iraq) and struggled to keep abreast of the United Kingdom's relentless lobbying in the run-up to the Maastricht summit (which turned the European Community into the European Union), I tried to keep a tally of how many countries I had visited.

I gave up partly because the very idea of what it meant to be a country was in such a state of flux. Some disappeared – the Soviet Union, Yugoslavia. Others reunited – East and West Germany. Some emerged after decades in eclipse – Georgia, Bosnia, Croatia and Co. Still others – the Asian Stans, for example – reinvented themselves as modern nation states for the first time. Our home is still marked by a legacy of this frenzied period of state-shifting: pull open a drawer of the desk or a cuff-link box on the dressing-table, and you will find tattered wodges of foreign banknotes, many of them bearing the name of a country that no longer exists.

History was on speed-dial during those early years in the 1990s, and I saw quite a lot of it being made. But I was moving around so fast that I seldom had a chance to absorb the meaning of what I witnessed, let alone to appreciate the place to which history had brought me.

When the Soviet flag came down over Red Square for the last time as the Soviet Union dissolved, I watched it lowered. All I can remember is the cold – so intense that I could not make my lips move when I tried to deliver a few words to camera. It reduced me to silence at the closing of one of the most significant chapters in the human story.

When Checkpoint Charlie, that chilling symbol of Cold War tension, star of so many spy books and films, was finally cleared from its Friedrichstrasse junction, I was there. I recall a brilliant soundbite, but little else. Douglas Hurd, Britain's foreign secretary, delivered an elegant epitaph for the dead of the Berlin Wall: 'And now, Charlie,' he declared, as the jaws of a great crane descended on the checkpoint's roof and swung it away to its new home as a museum attraction, 'we are bringing you in from the cold.'

The memories are so fleeting because these moments of history were almost always followed by a scramble edit for *News at Ten*, a hasty car journey to the airport and a plane ride to the next story that would make a lead. I did my best to recollect in the tranquillity of a club-class seat on the way, but most of it was just a blur.

Very occasionally, and usually because something went wrong, the pace slowed down enough for me to catch more than a glimpse of where I was. When it happened it was, because of those strange, tumultuous times, especially rewarding.

Churchill's Iron Curtain was more than a metaphor. Until that miraculous year of revolutions, 1989, huge swathes of our continent were hidden from us. Jewels like the great Polish city of Kraków and the charming old capitals of the Baltic States, now so familiar to stag weekenders, were forbidden territory, simply inaccessible in the ordinary way of things. So when the Curtain was drawn back, there was a feast to enjoy.

In some areas of Russia, foreigners were specifically banned by Soviet law – for reasons of state security. When the chance to visit one came up I found it irresistible. The city of Saratov lies on the Volga river some five hundred miles to the south-east of Moscow. It was an industrial centre, stuffed with technical institutions, scientific research centres and laboratories, and there was an air force base nearby – in other words, it had everything the Soviet state liked to hide from the prying eyes of outsiders. But while we were preparing a profile of Boris Yeltsin, newly emerged as the dominant figure in Russian politics, he decided to make a trip there, and when we enquired whether we could cover the visit his office agreed without demur.

It was February: the Volga was a vast frozen steppe, and right across the river, as if arranged by Lowry, dozens of dark figures fished through the ice. Parts of the city looked as if they had not changed since the 1917 revolution; old wooden houses, gaily painted, leant crazily across narrow streets. Even on the journey from the airport we saw enough to know that this was a different Russia, one none of us had seen before. The cameraman straightened up in his seat in the car, like a spaniel sniffing the breeze before a shoot.

But when we arrived at the hotel we had booked, the receptionist looked at us in surprise – and not in a good way. 'You are foreigners,' she stated flatly, as if it was the worst possible charge she could make. We explained that we had come to film Boris Yeltsin, who was, in theory at least, running the country, and that we had his permission. To no avail. 'You must speak to the KGB,' she declared, handing a phone across the desk to our Russian translator.

This brought us up short. The notorious security service had been formally abolished a couple of months previously, in early December. But there was no arguing with the voice at the other end of the line. We were told we must spend the night in a KGB safe house and report to the local Lubyanka, as KGB offices were known, in the morning, and since there was no budging the receptionist – the modern comforts of our brutalist Soviet hotel suddenly seemed very appealing – we piled back into a van and made our way through dark, frozen streets.

Our lodgings – which were indescribably squalid – were presided over by a *babushka* who informed us, 'This is where they put all the strange foreigners.' Dinner that night consisted, eccentrically, of two slightly mouldy apples and a bottle of vodka between four of us. We were given rough blankets and camp beds to sleep on. Our Russian translator was more shocked by this turn of events than any of us: she was a daughter of the *nomenklatura*, the Soviet equivalent of the Establishment, well-educated and always smartly dressed. She was not accustomed to this kind of treatment.

The *babushka* in charge handed me a bill in the morning; the value of the rouble had collapsed so completely that when I came to claim the money back on my expenses I found that the cost for the four of us came in at under a fiver.

The colonel who greeted us at KGB headquarters was dressed entirely in leather, and her impersonation of a James Bond villain was pitch-perfect. She brushed aside all our talk of permissions from the president's office – 'Boris Nikolayevich can do what he likes in Moscow, but down here I run things' – threatened us with everything from arrest to deportation and solemnly filled out an official report detailing the transgression we had committed simply by being in the city.

Finally she instructed us that we must take the next plane back to the capital, which left at four that afternoon. Then came the kicker: 'If you miss the plane,' she warned us, 'no one will take you in – I shall make sure of that. The nights here are very cold [minus 15 centigrade], and you will almost certainly die.' There was not a flicker of a smile.

Being detained and threatened with death by exposure felt like a badge of honour – especially since the threat came from a notorious security agency that had been formally abolished. The surreal nature of the experience quickly took over from our disappointment at having our wings clipped. In a diary piece for a weekly magazine I described our KGB colonel as a 'functionary dutifully performing a function rendered entirely worthless by change'. How wrong I was. Today's Russia suggests that Yeltsin, not the colonel, was on the wrong side of history.

There was another telling – though fleeting – moment at the airport before we left. The four of us – our Russian translator and three very obviously Western men – were spotted by a group of local young women. Any one of them, with their furs and hats and glowing cheeks, could have played the part of Natasha in Tolstoy's *War and Peace*. The look that lit up their faces at the sight of us revealed that we were, without doubt, the first foreigners they had ever seen, and for a beat or two I felt like Ferdinand when he is spotted by Miranda in *The Tempest*: un-bathed and unshaven we may have been, after our night as guests of the Committee for State Security, but to them, just for that moment, we were the 'goodly creatures . . . beauteous mankind' of their brave new world.

It was the oddest of trips, and produced absolutely nothing worth broadcasting. But it taught me more about Russia – about its subterranean power structures and its dangerous seductiveness – than almost anything else I did there.

And there were moments when the job gave me travelling experiences denied to most other people – sometimes even the locals. When Nelson Mandela was released after his twenty-seven years in gaol, my assignment was to stand on a flatbed truck outside his home in Soweto to report reaction there for a live ITN programme. The day began well, with thousands of ANC supporters jamming the streets, chanting '*Amandla*', power, and stomping out a Toyi-toyi, the half dance, half military march that had become the movement's signature form of protest.

But the great man's actual release was delayed by several

hours, during which a drenching rainstorm cleared the streets. We had arranged for a senior ANC official to stand with me on my truck and bring to the crowd the joyful news that Mandela was free, but by the time it actually happened the crowd had melted away, and the two of us were very wet.

That Soweto sojourn did, however, bring an enjoyably unscripted moment that reflected the emotions of the occasion. The following day, Desmond Tutu agreed to appear on *News at Ten*, and one of ITN's senior editors – who was there just for the thrill – offered to make himself useful by escorting the archbishop to the live point from his house just up the road. The streets had filled again by this time, and the whole of Soweto was one swinging party. When Tutu appeared at his front door he was immediately hoisted shoulder high by the crowd; our editor, determined not to lose the evening's star interviewee, kept a firm grip on the archbishop's arm and was hoisted up by the crowd too, borne along on this tide of celebration, like a Roman emperor in triumph.

Later I felt in need of a soft drink and a snack to keep me going, so I nosed my way through the crowd to a convenience store at the nearest junction. It was a balmy South African evening, and although the excitement of the day had begun to subside, the streets were still alive with what we might, in Mediterranean cities, call a *passeggiata*. One or two faces registered surprise at the appearance of a white face in this Black heartland, but happiness had set the tone of the evening, and no one questioned my presence. There was cheerful chatter everywhere, full of hope.

The following day I had a cup of coffee with an old friend from my Ghana years who had married a South African and settled there. When I described my Soweto evening the colour drained from her face: she had lived in Johannesburg for years but had never set foot in the Black suburb just a short drive from her home.

She found the idea of spending time in Soweto after dark simply terrifying. We have lost touch, but I do not imagine she feels very differently today.

Mandela's release was a truly momentous moment. It began the unwinding of all those coils of destructive passions apartheid had spun, not just in South Africa but in the United Kingdom too. And if I think back to that day it is my walk to the local shop that comes most readily to mind. It is easy to forget what a privilege it is to be given the kind of glimpse behind the curtain that travel as a journalist offers. And it is the moments of ordinary life in extraordinary situations and places that I treasure most: they bring home the 'true-ness' of other peoples and nations that so perplexed J. B. Priestley's daughter.

In Britain after the Brexit vote the idea took hold that if you spend too much time away from your national home you become deracinated, that, as Theresa May famously – or infamously, depending on where you stand on these matters – put it, 'If you believe you are a citizen of the world, you are a citizen of nowhere.' My experience has been precisely the reverse: because I have travelled so widely and moved so often, I treasure the sense of home more than ever, and make one wherever I am.

When Ariel Sharon suffered a massive stroke in January 2006, I jumped on the first flight I could find to Tel Aviv to report the story for the *Today* programme. The Israeli prime minister was to linger on in a permanent vegetative state for a full eight years before finally succumbing to kidney failure. At the time, of course, we had no idea of what was in store, so I stayed on for a few days on a death watch. He was such a massively dominant presence in Israeli politics that it was difficult to imagine the Middle East without him.

A period of enforced idleness in the American Colony Hotel in Jerusalem was not an especially arduous assignment. It is extremely comfortable, looks like the set of an Agatha Christie costume drama, and is full of history – everyone from Lawrence of Arabia to Tony Blair has stayed there, and the last Ottoman governor of Jerusalem pinched one of its bedsheets when he wanted to raise a white flag to the British in 1917.

On Sunday, with no professional duties beyond keeping my phone switched on in case the comatose prime minister took a turn for the worse, I decided to go to mass – this was, after all, where the central act of Christian worship had been invented. But going to mass near the place where Jesus and his disciples had gathered for the Last Supper proved more difficult than you might imagine: if you look at the skyline of the Old City you will see plenty of church towers and spires, but once you step into the rabbit warren of streets within its walls you lose sight of them, and finding a church from ground level is a real challenge.

I spotted, serendipitously, an elderly Palestinian woman carrying a prayer book and a rosary, and since she had the harassed look of late mass-goers everywhere I followed her – I hope not too creepily. We ducked under an archway, then through the ancient doors of what I now know to be the Franciscan Church of St Saviour, a blaze of marble and gold that would have looked harmoniously at home in Tuscany.

The mass was said entirely in Arabic – naturally – and since my knowledge of the language is limited to greetings and thank-yous I could not understand a word of it. But the form of the liturgy – again, naturally – was exactly as it would have been in the parish church on Brixton Hill back at home, so it was both completely foreign and completely familiar, the experience at once alienating and comforting. And that sense of connection between two worlds was sealed by the weather: it was January, and I walked back to the Colony through a damp chill of precisely the character you are likely to experience on a wet winter's day in south-west London.

World citizenship entails civic duties as well as privileges. Wherever I go, and no matter how pressed I am, I always now try to escape the convenience bubble of Western-style hotels and dig around a little bit for what the ancient Romans called the *genius loci*, the spirit of the place. This is my nod to – if the concept is not too abstract and pompous – 'moral travelling'.

Radio is a more modest medium than television. When all you carry is a microphone you do not need to colonize your environment in quite the same way. And radio gave me a whole sequence of travelling experiences that involved searching for a *genius loci* wherever I went, assignments that were the precise opposite of all those deadline-driven years as a diplomatic editor.

These treats came about as the result of an epiphany experienced by a BBC producer, Phil Pegum, while on holiday in Cyprus. Visiting a church in Paphos, the town where St Paul is said to have out-foxed and blinded the false prophet Bar-Jesus, Phil had the inspired idea of a Radio 4 series following in Paul's footsteps around the Mediterranean. The BBC owed me a favour or two at the time, and I got the gig as the presenter.

Over a period of weeks, and moving at an altogether statelier pace than, with my news background, I was accustomed to, we wound our way from Jerusalem to Damascus (a much more complicated modern journey than Paul would have known, owing to the settled enmity of Syria and Israel), along the via Egnatia to Philippi in Greece, on to Ephesus in Turkey and back to Greece to explore Paul's time in Corinth and Athens, finally finishing up in Rome.

We made our pilgrimage in the aftermath of 9/11 and the defeat of the Taliban in Afghanistan, and much of the region felt edgy – it was pretty clear that the War on Terror had a lap or two to run – so we mixed current affairs with history as we went. The resulting radio series brought home how important a sense of place and its

135

past can be when you are trying to understand the big stories of today.

Programmes like these can only work if you take your tourism seriously. The places we visited illuminate Paul's story and bring it alive. The 'street called Straight' still cuts through the heart of Damascus – or at least it did in those pre-civil war days – and we found it every bit as busy and noisy as it must have been when Ananias was sent down it to find Paul after his Damascene conversion. In Ephesus the amphitheatre, where silversmiths rioted because they feared Paul threatened their trade in pagan effigies, still stands. My job was to take the listener with me as I walked through these places, giving new life to the old tales, and to do that I had to watch and listen and absorb.

The series proved such a success that we turned it into a franchise, and subsequently followed the footsteps of Moses, Muhammad and Jesus.

Muhammad presented a particular challenge as we could not, being non-Muslims, follow his footsteps to Mecca. In our striving for authenticity, we spent a good deal of time in the Saudi desert. The opportunities for wordsmithing in a desert – once you have done the sun and the sand – can be limited, but sound, of course, plays as much of a role as words in radio tourism. I took a photograph of Phil sitting – uneasily – on a camel, with his microphone cable dropping down to ground level, the mic up close to record the authentic sound of hoofs sinking into soft sand. Only at the BBC will you find such meticulous attention to auditory detail.

Radio allows you to weave ideas as well as history into the description of what you are seeing and where you are, and that can give new meaning to familiar texts.

I had, of course, read the Quran before setting out on the Muhammad journey, and was struck by how often water features in its descriptions of paradise. The reward for the blessed is 'Gardens graced with flowing streams' in Sura 48; it has 'shading branches' and 'a pair of gushing springs' in Sura 55; and those who gain entry will enjoy 'spreading shade, constantly flowing water, abundant fruits' in Sura 56.

We arranged to interview an Islamic scholar from Jeddah under a Lote Tree (Lote Trees also feature in the Quran) amid the dunes just outside the city. The scene was almost a cliché: a herd of camels grazed rather disconsolately off the few bits of scrub poking through the sand, there was a backdrop of dun-coloured hills, and otherwise nothing but sand as far as the eye could see. In this cauldron-like heat, those paradise passages suddenly made more sense than they had done when I first read them, looking out at my soggy garden in south London. If you lived beneath this blistering sun, of course you would dream of a heaven of streams and shady bowers.

Phil Pegum was one of the last truly great stokers on the BBC gravy-train. When Radio 4 pointed out to us that we had done the full set of big figures from Christianity, Judaism and Islam, he took us in the footsteps of missionaries – we collected air-miles to Central America, West Africa, Japan and Washington – and then of Chairman Mao on his Long March across China in the 1930s.

Back in the Middle East, water proved an especially productive way to keep this gravy-train on the rails: we tempted the commissioners with the idea of sacred rivers, and they took the bait. A river journey is a wonderful narrative device – you simply let the flow carry you onwards.

The Jordan turned out to be a sadly diminished and often muddy stream for much of its journey from the Golan Heights to the Dead Sea, but its banks proved wonderfully rich in history. The Nile was every bit as majestic as it should be, and since Egypt was in the middle of a revolution we had it largely to ourselves.

There was a moment in Cairo, at the end of our Nile journey, when I realized that I really had managed to shake off the news-hunger that had dominated and sometimes distorted so much of my travelling. Phil and I were dining at Shepheard's Hotel, or at least at the replacement built after the original landmark building was destroyed by nationalist riots and fire in 1952. We had come partly because of its history – Shepheard's features in *The English Patient*, an Agatha Christie yarn and even a Trollope short story – and partly because of a rather romantic memory of my mother's: she had stayed at Shepheard's for three weeks on her own when she was a very young girl.

In 1946 she was allowed to visit her parents in Addis Ababa for an extended stay. She took off from Poole Harbour in Dorset aboard a Sutherland seaplane, touching down briefly off Nice to refuel on the way to Cairo, where she was due to change planes. But the second leg of her journey was delayed because she could not find her yellow fever certificate (health passports were a familiar feature of African travel long before Covid).

Temporarily orphaned and still, as she tells the story, wearing her tweed school skirt, she was delivered into the care of one of King Farouk's nieces. And the princess, having little use for an English girl, booked her a room at Shepheard's and gave her a groom and a horse. While things were sorted out my ten-year-old mother spent her days riding in the desert around the Pyramids, and her nights in the glamour of the most famous watering-hole in North Africa. The certificate was eventually discovered pinned to the inside pocket of her jacket, and she was able to complete the journey.

In the middle of dinner word reached us – from an anxious waiter – that there was more violence in Tahrir Square, the heart of Egypt's revolution and only a short walk away. Most tourists would, in such circumstances, no doubt have removed themselves from the area of danger; most journalists would certainly have done the opposite, because trouble usually offers a story. Phil and I paused to wonder which we were, tourists or journalists; in the end it seemed simplest to stay put and order another bottle of wine.

The last of our water-borne adventures took us to Istanbul. The Bosphorus is not, strictly speaking, a river but, like the Jordan and the Nile, it has defined the history and culture of the lands around it. And it gave me a word that eloquently echoes the kind of relaxed and receptive travelling style we were aiming for.

An American writer, who had been seduced into permanent exile here by his view across the water to Asia, gave me a definition of what he called Bosphorizing: 'giving way to the beauty of the place and watching your will and ambition, which were formed in the West, suddenly dissolve'. Istanbulites informed us that this happy state was best achieved with a plate of grilled fish and a glass of arak.

12 · 10 BEDWELL ROAD

Sometimes on these journeys I had to pinch myself in case I was in a dream. Could it really be true that I was being paid to indulge my curiosity about places I had always longed to visit? I feel special gratitude that my trade has taken me back to the land of my birth.

In conversation, my parents routinely referred to places like Port Harcourt, Ibadan and Kano as if they were talking about Guildford or Sunningdale, so Nigeria always felt as if it was familiar territory. But I had to wait for some forty years after that Junior Jet Club journey from Lagos to London in 1958 before I went back as an adult.

The first trip nearly ended in disaster – precisely because it involved bending the world to fit my own needs, a colonizing journey in the best telly tradition.

In the late 1990s I presented a BBC Two foreign affairs programme called *Correspondent*, and spent much of my time travelling to glamorous locations that would provide striking backdrops as I introduced reports. One week the choice fell on Kano in northern Nigeria. My diary was extremely tight, but the production team and I worked out that, if all the flights fell right, I could just manage the day of filming that was needed.

The BBC driver who met me at Lagos international airport and drove me to my connecting flight at the domestic hub tipped off the airport authorities that I was there – I am sure his intentions were the best, but it turned out to be a tactical error. A passing BBC man proved a tempting target.

While waiting for my flight to Kano I was approached by an

airport official. The harmattan – a sandy wind that comes down from the Sahara – had, he informed me courteously, blown especially hard the previous day, and all flights had been cancelled. Yesterday's passengers had been transferred to today's plane, and there was no room for me. My carefully worked schedule was about to collapse, and I exploded. There was a beat before he said, 'Unless you can help me with a dash.'

The word 'dash' is used across West Africa to mean a gift or, in circumstances like this, a bribe. When I asked how much dash he wanted, he gave a figure that was rather larger than the cost of my plane ticket. The rules about this kind of thing were less rigorous then: because of that super-tight schedule, I swallowed and agreed.

The flight was called and he duly appeared at my side, whisking me through security at the head of the queue. So far so good. But as we walked across the tarmac it became apparent that very few passengers were heading for the plane. When I pointed this out I received a reply that was less than reassuring: 'That is true, but the plane only has enough fuel to carry these numbers.'

When we reached the boarding steps I turned and challenged him, politely of course: 'Look, you have been very helpful, but it's perfectly clear that I could have got on this plane without dashing you.' I was smiling in a reasonable way. 'Why don't I give you half the sum we agreed and we'll call it quits?' Again, one of those unnerving beats, as he looked over my shoulder at a plane a couple of hundred yards away on the tarmac. It was also loading up – but for a flight to a different northern destination. 'If you pay me in full,' he smiled back, 'I shall make sure your luggage doesn't go to Kaduna.' Game, set and match. I dug out the dollars.

A later, slightly more relaxed, Nigerian assignment gave me an opportunity to hunt my past. I arrived in Lagos armed with a couple of addresses, and on the day before flying back to London I had leisure to track them down.

Temple Road, where my parents had lived and so my first home, had been renamed after a Nigerian politician, and I found that number 18, where our house had once stood, had been turned into an office block. But my paternal grandparents' house at 10 Bedwell Road was still standing, a whopping great whitewashed statement of colonial confidence set in an acre or so of grounds.

The house would have belonged to the British colonial authorities when it was Grandpa's official residence, and was presumably inherited by the Nigerian state at independence. Bedwell Road is in Ikoyi, one of the snootiest neighbourhoods in modern Lagos – it is sometimes described as the city's Belgravia – but the property had been left to rot: the veranda on the first floor was boarded in and the grounds had run wild, although the remains of a rose garden were still discernible.

I was able to see it close up because, although the building itself was locked, the gates hung open. A family had made their home in the gatehouse, but they had no idea who now owned the property or whether there might be any plans for its future. There was a man snoozing the day away on an old mattress under the vast coaching porch over the front door, but I could still imagine my grandfather – who was always immaculately turned out – striding out to his official car in his crisply pressed uniform.

He was the inspector general of police here in the 1950s, and the way his home had been abandoned – but not knocked down – struck me as an evocative metaphor for the way that period of history has been, rather awkwardly, parked out of sight.

In Britain we have – at least I think we have – come to a collective understanding of some of the sins in our imperial past: you will not find many people today willing to defend the Amritsar massacre of

1919, when General Dyer ordered his troops to fire on an unarmed Indian crowd, killing several hundred, or, to take another example of British barbarity, the 1860 sacking of the Summer Palace* in Beijing. But our understanding of the more recent period of post-war decolonization is messier, blurred partly by its proximity.

My grandfather was a very decent man and a dedicated public servant, and his role in the final chapter of that process has always intrigued me. He was the penultimate leader of the whole colonial police force, and in the early 1960s, as the Labour government accelerated the process of decolonization, his job was to dismantle the service to which he had given his working life. Inspired partly by curiosity about that experience, I considered attempting a history of colonial policing – having written a book about the BBC during the Second World War, plus an official history of a publisher, and edited one about my Cambridge college and another about the *Today* programme, I had come to enjoy institutional history.

Part of the challenge with projects like this is the awkward fact that the heroes you find in these stories are likely to seem deeply flawed to today's readers because of prejudices and views we now abhor. Many of the Second World War BBC types I met in my researches, for example, showed great physical and moral courage in their pursuit of the truth, but their world was, of course, soaked in sexism and snobbery.

My solution has been to dig deep into personal diaries and autobiographies, which help explain the attitudes of the day: I found that allowed me to tease out my heroes and their times, putting a little distance between them and me without squashing them altogether with censorious twenty-first-century judgements.

---

* During the Second Opium War, British and French troops captured, looted and then destroyed the historic residence of Qing dynasty emperors.

So, part of my research for the new project – alongside grim duties like studying the searing story of the Mau Mau emergency* – was to dig out similar material written by police officers serving in far-flung corners coloured red on the map, and I tracked down what promised to be a small gem: a slim volume called *The History of the Nigerian Police*, written by a serving officer and published in 1950 by the government printer in Lagos, price three shillings and sixpence.

The book includes some fine photographs of officers in an array of astonishingly elaborate uniforms – testament to the British Empire's love affair with fancy dress – but the most compelling section is dedicated to what is described as 'Constabulary Duty'. This covers occasions when the police operated as a paramilitary force sent to assert British control over rebellious civilians. These episodes all involved violent confrontation – the police armed with guns, the 'pagans', as they are weirdly described, armed with poisoned arrows, spears and stones. And the most startling fact to emerge from these stories – to me at least – is that the destruction of individual houses or sometimes whole villages was apparently regarded as an appropriate response to the non-payment of tax.

Occasionally things go badly for the authorities. A Corporal Amadu Panda tells the story of C. M. Barlow, an assistant district officer, who was so preoccupied with the destruction of a tax evader's house in the Dimmuk hills that he ignored the warnings of his police escort: 'Then from a house on a hill to the north a pagan emerged and blew a horn,' Panda reported. 'I heard Mr Barlow ask

---

*   During the Mau Mau uprising (1952–1960), the British suspended civil liberties in Kenya and detained tens, possibly hundreds of thousands of people. Many of them were brutally tortured while being interrogated. The Mau Mau were also guilty of numerous war crimes and murders.

Kworbai, "What are they doing?" To which Kworbai replied, "They are going to kill us all." "Let's get on with our work," said Mr Barlow, and the police continued knocking down the house.' Shortly thereafter the local people began stoning Mr Barlow's detachment, and he was struck on the back of the head, dying the following day without regaining consciousness.

More usually, however, superior weaponry delivered the desired effect. In 1932 a substantial detachment of police was sent into Zinna, a district of what was then Adamawa Province in northeast Nigeria, to pacify the inhabitants of two mountain villages who had 'refused to be counted for the annual tax assessment'. Despite attracting 'a few poisoned arrows', the police dealt with the first village in the approved manner for managing recalcitrant contributors to the Revenue: 'The patrol searched the hilltop area, and, in view of the resistance encountered, destroyed the houses on the hilltops, leaving those on the lower slopes as an object lesson that hilltops, however difficult of access, do not confer immunity on their inhabitants nor valleys leave them especially vulnerable.'

In the second village, Debu, there was a similarly 'exemplary' approach: 'A final message was shouted to some of the inhabitants, who could be seen on the hillside, to tell their headman to come in and submit or they would have their huts destroyed. The message was greeted with jeers, so the patrol moved up the hillside and destroyed the headman's compound.' The casualties on the police side during these two operations were recorded as 'one carrier killed [by a poisoned arrow], one constable wounded by a stone fragment, and three carriers and three constables staked in booby traps'. The number of dead among the local people was estimated at twenty-four.

There is quite a lot to be shocked by in *The History of the Nigeria Police*, but I was perhaps most shocked by the tone in which the book is written: there is no acknowledgement at all that there is anything uncomfortable about the way these stories are told – far from it. In fact, the writing assumes that readers will share the view that these were police achievements deserving celebration.

In his opening Note the author regrets that the police no longer had to get involved in episodes like these:

> There are few districts today where we provide an armed escort to touring Administrative Officers, and a patrol is a rarity, and in the transition we are losing a priceless asset. Gone is the easy comradeship of march and camp, which brought officers and men so close together and provided such an opportunity for the understanding and appreciation of one another. Nearly gone is the opportunity for the men to show their magnificent loyalty, in times of stress and danger, to their leaders and training.

These were the assumptions behind an officially sanctioned publication that came out at the beginning of the decade of Nigerian independence, just seven years before my birth in Lagos. That brings this world view very close to home. In the end I gave up on the colonial police book, partly because I realized what a vast canvas I would need to cover, but also because I simply did not feel I could bridge the abyss that divides my world from that of Corporal Panda and Mr Barlow.

I also sense that feelings among Nigerians about this period are more complex than one might imagine. In the aftermath of the 2019 British general election, I recorded a Radio 4 *Analysis* programme about the Labour Party and patriotism, and we interviewed my newly elected local MP in south London, Florence Eshalomi, who is of Nigerian heritage.

She explained that when it came to love of country, she made a critical distinction between Englishness and Britishness. The former she dismissed with a laugh: 'Englishness, I think for me personally, is something that I wouldn't associate myself with. Instinctively, when you talk about Englishness, I think there's that vision of the English upper class and I want to think back to Shakespeare and Dickens's days!'

But she was very happy to sign up to the idea of Britishness. 'For me, British is about Britain being open, Britain being inclusive, Britain, you know, welcoming a number of people, whether it's from the *Windrush* generation, the men from Burma, the Sikhs, everyone that contributed and helped Great Britain during the wars – First World War, Second World War. That's what I hold on to. Britain can still be Great Britain, has to still be great. As a British woman, I want it to be great, but I want Britain to be great for everybody that currently lives here, and people who want to come here as well.'

'Who on earth,' enquired our editor when we played him the programme before it was broadcast, 'are the men from Burma?' I suspect most of our Radio 4 audience were similarly perplexed, but any Nigerian listener would have known immediately whom Florence Eshalomi meant – and so did I, because I came to know one of those 'men from Burma' very well.

My late father-in-law's journey to Nigeria is a challenge to conventional ideas about builders of the British Empire. Brought up in the Welsh valleys, he left school at fourteen so that he could contribute to the family budget – his father was a village policeman. He joined the army in the Second World War as soon as he was old enough, and – how this happened is not quite clear, but he was a clever man – found his way to Sandhurst and an officer's commission.

Active service took him on secondment to a Nigerian regiment, and he was dropped behind Japanese lines in Burma to fight with

147

the Chindits. His troops were Hausas, from northern Nigeria, and he learnt to speak their language with them in the jungle.

After leaving the army at the end of the war – with a wound and a 'mention in despatches' – he offered his language skills to the Colonial Office, and was duly sent to northern Nigeria as a district officer. Nigeria was his home for the next twenty years, and at independence the new Nigerian administration asked him to stay on. For a further three years he served as a permanent secretary in the Nigerian civil service.

John King's story was a remarkable example of the way war and empire could transform lives, and his jungle service made him part of a history that is every bit as Nigerian as it is British. Forty-five thousand Nigerian troops served during the Second World War, and the 'men from Burma' are part of Nigeria's sense of its own identity. They are much more prominent in Nigerian culture than they are in our own, and, as Florence Eshalomi's comments suggest, they reflect the complexity and depth of the relationship between Nigeria and the United Kingdom.

John's time in Nigeria overlapped with my grandfather's; I am often surprised by how many British still count Nigeria as part of their family story. It is a decade since that visit to my grandfather's house at 10 Bedwell Road, and I have no idea what has happened to it since. It was a handsome building, and it would be nice to think that, rather than being knocked down, it has found a purpose, despite all the contested history that swirls around it.

I felt nervous on my Nigerian trips about confessing my colonial connections. But I should not have worried. No one showed the least personal animosity when I mentioned that I had been a colonial child – quite the reverse, in fact.

On the drive to the airport after my Bedwell Road expedition, our van driver got stuck in the traffic that is Lagos's curse. As we stewed in the lines of stationary, hooting cars, he turned and asked me in exasperated tones whether I had ever visited the city before. When I somewhat sheepishly admitted that I had indeed first seen the light of day there he was so thrilled that he rang up his girl-friend: 'I've got a whitey born in Lagos in the car,' he told her. 'You've got to talk to him.'

The Nigerian government has not always welcomed the attention of foreign journalists – the long period of insecurity in the north created by Boko Haram is an especially sensitive issue – so getting a visa to cover the 2019 presidential election was not easy: there was a great deal of form-filling and a long wait before permission came through. But after weeks of uncertainty, I was told to present myself at the visa offices in the Strand.

A Nigerian consular official looked down my form, and his eyes alighted on my place of birth. 'You are from Lagos,' he remarked. 'I shall put your race down' – he was smiling broadly – 'as Black African.' And he did.

That really felt like being a Citizen of the World.

PLYING MY TRADE

13 · A TRIBE WITHOUT A TENT

My trip to cover the Bosnian war marked a tipping point in my reporting career. It was so packed with coincidence, comic mishap and blind terror that any decent fiction editor would have put a blue pencil through the whole episode.

It began on a routine weekend newsreading shift in ITN's offices in Gray's Inn Road. It was June 1992, and the BBC bulletins brought the unwelcome revelation that their correspondent Martin Bell had managed to penetrate the Bosnian Serb lines to get into Sarajevo, where one of the most brutal sieges of the late twentieth century had just begun. As diplomatic editor, I was supposed to know about foreign parts so the duty editor on the foreign desk pottered over to ask for my advice on how to match the competition.

Like some First World War general, I pulled out a map of the Balkans and studied it, eventually suggesting the possibility of sending two teams to the region – one to Split, in Croatia, one to the Bulgarian capital, Sofia – and instructing them to race one another overland to the besieged Bosnian city. 'Brilliant,' said the duty foreign editor.

A few hours later she called me over as I prepared to head home and suggested I might like to lead one of the teams. 'Brilliant,' I said, with slightly less conviction.

Bulgaria had only recently emerged from the clutches of Communism, and Sofia had yet to learn fluency in its interactions with the outside world. It rapidly became apparent that the 'international hotel' the foreign desk had booked for us was in fact a brothel: the bathrooms were copiously equipped with condoms, and when we went down for dinner, we were invited to choose a companion from a line of young women dressed in elaborate peasant costumes.

We had hired a Serb 'fixer'* from Belgrade to help us, and, perhaps because he had a better idea than the rest of us of what awaited us if we succeeded in this slightly madcap mission, he stayed sober at dinner. I am afraid that the rest of the team put away a good deal of wine. The circumstances seemed so incongruous that one could only surrender to the bizarre comedy of the moment.

Towards the end of the meal, someone suggested we should simply set off in the general direction of Bosnia. There was nothing to keep us in Sofia, and even after copious quantities of alcohol no member of my team was tempted by the peasant smocks. So, we piled all the big tin boxes that television crews use back down to Reception, and the sober Serb took the wheel.

We reached Belgrade, the Serbian capital, the following morning, and thought we should catch a few hours' sleep. Our fixer found us a hotel – a real one this time – but just as those tin boxes were coming back out of the minivan, I noticed a column of military vehicles grinding up the dual carriageway flying United Nations flags. Since the nearest UN mission we knew of was in Sarajevo, we concluded – impressively quickly, given the drink and the lack of sleep – it was almost certainly heading for our intended destination.

Back into the van went all the boxes, and we tagged on to the back of the convoy, following it deep into the Bosnian mountains. We took shifts at the wheel, and there was a bad moment while I was driving: we reached a checkpoint marked by a chicane of landmines placed along the road, and the van seemed unnaturally wide

---

* Fixers are the local helpers hired to translate, book hotels, organize transport and so on.

as I wove it through. When the convoy made camp that night we slept in a field, and woke soaked in mountain dew.

A British Army doctor working with the UN, Major Vanessa Lloyd-Davies (she became one of the real heroes of the Balkan conflict), was sent back to parley with us: the convoy commanders were not, it seemed, particularly happy to have picked up a bunch of strays. But we were now too deep into the middle of a shooting war to be abandoned altogether. The following afternoon we arrived at the final Bosnian Serb checkpoint in Sarajevo's suburbs. Sticking close to the tail of the convoy, showing our best military swagger and looking as confident as we could about our right to be there, we brazened our way past a puzzled-looking soldier – a 'Serbski sniper', as we would soon learn to call them.

When we reached the Holiday Inn – still, amazingly, operating as a hotel – the tin-box ritual discovered a mysterious suitcase that no one claimed. A card inside revealed that it belonged to a Macedonian citrus-fruit trader, and we realized we must have swept it up along with our gear on that drunken evening in Sofia. We called him on the satellite phone – introducing ourselves carefully, as he might not have wanted to advertise where he had been staying – and gave him the good news: his suitcase was safe. As for the bad . . .

He eventually got his luggage back – and sent the foreign desk a case of oranges by way of a thank-you.

The hotel car park was across the road from Reception, and every morning, without fail, the 'Serbski snipers' enlivened the day by shooting at us as we ran to collect our van. The bullets were close enough for us to hear them fluttering as they sang above our heads.

The airport road was an especially notorious snipers' alley, which we quickly realized was best avoided if at all possible. Our usual practice was to cover this ground at speed, weaving across the lanes to make the car a more difficult target, but on a return trip

I was caught behind a slow-moving UN armoured personnel carrier. The trundling pace gave our regular sniper time to line up his shot, and he put a high-velocity bullet dead-centre down the middle of the car. It passed between my head and that of the cameraman sitting with me on the back seat – so close that I felt the bullet's breath on the back of my neck – and smashed neatly out through the middle of the windscreen.

The moment of the shot was infinitesimally small in lifetime terms – high-velocity rounds cover at least a thousand metres a second. Its trajectory was decided by the laws of physics, and the closeness of the bullet to my brain merely underlined the fact that the sniper did not quite master the variables – the angle of the barrel, the speed of our car – to achieve the intended outcome (it seems reasonable to assume that he intended to kill someone). Despite all that, I cannot resist the temptation to look for meaning in that moment.

The people of Sarajevo had to endure risks like that every day. One of the oddest aspects of city life under siege was the way people sprinted whenever they reached a zebra crossing. You might see a besuited businessman sauntering along a tree-lined boulevard with his briefcase, apparently preoccupied with the cares of office politics as a member of his caste might be in any European capital, only to run – quite literally – for his life when he broke cover to cross the road. Bosnian Serb snipers had taken over the high-rise office and apartment blocks on their side of the front line, giving themselves clear lines of sight down the city-centre streets.

In one of my despatches – the scripts, scribbled on tatty notepaper, have survived in the attic ever since – I reported that 'In the river just behind General Mackenzie's office [he was the commander of the small Canadian UN force in the city], there is evidence of the brutality of this conflict: Serbian dead dumped in the river, bearing the marks of beatings.' I can still see the two bodies, their trousers pulled ominously below their knees and their heads dipped under the crystal mountain waters.

Even more unsettling were the random dead, people who had been killed while going about their daily business and remained unrecovered because their friends and family had no idea what had happened to them. One morning a car turned up at the Sarajevo television station where we had set up temporary offices – it somehow continued to function – and disgorged a grisly cargo: a sniper had put a bullet through both the passengers on the back seat, killing one and gravely injuring the other. The survivor was bundled into a press car and taken to hospital; the dead man was laid out on a stretcher and covered with a blanket. Since no one had any idea of who he was, he stayed there for the rest of my tour, a mute sentry at the foot of the staircase, greeting us each morning as we arrived for work.

We were a tiny handful of reporters and crews in Sarajevo that summer: Martin Bell, who can be proud of taking the Balkan wars seriously long before anyone else did, the brilliant radio reporter Alan Little (later a colleague on *Today*), a team from the Canadian Broadcasting Corporation (during this early phase of the siege the UN force was led by the Canadians) and the CNN star Christiane Amanpour.

The sense of being a small band of brothers (and sisters) was all the stronger when Christiane reminded me that I had once danced a vaudeville routine on stage at her English Catholic boarding school to raise money for charity; the Ampleforth First XV high-kicked to a chorus from *Thoroughly Modern Millie* in full match gear, and at the climax we threw bunny tails stuck to the back of our rugby shorts to the girls in the audience.

Christiane was insanely brave and sometimes drove the airport road on her own, but CNN still seemed too marginal to worry about in those days. So, after the sniper incident Martin Bell and I did a deal: only one team would risk that journey each day, and we pooled material to avoid unnecessary risk. No one back at base would ever know, and the deal significantly increased our chances of getting home unhurt.

After a couple of weeks – it felt like much longer, and my cigarette consumption hit eighty a day – the UN managed to open Sarajevo airport for aid flights, and I was relieved by Michael Nicholson, the reporter whose Cyprus scoop had so impressed me when I joined ITN as a trainee.

I had not had much of an emotional reaction to my near-death moment. I have dug out one of my later Sarajevo reports online, and I appear perfectly calm and coherent. But when I made it to Zagreb at the end of my tour – hitching a ride out in the back of a British Hercules – I poured most of the contents of the hotel mini-bar down my throat. In my notebook I wrote, 'No guns, no explosions. No fear. We stop at traffic lights and drive calmly. After sleeping I went for a long walk – simply for the pleasure of crossing roads without running to avoid the snipers.'

I got back to London just in time for a summer drinks party in Wandsworth, and made it only by going straight there from the airport, depositing my flak jacket in our hosts' hall. I found myself chatting over my Bucks Fizz to a woman smartly dressed for the current chapter in the English Summer Season: 'I have just come from Wimbledon,' she said. 'Where have you come from?' She struggled a bit with my answer.

The trip marked a tipping point partly for personal reasons. Inevitably it scraped away any youthful sense of invulnerability – I was in my thirties at the time. And it finally convinced me, a little late in the day, that you cannot be a reporter and pretend that it's just another job, like that of a banker or a lawyer – so it cut another link in the chain that would otherwise have connected me to contemporaries who had followed more conventional and comfortable career paths. But it was a professional tipping point too: it was around this time that the character of reporting changed.

Everything about that trip would now be condemned as an object lesson in worst practice.

There had been absolutely no planning, let alone a risk assessment, and the decisions I took in the field were made on the hoof without any reference to my bosses in London. Plus, drinking anywhere near a war zone is a terrible idea – that lesson was, ironically, driven home by some of the Bosnian volunteer fighters we interviewed as they crouched in the basement of a shell-blown building close to the Serb lines. They were smashed on slivovitz at breakfast time, which was perfectly understandable in the circumstances but had clearly not improved their capacity for frontline alertness. And, in those pre-mobile days, we had no mechanism for keeping London informed about our progress. The satellite phone took a bit of time to set up, so while we were on the road and keeping up with the UN convoy, we simply disappeared off the radar for a couple of days. There was no agreed back-up schedule to trigger alarm bells in London: they just hoped and waited until we popped up on the line from Sarajevo. None of us had first-aid training – today anyone going near a conflict zone will know basic battlefield medical skills.

We had flak jackets and helmets, but we were using a thin-skinned vehicle – five minutes' thought would have told us we needed an armoured car, and not long afterwards both the BBC and ITN began using them routinely. There was no protocol at all for managing risk. The cameraman Sebastian Rich – who, in a different and less stressful life, had been involved in my Anthony Blunt debacle – took a ricochet bullet in his flak jacket outside the Holiday Inn. I got shouted at by the foreign editor in London for allowing this to happen, but that was about as far as it went.

No one remotely worried about our mental condition when we got back, largely because the concept of post-traumatic stress disorder simply did not feature in our thinking. The nearest I had to an understanding of PTSD was a memory of the return journey from one of my Lebanon trips in my mid-twenties. It was early evening as the cab from Heathrow drove up Regent Street on the way to the office, and when a shop-keeper brought his metal grille down with a crash at closing time the driver asked me what I was doing on the floor in the back of his car. Hitting the deck after a big bang had become instinctive.

And I compounded these multiple procedural crimes in the management of that Balkan foray by committing a mortal sin against journalistic impartiality. Without asking my bosses for permission, I wrote a ferociously opinionated piece for the *Daily Telegraph* arguing that the British government should send troops to Bosnia to stop the fighting.

Western policy makers at the time were in a complete funk about what to do in the Balkans. The daily briefings my diplomatic colleagues and I had had from the pinstripe brigade at the Foreign and Commonwealth Office in King Charles Street (as diplomatic editor my long-suffering suit felt at home) involved a great deal of teeth-sucking and increasingly imaginative reasons for turning a blind eye to the whole sordid business. The foreign secretary, Douglas Hurd, whom I otherwise greatly admired (not least for his superb Trinity style of dress, manner, and intellectual elegance), seemed to take the view that the peoples of the former Yugoslavia should be left to kill one another until they exhausted themselves.

It was characteristic of the European approach to the crisis to appoint the ever-dutiful former foreign secretary Peter Carrington as the EC's envoy to the region, without giving him any of the diplomatic – let alone military – muscle that might actually have stopped the fighting. Lord Carrington combined this role with the chairmanship of Christie's, and would issue statements from his office at the auction house in St James's.

When the airport opened up during my spell in Sarajevo he flew in on a military plane – he was extremely brave, with a war-time Military Cross to show for it – to hold talks with the Bosnian president Alija Izetbegović, and the two held a brief photo op for the press. Carrington looked around the shattered windows of the presidential palace – the shells had been raining down right up until his arrival – and remarked to his host, 'I do hope you have a decent cellar here.' He was, of course, expressing concern about the president's safety, but as that unmistakably aristocratic drawl sang out across the room it sounded very much as if he was asking about the supply of claret.

Carrington, like Hurd, was from the old-school tradition of British public servants – men who concealed their cleverness with charm and remained cool in the most stressful of circumstances. My fascination with this caste was finally exhausted by experiencing the reality of an almost medieval city siege.

As Foreign Office officials put it, this is a 'nasty little war and no one respects the Geneva conventions governing casualties' [I wrote in the *Telegraph*]. In Sarajevo, bodies turn up in the most surprising places, and many remain uncollected because they cannot be identified or their families cannot be found. Estimates of the number of dead in last year's fighting in Croatia vary between 10,000 and 15,000, and the figure for Bosnia is now thought to be approaching the same level – the Bosnian government puts it at double that. The estimate of 2.2 million refugees is generally accepted as reasonably accurate. Nasty this war is: little it is not . . .

The current Foreign Office response to almost any initiative on the Balkans is that it falls into the 'something must be done' category of gesture politics, but something *must* be done, and only full-scale military intervention can make a difference. The principles of decent human behaviour and the national interest in a peaceful Europe are worth the risks.

Only a few months later the British government came round to a similar way of thinking: British troops went into Bosnia that autumn. But at the time such views were heresy. I got a bollocking from my editor, Stewart Purvis, from the Foreign Office minister Douglas Hogg, and even from my old university friend Andrew Mitchell, now a government whip. The former Labour MP and talk-show host Robert Kilroy-Silk took a pop at me in his column in the *Express*: 'Will they, the Stourtons of this world, be there to comfort the women when their men come home in body bags?' he demanded rhetorically. 'I doubt it. They are ringing the bells today all right, but they will be wringing their hands tomorrow.' They were all quite within their rights: as a broadcaster covering a highly contentious subject, I was well on the wrong side of the line. Today I would be taken off the air for much less.

But I do not regret having written the piece. I was angry, simply boiling – if you will forgive me mixing the metaphor like this – with an icy rage at what I had seen in Sarajevo. The targeting of civilians was unconscionable, something that quite simply should not be allowed in late-twentieth-century Europe.

And if, as a reporter, you lose the capacity for rage, if you are not at least tempted to overstep the mark from time to time, you should give up, go home, and get a different, more useful job. And spare us your views, no matter how judicious they may be: trenchant analysis is not enough. In journalism, passion and fellow feeling for those you report on really matter.

Of course, no story is worth dying for: no one would want to return to the cavalier, macho, risk-taking culture of war reporting in those days.

The Bosnian war had an especially powerful impact on the way journalism dealt with risk because it was one of the first conflicts in which journalists were routinely treated as targets. Putting 'TV News' in large letters on your vehicle became an invitation to be fired on rather than a form of protection.

As the nineties advanced, broadcasters became increasingly attuned to the reality of just how dangerous modern wars had become. Armoured cars, risk assessments and training courses eventually became the norm. And I am pleased I have now been taught basic first aid – I even used it once to help someone injured in a traffic accident.

But I am still glad to have experienced the days of wild adventure, and there are things I miss. One, oddly, is the sense of complete freedom that covering a war then offered. I tried to catch the Sarajevo experience in my notebook as soon as I had left the city:

What a high to cover raw news like that – especially when I first arrived and there were so few of us, all feeling our way. You could go where you wanted to – as long as you were prepared to take the risk. No tiresome press officers at the UN – you just walked into the offices and talked. And everywhere you went the story changed in front of you – you didn't know when the Serbs would withdraw from the airport, but you turned up and watched the tanks roll away. You didn't know when the guns would start – it just happened around you. And everyone you spoke to had his or her human drama to tell.

No one was going to give you a parking ticket, insist on the correct form of press accreditation or tick bureaucratic boxes to decide when you were clocking on and off. And you felt trusted at home because, in such dynamic circumstances, the office in London could do very little to assess what was happening around you, much less tell you what to do.

Alongside that freedom came a focused clarity of thought not unlike that I still enjoy when broadcasting live but more intense because the stakes were higher. The risk sharpened your judgement and even your writing, and that helped meet some of the challenges. The year before my Balkan adventure I had covered part of the first Gulf War from Baghdad, where the overriding challenge was enemy censorship.

Logic said that this assignment was not really dangerous at all: I was sent in halfway through the American and British bombing campaign, and by the time I set out on the day-long drive across the desert from the Jordanian border the astonishing accuracy of the Allied bombing arsenal was well-established. All the foreign press were corralled into the Al-Rasheed Hotel in the centre of the Iraqi capital, and everyone knew where we were; it seemed unlikely that Washington or London would deliberately wipe out a large cohort of their own reporters.

Such was our collective confidence that many of us would step out into the hotel grounds in the cool of the evening for each night's awesome sound and light show. Watching the country's infrastructure systematically laid to waste was like spectating at an especially elaborate Guy Fawkes display. In the morning you might find the odd bit of cruise missile in the shrubbery, but I never felt in any danger of being blown up.

On the other hand, we were in the heart of the enemy camp. An unexpectedly large number of the Iraqi censors who 'minded' us had been educated at Edinburgh University, and enjoyed dropping into our makeshift offices in the evenings for a splash or two (or three – many Baath Party members were aggressively secular) of Scotch, but none of us doubted the ruthless character of Saddam Hussein's regime. And the pressure from home audiences – and therefore from our bosses – was intense: in the United Kingdom especially there was a widespread view that we were betraying our country by reporting the enemy's side of the story.

Every report we transmitted became a sophisticated high-wire act: I had to construct my pieces so that they reassured the audience at home they were getting something more worthwhile than unfiltered Iraqi propaganda, but each report also had to pass a viewing by an Iraqi censor before the authorities would allow it to be sent by satellite to London.

We played what we thought were sophisticated games. There was an anti-aircraft gun emplacement in a park just across the way from our hotel, and the censors always insisted that, for reasons of military security, this image should never appear on Western television screens (in reality there was very little doubt that the Americans and the British knew its location perfectly well). So we deliberately put this shot into almost every report, confident that the censor of the day would insist it be cut out, and hoping that would distract his (they were all men) attention, allowing us to smuggle through cleverly phrased little pieces of seditious commentary. It worked for a while before the Iraqis rumbled the game, and the daily struggle resumed with ever greater intensity as the conflict ground towards its conclusion.

It was especially difficult to keep your head straight in these circumstances because we inevitably developed cordial relationships with some of the 'minders' who censored our material. Enduring the privations of a Blitz-like assault together naturally created fellow-feeling, and not all of them were hard-line Baathists. The Iraqi Ministry of Information had trawled through the country's universities to find the most fluent English-speakers, and many of them were academics.

We were often censored by a gentle, elderly poet with a sly sense of humour. There was a ferocious storm one night with winds that whipped through the city and took some of our broadcasting equipment with it, including the bivouac that kept the satellite equipment dry. Our poet sidled up to the producer the following morning with the words 'ITN – the tribe without a tent', and with no elaboration, went chuckling on his way. He always appeared dressed in a jacket (well-worn tweed) and tie topped off with a freshly ironed black-and-white *keffiyeh* – like an exotic Oxbridge don – and I liked him very much. But he was, of course, part of the enemy apparatus.

It was exhausting but exhilarating, and when the Iraqis eventually threw us all out – polishing off the Scotch during an 'end of era' evening of strangely abandoned parties before we left – I thought I had done the job quite well.

Not long afterwards, however, the Queen came to open ITN's new offices in Gray's Inn Road, and four of us who had done front-line reporting tours during the conflict were lined up to meet her. David Manion, my immediate boss, introduced me with the words 'This is Edward Stourton, who reported for us from Baghdad.'

I was expecting some banal chat of the 'Have you come far?' kind, but Her Majesty had other ideas. 'I expect,' she said, looking as if she had just bitten into a lemon, 'that the Iraqis found you very useful.' I put the photo up in the loo anyway, because that was what one did.

14 · THE TRADITIONAL LIFT, SPIN, BEND OVER, SPREAD BUTTOCKS

Most news interviews for television are done at speed and on the hoof. If you miss your deadline it does not matter how elegant your report looks, so a workmanlike job will often best fit the bill. It is easier outside (not so much faffing with the lighting) as long as the weather is clement, and half a dozen questions should do the trick. Noisy traffic and planes cause problems, but as long as the audio is clear enough to hear you can probably put up with that.

Interviews for longer current affairs or documentary television programmes are an altogether different proposition, and I learnt to take a book – ideally something Russian and long that would keep me absorbed for lengthy periods – whenever I did one.

Dressing the set – sometimes involving the most minuscule adjustments to pot plants and pictures – can take for ever, and cameraperson and director will often disappear into long debate about the 'mood' and 'tone' of the backdrop.

The interview itself is likely to take well over an hour, and will almost certainly be interrupted several times. If the sound recordist hears the merest mouse-squeak in the headphones, he or she will stop the show, and some directors and producers like to get interviewees to say the same thing in several slightly different ways, just to be sure. Then there are what used to be called the 'noddies', when the camera is reversed to film the interviewer, who is required to put on a variety of expressions that can be used to cover the joins when the interview is cut together.

All this can be extremely trying for the interviewees, especially if they are ordinary people rather than those – like politicians – who have had to get to grips with the ways of telly for professional reasons. And I often became frustrated too. Your job as an interviewer is to drill down to the difficult subjects, and sometimes that means a bit of gentle bullying. It certainly means listening hard, so the endless stopping and starting can be tiresome in the extreme.

I have found one interview transcript in which an American prison warder was required at least three times to detail the unsavoury business of body-searching a death-row inmate. 'So he's in the nude in there,' Lieutenant Hood explained, 'so he does the traditional lift, spin, bend over, spread buttocks, shows me the bottoms of his feet, hands. I'll look in his mouth, move his tongue—' *Interruption*, shrieks the transcript, with no indication of why, so perhaps the sound recordist picked up some extraneous piece of domestic sound.

The lieutenant tries again: '. . . lift, spin, bend over—' *Interruption*, again. This time the producer can be heard off mic asking me to clarify the 'lift' element of that litany. 'Lift,' the lieutenant continues gamely, 'means he will lift his genitals, where the officer can look underneath between his thighs, and he will turn around a hundred and eighty degrees, bend over and spread his buttocks so that you can see there's no contraband items placed in the area . . .' We got there in the end, but neither of us enjoyed these grisly details, and by the time the producer called a wrap we were both sweating profusely.

In those pre-digital days, each interview was transcribed, printed off and circulated to every member of the production team. Once we had read them all I would sit down with the producer for an exercise known as 'pulling synch' – agreeing which chunks of interview we should include, and assembling them like a jigsaw. From this sometimes exhausting process the basic shape of the programme would emerge.

The ring-binders we used were always bulging – they held

hundreds and hundreds of pages of speech, and the BBC transcribers were meticulous about including absolutely everything. I have kept many of them, along with other boxes of the notes, old newspaper cuttings and sundry research material I used for my scripts, a ridiculously inconvenient archive I have dragged along from one house move to another. Why? I am not absolutely sure.

Part of my motivation has been a natural affection for paper archives, and an instinct that they should be preserved. But this compulsion also reflected a reluctance to wave goodbye altogether to people I had got to know quite well. Those long current-affairs interviews took me to sometimes intense places, and we would often spend several days filming with our main characters. If you make a current-affairs programme today it will almost certainly live somewhere on the internet; twenty years ago, your programme was likely to disappear once it had been broadcast. I found I did not want to forget so quickly – all those hours of agonizing to get the film right, and then it was gone.

The 'lift, spin, bend over' conversation with Lieutenant Hood, for example, took place while I was following the last days of a death-row prisoner. We decided to cover the story because he was the first for many decades who was due to die for a crime he had committed as a teenager – we called our film *Dead Kid Walking* – but sophisticated human-rights considerations about his age were quickly overwhelmed by the brutal logic of the way a modern state sets about killing one of its own citizens. I wrote a newspaper feature when the film was broadcast and, because of the wrenching rawness of the experience, I kept the tone on a tight leash. It was done as a diary, and began like this:

25 January 1999

'Good morning, is that the Oklahoma Cremation Society?' Steve Presson was on the telephone arranging for the disposal of his

client's body when I walked into his office. The client in question was still alive at the time of the call – twenty-nine years old, well-built and healthy. But his execution was scheduled for the following week.

During the next ten days I was again and again brought up short by the finality of that deadline.

Steve Presson, an ex-cop turned lawyer, has devoted his professional life to saving convicted killers from the execution chamber – not a popular vocation in a state where the death penalty is an article of faith. There is plenty of work to keep him going. Oklahoma has nearly a hundred and fifty men on death row. Many of them are nearing the end of the appeals process, so the pace of executions is picking up. For most of this decade the state carried out only one or two executions a year; last December there were two within a month, there was one in January and another at the beginning of February.

The stress has taken its toll – Steve Presson looks like a man who eats too much and sleeps too little. Every case is emotionally exhausting, because the stakes are so high, but this one stood out from the rest. Sean Sellers, his client, committed his crimes when he was sixteen years old. America is unique in the Western world in sentencing juveniles to death – it is, as Presson points out in a wearily well-rehearsed litany, a practice it shares only with Iran, Iraq, Pakistan, Nigeria and Saudi Arabia. China – which kills more of its citizens than any other country in the world – used to do it but stopped two years ago.

I had come to Oklahoma to investigate an abstract idea, a point of legal principle: at what age can a child be held fully responsible for what he or she does?

I found myself sucked into a story instead of a debate. Most stories I follow as a news journalist are made rich by uncertainty: who will win with this election, and will the heads of government reach agreement at this summit? In this case everyone knew that the *story would end with a couple of hundred pounds of dead human flesh being humped into a van at the back of the Oklahoma State Penitentiary. Steve Presson fought for his client until the final hours of his life, and we all went along with the fiction that it might make a difference. But the appeals and the carefully drafted legal briefs were little more than displacement activity.*

That sense of inevitability haunted me throughout the days that followed. It was especially acute when I conducted the last television interview Sean Sellers gave before his death. It was, I suppose, a scoop in a grim way, but I felt guilty about the ghoulish fascination it inspired, and it seemed cruel to be taking up even an hour of the time that must by then have seemed such a precious commodity to him. I also knew that I had to ask him some tough questions.

He was, after all, guilty of three murders. The first was as whimsical in its conception as it was brutal in its execution. He gunned down a cashier in an all-night store – a man he had never met before. He told a friend he had done it 'to see what it feels like to kill someone', and for six months after the killing he continued to live like any other teenager – going to school and falling in love as if nothing had happened.

Then, in May 1986, he slipped into his parents' bedroom and killed them both – he shot his mother twice in the head, his stepfather once. He faked a break-in and left to stay the night with a friend, pretending to discover the bodies the following morning. They were the kind of killings that haunt the modern American imagination and feed the national appetite for execution. Sean Sellers was no honey.

H Unit, Oklahoma's death row, was designed by the prison staff for maximum security, and the sense of unreality I felt as I arrived for the interview was augmented by the way the place had been built. The earth had been banked up around the walls on all sides, so once you stepped in it was as if you were underground.

We had to conduct our interview separated by reinforced glass, and the technical difficulties that presented meant the process of 'setting up' was even more time-consuming than usual. While we waited, I chatted to one of the guards, a man who had often done duty in the holding cell where those due for execution wait out their final sixteen hours. I was curious to know what they talked about. 'Not much,' he said. 'They know they don't have a tomorrow, and that limits the topics for conversation.'

He showed me the execution chamber and explained the machinery of death in matter-of-fact tones. The condemned man is allowed to choose a last meal: Sean Sellers had already decided he wanted Chinese. But – this was said with an indulgent chuckle – 'We have a fifteen-dollar limit on what we feed 'em with.'

I was allotted an hour for my interview, and kept an eye on the clock with a view to covering the ground necessary to make a good television programme, but I was also uncomfortably conscious that Sean Sellers was watching eternity hurtling towards him. He did not fit the death-row stereotype. He was highly articulate, middle class and white, and had been 'born again' as a Christian soon after being sentenced.

Those campaigning to see him die – and there were many of them – argued that he had found God simply to escape execution. Whether or not his conversion was sincere, his plea that it be recognized has stayed with me: 'I have one question that I have been asking everybody, and it is this. After a man has done something horrible, after he's killed, is there anything he can do to make up for it? No one has been able to give me an answer to that yet. I would really like to have an answer to that before I die.' When asked by someone with eight days to live, it is not an academic question.

Religion loomed large in the debate about his fate, as it does in so many areas of American public life. For much of the previous week the news programmes and newspaper headlines had been dominated by stories about Pope John Paul II's tour of Mexico and the United States. The pope had spoken loud and clear against the death penalty on almost every occasion he could, and in the state of Missouri next door he had even persuaded the governor to spare a triple murderer scheduled for execution during his visit.

Oklahoma's governor, Frank Keating, was a Catholic, so I asked him whether John Paul's campaigning zeal on this issue had made a difference. 'The Pope is a wonderful human being,' the governor replied, 'far greater than I could ever be. But on this issue he's wrong.'

Like many conservative Catholics in the United States, Keating was a ferocious opponent of abortion; his 'pro-life' stand on that issue was matched by an equally ferocious 'pro-death' position on crime and punishment. Oklahoma law allowed Sean Sellers one last shot at staying alive: he had the right to plead for clemency before the state's Parole Board. But Keating had tipped the odds by ensuring that all five members of the board were enthusiastic death-penalty supporters, and he stated publicly that if the board did recommend clemency – something they had never done before – he would reject their advice.

The clemency hearing, which was held in the prison chapel, really shook me. I noted at the time that 'It was conducted in the manner of a public inquiry into a rural bypass, and the five members of the Pardon and Parole Board looked and sounded as if they were dealing with an especially recalcitrant late-returner of library books.'

Steve Presson, Sellers's lawyer, had produced a glossy brochure detailing his client's virtuous achievements during his long years on death row, and erected a small display of Sean Sellers's pictures (he had become an enthusiastic artist during his time inside) and writings, like a shrine around the Formica table that served as a witness stand. The assistant attorney general, who had come to make the case for the execution to go ahead, treated this with chilling irony, remarking that the art world would not miss Sean Sellers because 'there are plenty of other painters of mediocre ability who are not also triple murderers'.

The only people who seemed to take the occasion seriously were the family of Sellers's murdered stepfather, the Bellofattos, who came to drive home how badly they wanted his capital sentence to be carried out. The most effective was Sellers's stepsister, Noelle Bellofatto, who was a school teacher and used to speaking in public. I had interviewed her before the hearing, and she told me, 'Somehow I have to impact these people and make them realize that Sean is not entitled to have his sentence commuted because of the pain and grief he has caused my family – and I hope my emotions will allow me to do that.' She coped just fine.

Sellers himself was brought into the hearing in shackles. All his articulate self-confidence had gone, and he made a complete hash of the twenty minutes he was allowed to plead for his life.

The Parole Board's decision was no surprise, but I had imagined they might take at least a few minutes to discuss it in private. Not so: Sean Sellers was scarcely out of the room before the chair asked each to vote yes or no, and they decided unanimously to deny clemency. Sean Sellers heard the result on the radio in his cell.

I described his final day in my newspaper article like this:

3 February

There is a script to be followed on execution days, and everyone's part is laid out with precision.

For the Bellofatto family, it began with a four-hour drive to the State Penitentiary. Seven of them had decided to exercise their right to witness the execution, and when they arrived Gary Gibson [the senior prison warden] gave them a tour of the execution chamber, and explained how lethal injection works.

The press were required to pick up accreditation at the media centre that had been set up in the prison grounds. We were given a 'Media Kit', which contained full details of Sean Sellers's crimes and a chronology of the progress of his case through the appeals system, and an 'Information Packet', which included a 'Schedule of Events', 'Media Centre Guidelines', and a helpful list of other inmates nearing execution. The local press drew lots to decide which of them would witness and report back to the rest of us; the opportunity fell to a cheerful young woman from the McAlester New Capital, *the local paper, who had watched four executions in the previous six months. Lest anyone seek to escape complicity in this killing, we were part of the process.*

For Steve Presson the script dictated a day of frantic faxes taking Sean Sellers's case all the way through the legal system one final time.

The Bellofatto family dined at the only decent Italian restaurant in town before leaving to watch the execution. Pete's Place does brisk business on execution evenings, and we sat down to our starters at a neighbouring table as the news came through that Sean Sellers's last appeal to the Supreme Court had failed.

Lorne Bellofatto [Noelle's brother] was looking forward to watching Sean Sellers being killed. 'I regard it as the next best thing to doing it myself,' he told me. His views on the use of lethal injection are beyond caricature: 'I think it's too easy,' he said. 'They offer you a sedative before they take you in . . . Sit back, relax, enjoy the ride, close your eyes, when you open them again you're before whatever god you worship. There's no pain to it, no punishment.'

Pro and anti death-penalty campaigners have their ritual roles to play too – both groups held vigils outside the prison as darkness fell. Both groups brandishing Biblical quotations – the first from the Old Testament, the second from the New.

To Sean Sellers the script gave that final fifteen-dollar Chinese meal – which he declared delicious – and a day of goodbyes. He was allowed to make telephone calls until 10 p.m., and Steve Presson had hired a room in the local Ramada Inn where Sean Sellers's friends and supporters talked to him in turn. The last conversation was with his lawyer, and Steve Presson cried as he hung up. Sellers then went back to writing his journal, and the final entry reads, '11.27: they have come for me.'

He was allowed to make a brief speech before the drugs were pumped into his veins, and from the gurney he addressed the members of the Bellofatto family by name. He told them they would still hate him in the morning, that his death would change nothing, and appealed to them not to waste their lives in hatred. Then he turned to the warden with the words 'Let's do it, Gary. Let's get it on.'

Afterwards the Bellofatto family came to the media centre to give a press conference. I asked Noelle how she had felt when Sean Sellers addressed her directly. 'It made me very angry,' she snarled, 'that he taunted us with his last breath.' For thirteen years her life had been corrupted – first by the murder of her father and then by the wait to see his killer killed. There was nothing to suggest the evening had brought her any kind of resolution.

A long love affair with America, which I regard as the freest, happiest, most creative and energetic society mankind has yet produced, suddenly felt uncertain. I settled in the United States for several years in the 1980s, and came to think of it as home. On death row I felt a foreigner for the first time.

From the prison Sean Sellers's body was taken to a hospital before it was released for cremation. Because he did not die of natural causes the state that killed him requires an autopsy. On his death certificate the cause of death is recorded as 'homicide'.

Looking back at my notes and transcripts I am struck by how desperately Sean Sellers clung to the idea that his life and death had some kind of enduring significance. In that final telephone call with his lawyer, one of the last things he said was 'I'm never going to be forgotten. My life has been surrendered to God, and God's not done yet. And I think that in ten years more people will know about who I was than they do now.' (The remark was shortly followed by the automated prison operator coming across the line to warn, 'Thirty seconds more on this call,' one of the most chilling moments of the evening.)

He also wrote a poem to inspire his followers; it was terrible ('Let the bronze bells toll my friends/Ring them loud and clear/The man you knew who loved and lost/Is no longer here/No more words will sprout anew/From voice to pen to page') but it was a very self-confident manifesto. And Sean Sellers did manage to attract some high-profile supporters – Desmond Tutu and Bianca Jagger both campaigned for his sentence to be commuted – which he clearly enjoyed.

But I do not imagine his poem or those last words to his lawyer exist almost anywhere outside my box files now, and his death did not really change anything, certainly not immediately: two years after his execution Oklahoma killed eighteen people, the highest tally in the state's history. The death penalty there was put on hold in 2015 after some hideously botched executions (two prisoners were given a chemical used for de-icing the wings of planes), but at the time of writing the state is preparing to start it again, and there are forty-seven people waiting on Oklahoma's death row.

Six years after Sellers's death, however, the United States Supreme Court did rule against death for a crime committed when the perpetrator was under eighteen, and Sellers remains the only murderer (in modern times) to be executed in the United States for a crime committed when he was under seventeen.

Looking back on this bleak story, I cannot help reflecting on the value of making programmes like *Dead Kid Walking*. The director, Bill Treharne Jones, and I poured ourselves into the production, while the camera team and editor took meticulous care over the way the film was recorded and put together. But what, really, did we achieve?

The article I have quoted above appeared in the *Daily Telegraph*. The editor, Charles Moore, dropped me a note afterwards to say that he had been uncertain about the death penalty – he had converted to Catholicism since we both left Cambridge – and that my piece had convinced him it was wrong. It was characteristically courteous, and it mattered. Experiences like my week with Sean Sellers change you: it is rewarding to know that reporting them can change a friend's mind, even if it does not change the world.

15 · NOT ON THE MOON

I was lucky to settle into a berth in current affairs around the turn of the century. BBC Two's international programme *Assignment* – later rebranded *Correspondent* – was guaranteed plenty of airtime and blessed with generous budgets. News reporting, meanwhile, was undergoing a transformation and, though I was only around forty, I had begun to feel like a creaky old warhorse on the road.

It was not just the new grown-up discipline and professionalism with which the big broadcasters now addressed the task of preventing their people getting killed: technology changed almost every aspect of news reporting. The mechanics of sending material back from remote locations became infinitely easier, television teams were smaller and cheaper to run, and the number of broadcasting organizations mushroomed. Many of the changes were, I was forced to recognize, benign – however much I might yearn nostalgically for the wild old days.

One consequence of the revolution was that the fibbers and fakers were cleaned out. In the days when reporters often found themselves alone in some far-flung place they could – if they were so minded – polish things up a bit when they put together their stories.

During the Balkan wars one of my ITN colleagues came under anti-aircraft fire while flying in a UN helicopter; once it had landed safely, he tried to persuade his cameraman to stay on board a little longer so that he could film while artfully shaking the camera, simulating the impact of the chopper pilot's evasive action.

Another of our more roguish stars at ITN had a habit of using his 'fixers' to play the part of commentators, handing them a piece of script to deliver then giving them the caption of 'economist' or 'political analyst' on screen – so much easier than arranging to interview a real expert!

Tricks like these became increasingly difficult to get away with when the chancers were surrounded by ballooning numbers of bright young reporters, most of them with old-fashioned ideas about truth. Technology also – you probably didn't notice this as a viewer because it happened gradually – broadened the geography of your news diet.

I had clocked the way technology distorted the news agenda during my time as a Washington correspondent: the United States dominated the news bulletins for the simple reason that bringing reports back across the Atlantic via satellite was cheap and reliable – we just popped the day's offering into the player in our bureau. In the 1980s getting something back from, say, Beirut, meant handing your precious material to a taxi driver willing to drive over the Chouf mountains, through the Bekaa Valley and all the way to the nearest satellite link in the Syrian capital Damascus – a journey of several hours in the middle of a war.

Mobile news vans with satellite 'up-links' and 'fly-away' systems, which could easily be sent overseas, changed all that. By the end of the 1990s it had become possible to transmit material back to base from almost anywhere. Wi-Fi has since made it even easier.

The downside of this revolution – especially to an olden-days reporter like me, who once enjoyed long lunches – was twenty-four-hour news. CNN blazed the trail, broadcasting first right back in 1980, just a few months after I began in journalism. A decade later the Gulf War made the channel a must-have source for viewers addicted to bombing raids on Baghdad and Scud missile attacks on Israel. And not long afterwards the 'CNN effect' became a recognized political phenomenon.

The term was coined following the cable broadcaster's coverage of the 'Black Hawk Down' episode in Mogadishu. CNN's bloody images of the humiliation of American forces by the Somali warlord Mohamed Farrah Aidid shocked America, and President Clinton altered his foreign policy accordingly. Twenty-four-hour news had become a force in global politics, and by the time the new century began, everyone was at it.

There are, of course, plenty of good arguments for offering a twenty-four-hour news service: flicking on the telly in your hotel room is a much easier way to keep up with the latest developments than pressing your ear to a scratchy shortwave radio in the way we once had to do. But plenty of students of media culture have noted that responding fast and getting good pictures on the air first wins large audiences – which, of course, in turn brings financial rewards. This, so the argument runs, encourages sensationalism and leads twenty-four-hour journalists to worry more about speed than getting facts right.

For reporters, the real challenge is the way twenty-four-hour news consumes your energy and time. It is a hungry beast, and if you devote your days to its voracious maw you are likely to be tied to a single spot, standing eternally in front of a striking backdrop and, like some journalistic Sisyphus, endlessly updating your story on the basis of other people's information.

You cannot gather news – that fundamental step in the reporting process – if you are never allowed off the air for long enough. You certainly cannot investigate the kind of leads that might prove revelatory. Original reporting takes time, and means accepting the risk that you will waste it and lose your way in a blind alley or two. Time, indeed, is the most precious of all journalistic commodities: you need it to talk to people.

There are, of course, some brilliant practitioners of the twenty-four-hour reporting art – quick-footed and vivid broadcasters who can convey the drama and immediacy of events. A very long time ago I might have enjoyed the role myself. As a young reporter I prided myself on my ability to speak with fluency and a good measure of gravitas, sometimes about nothing of any substance at all. But after a couple of decades, broadcasting dexterity and simply 'being on the telly' began to pall. The process of finding things out – especially things that someone wanted to keep secret – became much more of a motivation.

News moves at a furious pace. Looking back through my ring-binders and box files reminds me that even in my ITN reporting days – positively languid compared to the frenzied pace of twenty-four-hour news – it was not unusual to cover a different story on every night of the week. Current-affairs reporting, by contrast, lets you press the pause button on the rush of news to catch one of those transient moments, like a butterfly – to put it another way – and pin it down so that you can study it. Although our programme on Sean Sellers's execution did not, for example, linger long in the public domain, we did at least explore what his story meant.

I caught another butterfly fluttering out of the pages of *The Economist* magazine in May 2000 – part of its extensive coverage of Israel's withdrawal from southern Lebanon that month.

The withdrawal was a huge story. Israel's first big incursion into the area was right back in 1978, when the Israeli Defence Force, or IDF, crossed the border to drive back the Palestinian Liberation Organization. The whole area came under Israeli control after the Lebanon invasion of 1982, and when the Israelis pulled back from Beirut they retained a presence in what became known as the South Lebanon Security Belt. To help secure its hold on the Belt, Israel armed and financed a local Lebanese militia known as the South Lebanon Army, or SLA.

So, Israel's 2000 withdrawal marked the end of an occupation that had lasted for well over two decades. It led to the collapse of the SLA, which was unable to control the area without Israeli support, and several thousand Lebanese, many of them SLA soldiers, fled to Israel.

The Economist's sharp-eyed reporter – anonymous as always, but I salute her or him – had noticed that one consequence of these developments was the liberation of a shadowy but sinister camp in a place called Khiam, just north of the Israeli border. Built originally by the French as a barracks in the 1930s, since 1985, it had – so it was widely rumoured – been used as a detention, interrogation and torture centre by the SLA, with the collaboration of their Israeli allies. I persuaded my editor that we should go in search of it.

Amnesty International had been investigating the camp since the early 1990s, but no one really knew what was going on there because the whole South Lebanon Security Belt was a closed zone, a black hole on the map that no one could visit. The Israelis steadfastly refused to talk about the camp, much less acknowledge responsibility.

Amnesty organized a letter-writing campaign, but the camp existed in a truly Kafkaesque limbo: letters sent via Israel were returned with a polite note pointing out that Khiam was in Lebanon; letters sent via Lebanon were equally pointless, as the writ of Beirut's government did not run in the south of its own country. You could not fax, you could not telephone, you certainly could not visit. You just knew it was there.

And suddenly its gates were open and its guards were gone. Anyone could tour the place as they wished.

The simple fact of being able to travel to the area was a thrill in itself. We had no idea what we would find, and driving down to south Lebanon had something of the novelty of those early trips behind the Iron Curtain in 1989 and 1990. When we reached the camp, we discovered that immediately after the SLA abandoned it

Khiam had become a local tourist destination, visited by families at weekends, almost like an English country house or the Tower of London.

There were the squalid detention blocks with their slop buckets, and the tiny windowless solitary-confinement cells, concrete cauldrons in the summer heat. There were the watch towers and the barbed wire. And there were the instruments of torture, most strikingly, in the main yard, 'the pole' where, hooded and handcuffed to the ironwork and often naked, prisoners were beaten, doused in hot, then cold water, or simply left to hang for hours with their toes just touching the ground.

And in the towns and villages nearby our producer, Giselle Portenier, found the witnesses.

Ali Kashmar was fourteen when he was arrested by the SLA – he never really knew why, but thought it might have been because he had made anti-Israeli comments in the school playground (his father had been killed by the IDF). He told us that after arriving at Khiam he was tortured with electric shocks for eleven days, and eventually began making up stories to please his interrogators.

He was never put through any kind of trial – there was no real judicial process in the Security Belt – and was kept in Khiam for ten years. By the time he was freed – as part of a release of more than fifty Khiam prisoners traded for the remains of three dead Israeli soldiers – he had grown from a boy into a man, without, a poignant detail, a mirror to use as his appearance changed.

Ryad Kalakesh was seventeen when he was picked up by Israeli troops on a sweep through his village; his family were deeply involved with the Islamic group Hezbollah, and one of his brothers had been a suicide bomber. He told us he was tortured for eleven months, and gave us a graphic account of the way electric shocks were administered to his fingers and genitals.

Ryad's other brother Adel was detained in Khiam too; when Adel refused to tell the interrogators what they wanted to hear they hauled in his wife Mona and tortured her so that he could hear her screams. Mona's pain was also inflicted with electricity – through wires attached to her nipples. She spent three months in solitary confinement and lost her baby while she was in prison.

We recorded this testimony, then flew to Jerusalem to explore the extent of Israel's connection with the regime at Khiam. And we found ourselves in the middle of the kind of news story that is liable to overwhelm time-consuming investigative journalism.

I had arranged a briefing with the British embassy – I have always found the Foreign Office well informed and its embassies helpful to passing journalists – but the ambassador, Francis Cornish, whom I had come to know quite well during his stint running the Foreign Office newsroom in London, phoned me to cancel, explaining that a 'little local difficulty' required his attention.

He was a former army officer and a diplomat of the old school, and this was something of an understatement. That morning, the hawkish ex-general Ariel Sharon and a delegation of his Likud party, guarded by scores of Israeli riot police, visited the Haram al-Sharif, the third holiest place in Islam, where the Dome of the Rock and the Al-Aqsa mosque stand. Because the site is also known as the Temple Mount – the Jewish Temple stood there until it was destroyed by the Romans in AD 70 – the compound is a notoriously contested piece of land. In the aftermath of Sharon's visit the Second Intifada (uprising) blew up, and over the following five years of mayhem and murder thousands of Israelis and Palestinians were killed. If anyone else had thought of investigating Khiam, the Intifada would have squashed the idea: it was no longer news. But we plodded on – even as the daily headlines consigned the recent past in Lebanon ever more definitively to history.

We were greatly helped by an Israeli human-rights group who took their own government to court to force an admission that Israel had paid the salaries of all the Khiam prison staff. Eleven of the guards were sentenced to death *in absentia* by the Lebanese government in Beirut, and we managed to run one of them, the camp commander, to earth in a spacious penthouse with Mediterranean views in the northern Israeli town of Netanya. He would not talk to us, but we had at least established that Israel had given him asylum.

And then we secured, with just a little guile, an interview that yielded a decisive admission. Yossi Peled had commanded Israeli forces in Lebanon in the late 1980s, and was now responsible for looking after the SLA refugees who had fled their country with the Israeli withdrawal. We asked to talk to him about his refugee work, but once the camera was rolling I began to ask him about Khiam – a subterfuge I do not for a moment regret.

He very quickly realized he had been had but, to his credit, he pressed on gamely with a defence. Eventually he conceded, 'It would be very difficult, not clever, to say we were not involved in any way. We were sitting in the Zone for so many years, and inside the Security Zone Khiam was located. It was not on the Moon.' Bingo, case closed, the fat lady was singing at last.

The programme won us an Amnesty Award for Best Television Documentary – never believe journalists who claim they do not care about such things – but the greatest compliment came, perversely, from the Israeli government. All sides in the Middle East conflict are notoriously energetic complainers – so much so that some editors would rather ignore the subject altogether, simply to avoid the hassle of answering the letters – and we expected plenty of protest from Israeli lobby groups and officials. We had given the programme the title *Israel Accused*, so it could not have been more provocatively sold. In fact it was met with complete silence – there was not so much as a peep from the embassy in London.

But, of course, by the time it was broadcast all the news bandwidth available in the Middle East was taken up by the Intifada and the terrifying phenomenon of the suicide bomber. The film went out on 4 November 2000. Two days earlier, a booby-trapped car had blown up in a crowded market in Jerusalem, killing two, and there were three bombings that month alone. The following year saw forty, which left 85 dead and 476 injured. It was only a few months since Israel's withdrawal from southern Lebanon, but Khiam had become territory for historians, not journalists.

So I was left wondering – as I was after telling Sean Sellers's story – what we had really achieved. The answer, or at least a kind of answer, was supplied by a novel I read while writing this chapter.

Alaa Al Aswany's *The Yacoubian Building* sold over a million copies and, as the flyleaf of his latest book proudly proclaims, 'was the bestselling novel in the Arab world for over five years'. Through the lives of a group of tenants in a Cairo apartment block it painted a devastating picture of Egyptian life under Hosni Mubarak, and Aswany was a passionate champion of the revolution that led to Mubarak's overthrow.

His 2021 book, *The Republic of False Truths*, uses the same technique to tell the story of the way that revolution unravelled. Through the eyes of a similar group of characters we experience the euphoria of revolt, then the relentless reassertion of old power systems, leading eventually to a new military strongman.

Midway through the book, there is a chapter of witness statements made by participants in a demonstration against the Military Council then running the country. They march peacefully chanting protest slogans ('Sons of Shubra, come on down! There's a million

Mubaraks still around!'), but are brutally attacked by the army and many of them are killed.

The witness statements are a very effective narrative technique, and Aswany has one of his characters begin his like this:

> 'First, let me offer my condolences to all the families of the martyrs and mourn all our Egyptian martyrs. I think of them as martyrs in God's eyes. Second: This is a testimony, not an analysis, meaning that I'm telling only what I saw, without analysis or inferences.'

Aswany is a journalist as well as a novelist, and that second declaration is a pregnant definition of good reporting. Campaigning journalism is something different, and it is not the BBC way, but we can broadcast 'testimony . . . without analysis or inferences'. Telling Khiam's story allowed our witnesses – Ali, Ryad, Adel and Mona, for they all deserve the dignity of their names – to put their witness statements on the record.

Perhaps the programme also helped to stop the Khiam episode – which was shameful and wrong – from dropping out of memory altogether. But recording testimony was itself worth doing. It matters to tell these stories, whether or not they have any impact. It matters especially to tell the stories of those – like the Khiam victims and Sean Sellers – who are left behind by the swirls and surging currents of daily news.

You have to believe in that principle to keep going as a reporter. And the truth demands that it is done well and accurately, even if your subject is a 'painter of mediocre ability' who is also a triple murderer. Story-telling is what still gets me up in the morning.

Aswany's book prompted another, more melancholy reflection on the reporter's trade. I interviewed him not long after the

Egyptian revolution – he is, on top of his other accomplishments, a dentist, so we met at his surgery in one of the elegant but slightly dowdy belle-époque apartment buildings that are such a Cairo feature. The country was in a ferment of debate about a new constitution, and the possibility of a democratic and free future seemed real. *The Republic of False Truths* is a heart-breaking reminder of how quickly those hopes were disappointed.

It made me think of all the other times reporting has taken me to places where hope has flourished only to be crushed.

I reached Kabul with a *Today* programme team a couple of days after the Taliban fell in 2001, and we broadcast the show live from a hotel balcony, enjoying the sunshine and the crisp air coming down from the Hindu Kush. Everyone was bubbling with optimism, especially for the future now promised to Afghan women.

A few years later my own daughter's soldier boyfriend (now her husband) was being shot at in Helmand by a resurgent Taliban. And twenty years on I was presenting *The World at One* as the Taliban closed on Kabul once again, and set about reinstating their regime. We played an archive clip from that 2001 programme to remind our listeners of all those high hopes of progress, which now seemed destined to be reversed.

I was in Baghdad for Iraq's elections in 2005, the country's first since the fall of Saddam Hussein and, indeed, the first free elections in its history. It was still a brutally violent city – one of my colleagues was startled when a spent round dropped neatly into the cup of tea he was enjoying on the veranda of the BBC guesthouse – but Iraqis turned out in their tens of thousands to exercise their right to vote. It was humbling to watch them risk their lives for something we take for granted, and it seemed to bode well for the future. A decade and a half later, democracy still has not delivered them from the deep flaw of sectarianism.

And hopes for a resolution to the conflict between Israel and the Palestinians have been raised and crushed more times than I can count. I am addicted to that troubled part of the Middle East – like most reporters who have worked there – but the prospects for peace now seem so bleak it is painful to make the trip back.

The madcap moments did not disappear altogether with the new reporting world. One of the maddest I enjoyed involved, not long after the Khiam documentary, a trip in search of the National Liberation Front of Corsica (or FLNC, to give them their French acronym) who were dedicated to separating their island from France. We were attracted to the group by widely quoted reports that they ran a terrorist summer camp, and had in the past included both the Basque separatists ETA and the IRA on their list of invitees.

My producer was an old friend, Ewa Ewart, who is Polish and had learnt her journalism while working as a fixer for foreign broadcasters during the Solidarity strikes, which helped bring down Communism in Poland. She is, in consequence, formidably determined and tenacious about achieving her objectives, and she lined up a most spectacular scoop.

The terrorists agreed to talk, and informed us – weirdly, it seemed to me – that the meeting should take place on an area of the island set aside for live-fire exercises by the French Army. We followed their instructions, and found that a gate in the barbed-wire fencing had indeed been left discreetly open for us. The *maquis* – the bushland that gave its name to French Resistance fighters during the Second World War – seemed entirely deserted until, in a miraculously well-coordinated moment, dozens of men wearing black balaclavas rose as one from the scrubby terrain. I was driving, and one of them leapt into the seat beside me, waving his gun and shouting orders to accelerate.

After some energetic bouncing over a murderously potholed track, we reached a cluster of abandoned farm buildings, and our hosts obligingly started blowing them up for the camera. They staged a variety of military manoeuvres – ambush, sniper fire, even a bit of drill – and then, just as suddenly and silently as they had appeared, they melted back into the *maquis*. My admittedly sketchy knowledge of the BBC producer guidelines told me we might have a bit of difficulty putting all this on air – we couldn't even pretend that it hadn't been staged for us – but it was impressive, and made for some wonderful footage.

The shine came off the day's outing when it became apparent our vehicle would not start. Later investigation revealed that in the wild rush up the track – my driving had been less than careful, an understandable lapse, I felt, in the circumstances – I had smashed some vital piece of the engine by bouncing over a rock. The truck was completely and irrecoverably immobile.

What do you do when you are *en panne* in the middle of a military firing range after a rendezvous with a group of armed outlaws, surrounded by miles of inhospitable terrain and with no idea of which way would lead you somewhere safe? Ewa did the sensible thing: she rang the local garage on her mobile. A mechanic arrived surprisingly quickly: he knew exactly where we were, because he had been there very recently himself, wearing a balaclava and brandishing a sub-machine gun.

TODAY

16 · A TERRIBLE MAN

To the audience the *Today* programme presenters *are* the programme. To some on the team who actually put the show together we were – when I was presenting – a group of cantankerous eccentrics who popped into the studio from time to time at anti-social hours and routinely made a hash of their carefully planned items. *Today*'s fiftieth anniversary fell during my time there, and in a piece in the *Observer* one of the producers anonymously compared our 4 a.m. arrival for each morning's show to being drenched in 'a bucket of cold sick'.

We almost never saw our colleagues in civilized hours. There were a few occasions at which fraternization was possible – political conferences, for example, the Christmas party and the annual skiing trip (of which more later) – but for the most part we visited the office at a time when most people were asleep or breakfasting.

But one afternoon in 2000, not long after joining the presenter line-up, I popped into *Today*'s open-plan area on the first floor of Television Centre after a meeting with another BBC programme. And my eyes were drawn to – who knows why? – a piece of paper lying on one of the desks. It was a memo from a senior editorial figure to the person in charge of the presenter rotas, and it read, 'If you need to fill a gap, try Stourton or Montague – they are cheaper than Humphrys and Naughtie.'

Sarah's pay dispute would later become part of a wider scandal about the way the BBC treated its women. I did not at all mind being viewed as a cheap date because it meant I got more shifts, which I greatly enjoyed. In financial terms I was also relishing the working hours of a job that liberated me just after nine in the morning: there was plenty of day left to make extra cash by doing something remunerative, like writing a book.

I suspect I also felt comfortable on *Today* because, despite its ambitions to be ahead of curves and to set agendas rather than following them, it was, in those days, a curiously old-fashioned institution, a journalistic version, in many ways, of the Pitt Club or the Ampleforth Monitors' Room. The physical environment, of course, was very different: the Green Room for guests at Television Centre was a small glass box furnished with a trolley of often tired toast, while in the roomy, stone-flagged Monitors' Room toast was made on an open fire and consumed on a vast oak settle. But the clubbiness and obedience to tradition were very much the same.

It reflected the fact that – like the Pitt and the monastery in North Yorkshire – *Today* had deep roots in history. Radio reigned supreme in the BBC's early years, and the medium emerged triumphantly from the Second World War as the nation's main source of information and entertainment. By the late 1950s, though, with the birth of ITV alongside the BBC's own television service, the Spoken Word (always capitalized in early BBC documents) faced a real challenge from moving pictures.

A 1957 internal report at the Corporation – *The Future of Sound Broadcasting in the Domestic Services* – concluded that early mornings, when most households were too busy to settle in front of a television set, represented radio's best hope of meeting the challenge, and the paper considered the case for a morning programme of 'news and information, weather, market reports, food news, press reviews, medical talks, household hints, etc'. *Today* went on the air that autumn.

Its founding mothers were two brilliant Oxford women, Janet Quigley, the chief assistant in the Talks department, and Isa Benzie, its first 'organizer'. Benzie's opening billing for the programme underlines how visionary she was: 'Today, whoever you are, wherever you are in the United Kingdom, face your own day more buoyant and stimulated for having heard *Today*, with something for you, wherever you work, and time checks! *Today*!'

Time-keeping habits have changed a bit since the 1950s, but Benzie's time checks endure even in an age when most younger listeners have moved beyond watches altogether, relying instead on their mobile phones. And the so-called 'programme furniture', which has grown up around them – the pips, the racing tips at the end of the sport slots, the courtesy of always mentioning your fellow presenter's name before your own when you 'ident' the programme – have acquired the sacred aura endowed by long tradition.

The Benzie–Quigley partnership was quirky as well as brilliant. Just before the programme went on the air Quigley raised an unusual suggestion: 'From time to time I am struck by the fact that, as a nation, we are so very bad about fish,' she wrote to her friend and colleague. 'We are ignorant about choosing it, unimaginative about cooking it, apathetic about eating it ... Some good ideas might occur if we thought about it hard. Meantime, what about devoting a regular item, however short, to it on Friday mornings? I mean just a flash – "The Fish of the Week".' 'Fish of the Week' did not have quite the staying power of the time checks, but the quirkiness is still there – and a mix of brilliance and quirkiness is the essential ingredient in most British institutions.

Even the journey to work had a ritual feel. I programmed my alarm to go off at 3 a.m., and the early starts took a little getting used to. In a diary piece I wrote for the *Journalist's Handbook* I recorded that 'One of the household cats, which always demands food at this ungodly hour, is unsatisfied by the dry stuff I have put in his bowl – the smell of anything else is too appalling to contemplate at this stage of the life cycle. He sits and stares at me with the unblinking inquisitorial eye of an unforgiving interviewer, and it is so unsettling that I have to move and finish my coffee at the desk in the drawing room.'

But I quite quickly established a routine, building in time for a good bath and shave, and at least ten minutes of contemplation over that restorative cup of coffee. Sometimes, on summer mornings, I even took it with me into the quiet of the garden, enjoying the rising rush of expectation and excitement amid the gentleness of the dawn, which I so relished during my reporting days.

At 3.40 a.m. I stepped into the sleek Mercedes waiting to take me to the office. A full set of papers was always placed on the back seat, so neat that I enjoyed a fancy they had been pressed by some mysterious BBC butler. It was exhilarating to be driven along the empty London streets while powering through the papers: I felt I could command the day ahead.

A pile of 'briefs' awaited me on my desk in Television Centre, carefully laid out in on-air sequence. Like lawyers' briefs, these were designed to provide the essential facts for each interview, and the presenting pair would spend the next two hours working through them and crafting quick 'cues' to introduce each item. Sharpening one's inquisitorial reflexes by being rude about the brief-writers was, I am afraid, part of the ritual.

In the studio the presenters sat alongside one another, like a tennis doubles team, facing interviewees across the desk. The two senior men had their settled places: John Humphrys always played forehand and James Naughtie manned the backhand court, their respective positions as reverently fixed as the library chair of any Pall Mall clubman. John insisted on old-fashioned Bakelite headphones, and a pair was always laid out on his desk.

Alongside all these time-honoured traditions, the programme was burdened with less attractive legacies from the past. The culture was undeniably sexist. Even when I joined at the turn of this century it seemed to be universally – and uncritically – accepted that the show should not, ideally, be presented by two women, because the audience 'wouldn't wear it'.

Much later I edited a book on *Today*'s history, and asked Sue MacGregor about her eighteen years on the show. 'I think the first pair of women to present was Jennie Bond [then the BBC's royal correspondent] and me,' she emailed. 'It was so extraordinary that the *Daily Express* came in to take a picture . . . and it didn't happen again for ages.' In her autobiography Sue quotes a survey which showed that in 2001 the main interview of the day went to John Humphrys on 77 per cent of his days on, while Jim Naughtie's score was 56 per cent and her own 38 per cent. 'Interestingly,' she added, 'Edward Stourton, a newer member of the *Today* team, had a figure of 61 per cent.'

I confess I was not aware of being a beneficiary of old-school chauvinism. The feature in the programme culture that most excited me was *Today*'s unembarrassed ambition to be intelligent. Most television newsrooms I had worked in were touched by cultural cringe, a fear of appearing arrogant to the viewers or talking over their heads. I found *Today* – and Radio 4 more generally – completely and wonderfully unabashed about being clever.

Just occasionally the cleverness got out of hand. Covering the G8 Summit in St Petersburg in 2006, I found myself in the hands of a notoriously literary producer called Peter Hanington (the father of the programme's long-running 'guest editor' scheme, and now a successful novelist). Just before the summit opened, war broke out between Israel and Hezbollah, and because the world's most powerful leaders were gathered with us, we were in pole position to cover the diplomatic fallout.

Peter, however, was not greatly impressed by this news imperative. He had discovered that Dostoyevsky's grandson worked in St Petersburg as a taxi driver, and conceived an ambition to interview him in the square where, in *Crime and Punishment*, Raskolnikov undergoes his conversion. Forget the summit, all our resources were directed towards achieving this ambition.

When we were eventually brought together with Dostoyevsky junior on the chosen piece of sacred earth, it emerged that our quarry did not speak English, and since we had no translator, we had to phone the BBC's Moscow bureau and relay the questions and answers through a native speaker. The questions themselves were even more of a challenge. What, when you think about it, does a St Petersburg taxi driver have to offer on Israel's need for a security zone in southern Lebanon? Somehow or other, Peter got something on air.

Moments of eccentricity like that apart, the commitment to cleverness provided the bedrock of *Today*'s sense of direction. We broadcast on the assumption that our audience are well-informed, thoughtful people with the capacity to understand complex arguments and ideas. That certainly did not mean being exclusive or – in the modern sense of the word – elitist. We would have been delighted if Mum in Wigan, that mythical figure of tabloid journalism I was taught to target in my early ITN days, had tuned in. If she did, we would certainly not have talked down to her.

Quite a lot of things made John Humphrys angry, but – and I greatly admired him for this – he became especially wound up at any hint of patronizing our listeners or guests. Woe betide any producer who suggested – on one of those briefs the team wrote up for our interviews – that an interviewee could be referred to by his or her first name simply because they were an 'ordinary person' rather than a politician or expert. 'You can't call her Doris just because she's in a care home,' John would thunder. 'She deserves the dignity of Mrs Snodgrass just as much as the prime minister deserves to be Mr Blair.'

I had done a little radio before joining the team – enough to realize that it required very different skills. A couple of years earlier I had recorded a big Radio 4 series on what were then called the Asian Tigers, the assertive economies emerging in places like South Korea, Malaysia and China. The producer, Sue Davies, took me to a sweatshop in Shenzhen where rows and rows of young women were stitching cheap clothing for export to Western markets. 'Describe what you see,' she instructed. That, of course, is the one thing you never do in television, because the pictures do the visual work. It took me time to learn how to include things like dimensions and colour, which you need to bring a scene to life with words.

But live radio broadcasting very quickly came to feel like liberation. Gone were the complicated cogs and wheels you need to master for live television, the endless worries about which camera to look at and how your hair and tie are holding up. And instead of the 'open talkback' of telly – which means the unfiltered chaos of the gallery constantly pouring into your earpiece – radio talkback is selective: all you hear in your cans are timings and, just occasionally, a suggested question from the editor.

Tony Whitby, the Radio 4 controller who, in the 1970s, gave the network its distinctive voice, pronounced this swaggering claim for the medium: 'In the realm of ideas, radio operates with uncluttered lucidity. In the realm of the imagination, it soars where other media limp.' I became a committed convert and, partly as a consequence, the over-controlling on-air anxiety of my telly newscaster days began to melt away.

Getting used to presenting a two-person show – especially such a long one – was a learning curve. Monsterish behaviour by presenters was an accepted part of *Today* life – very much of a piece, indeed, with the testosterone-fuelled and unforgiving on-air atmosphere that made programmes fizz.

Sledging in the studio was not unknown. An experienced presenter can, for example, quite easily trip a newcomer into the cardinal crime known as 'crashing the pips' – talking over those six short bursts of tone that announce the turn of each hour. And I quickly learnt to feel irritated when my partner pinched too much airtime for an interview, shrinking mine by doing so. There are usually two big interviews in the 7.30–8.00 section, for example, and when I was assigned the second I knew I was almost bound to feel my blood pressure rising as my colleague stole time for the first. As one of our editors, Kevin Marsh, liked to remind us, the Time Fairy does not exist, and no one is going to push back the eight o'clock news.

Today is a surprisingly easy programme to present competently. All the 'programme furniture' it has inherited may be daunting at first, but I quickly realized it provided useful props to hang on to. As long as you get your time checks right and remember when to introduce sport and Thought for the Day you can sound perfectly plausible. But it is a very difficult programme to present well: you need the confidence to take risks. And a solid relationship with your fellow presenters is key to that confidence.

John Humphrys, belying his fearsome reputation, welcomed me to the team with a piece of advice told as a joke. On a bad morning, when lines were going down and minds were constantly changing, the gallery could descend into chaos. 'Just occasionally,' John warned me, 'they'll fling you an interview at the last minute without telling you what it's about or who you're talking to. They'll just shout something like "Millbank – now" at you, and all you can really say by way of introduction is "We go live to our Westminster studio." My technique for dealing with this is to put on my gravest voice and say, "Minister, this sounds serious" – with a bit of luck he or she will tell you what the story is in the first answer.'

There was another version of this for dealing with complex foreign stories: if you felt you were getting out of your depth, you could resort to 'And tell me, what's the position now in the south of the country?' It never quite happened like this, but it sometimes came close.

I became – and I hope remain – friends with all my fellow presenters, but relations between us were not made any easier by the steady stream of newspaper commentary on our relative status and performances, plus advice on which of us should be sacked and which promoted. Leafing idly through the gossip columns before going on air, one was likely to chance upon charming little nuggets like this, from the Ephraim Hardcastle column in the *Mail*: 'As the published historian of Radio 4's *Today* programme, its former editor Tim Luckhurst writes about its decline. He says Sarah Montague is "struggling to cope", and regards Ed "Posh" Stourton as second banana to Humphrys, whom he sees as the only class act. Mr Luckhurst fails to mention presenter James Naughtie at all. "Mr Naughtie reeks of the politically correct bias that so damages the *Today* programme's reputation," he says.'

And when Mark Damazer, my friend from ITN days, took over as the controller of Radio 4, a former BBC editor offered him this in a long piece in the *Independent*: 'My advice: bolster James Naughtie and Ed Stourton, replace Sarah Montague with Carolyn Quinn, and sideline Humphrys. If he flounces out in a huff, so much the better.'

Reflect that when you read this kind of thing, a colleague who had received one of the more disobliging notices was likely to be sitting in the chair next to you. We would both pretend we had not read it, while both knowing perfectly well that we both had, and it rather took the shine off the studio atmosphere during that day's programme.

And, of course, we all took flak from time to time. The *Mail* later changed its mind about me. From the heights of being 'second banana to Humphrys', I became 'that blandly effete paragon of political correctness Ed Stourton'. My crime was being insufficiently rude to Tony Blair during an interview, and the paper devoted a whole op-ed* page to the questions I failed to ask. This jeremiad was written by a panel of heavyweight commentators, including one near-contemporary from university I had always got on well with, and a friend who had recently attended a party my wife Fiona and I had held to celebrate our marriage. Journalism is a rough old game at the top.

Looking through the cuttings – so many of them utterly inconsequential – I am surprised by how often the 'posh' label pops up. Almost every mention of my name is accompanied by a reference to 'cultured tones', a 'grand voice' or even, in one newspaper, 'the Stourton drawl, a product of Ampleforth and Caam-bridge'.

In the *Evening Standard* I read that '*Today* programme presenter Edward Stourton has been desperately trying to beef up his tough-man image at the BBC in an attempt to overcome internal prejudice against softly spoken toffs such as himself.' News to me, but as evidence the writer cited 'a recent media dinner when one senior BBC executive loudly proclaimed that Stourton, known as Posh Spice to his colleagues, should "do a Thatcher in reverse" to bolster his career prospects'.

The *Guardian*, meanwhile, invented a kind of High Court judge persona for me – aloof and comically ignorant of the modern

---

* Opposite the editorial page.

world – in their G2 section. They ran a fantasy interview in which I struggled with the news that Dizzee Rascal had won the Mercury music prize. 'Um, a bit of translation?' they had me plead, after hearing the rapper's acceptance speech. 'What does "big up" mean for a start?'

Politicians worry about this kind of thing. These were the Blair–Brown years, and it was not unusual for a thin-skinned senior cabinet minister to ring a journalist personally to complain about some trivial slight. We hacks all rather scoffed at this sensitivity, but the politicians were probably right: gossipy stories and flip labels do stick. I had always thought of myself as someone who reported on the doings of others, and did not take seriously the idea that I might be reported on myself. I probably should have done.

Rod Liddle, *Today*'s editor when I joined, saw the comic potential of the posh label. I found him a more complex character than the slightly monotone shouty voice he projects in his *Sunday Times* columns suggests. It is true that he dressed like a Goth, sporting black day and night, and that he drank and swore as if he had stepped out of a 1960s Fleet Street satire. But he could also be oddly courtly and old-fashioned: I did some trial shifts on the programme before I joined full time, and was surprised – and pleased – to get a thank-you note from him written with a fountain pen.

Rod had an unerring instinct for where Middle England liked to be tickled and scratched, and his antennae for the British class system were finely tuned. John Prescott, deputy prime minister at the time, was famously chippy about his working-class origins (when asked whether an MP's salary had altered his life he replied, 'I have changed. I no longer keep the coal in the bath. I keep it in the bidet'), and was also very sensitive about his inability to corral his speeches and interviews into meaningful sentences. The (late and great) sketch writer Simon Hoggart compared a Prescott speech to 'a man taking a big bouncy dog for a country walk. No matter how hard he tries, he can't help the speech racing off wherever it will, being distracted by a herd of cows, charging into undergrowth, tugging at its lead so it almost drags its owner into the mud.'

Rod calculated that he could push Prescott just a bit closer to the edge by assigning an alleged toff to his interviews. It was a good call. Almost all our encounters proved rich examples of those moments when, as Hoggart put it, 'the syntax crumbles and the *Today* team ducks under the table'. The first took place in the middle of a controversy about Prescott's enormous portfolio of power – his brief covered the environment, transport, housing and the regions, and his department was known as a 'super-ministry'. Throughout the interview the deputy prime minister referred to super-ministries as 'supermarkets'.

Prescott's tactical response to Rod's gambit was to refer to me as 'Eddie' on air – he was right in thinking that annoyed me – and on one occasion he delivered an *ad hominem* attack before I had even completed my first question. Sometimes he simply defeated me by leaving all sense and logic behind. 'I am asking you, if you give me these facts, you are supposed to give some factual analysis to it – I mean, you are not denying that these facts are wrong, are you?' he demanded on one occasion. If I had tried thinking that one through, I would have been lost for the rest of the programme.

Perhaps most enjoyable was this response during an interview in the autumn of 2002: 'You're a terrible man for asking the questions and not giving an answer,' he declared, with the confidence of a man delivering a knockout blow. I had always imagined that was the point of my job: silly me.

Preconceived ideas about the BBC in general and the *Today* programme in particular run deep, and the fact that they sometimes contradict one another does not stop them being firmly held. While taking flak for being an arrogant toff doing his best to undermine the Labour government, I also got a healthy crop of listener letters accusing me – and often all my BBC colleagues – of being a dangerous leftie devoted to the death of all that is sacred in British society.

At around the time of my duels with John Prescott, the BBC was caught in a PR maelstrom over the coverage of the death of the Queen Mother, confected almost entirely around the colour of poor Peter Sissons's tie when he broadcast the news. After an enjoyable on-air rough and tumble with the *Mail* journalist Quentin Letts on this subject, I got a letter from Chipping Norton attacking 'your aggressive and (characteristically) ill-mannered constant interruptions'.

There were a couple of paragraphs raging against me, and then my correspondent really got into his stride, leaving punctuation stranded in his angry wake: 'Your Director General [Greg Dyke] looking like a barrow boy is also a friend and supporter of Tony Blair and contributor to New Labour who, one must assume, supports if not promotes the filthy gutter language now so frequently heard on the BBC. The whole rotten organization staffed by Guardian reading republicans, many of whom seem to be self-promoting queers or at least politically correct supporters of sexual deviance . . .' You get the picture. Even more collectible was a letter from someone claiming they could 'see the hatred of the Tories in your eyes' during an interview with a member of the Conservative shadow cabinet – an impressive perception, since the interview was broadcast on the radio.

Listeners' letters – and most of the listeners, especially the angry ones, preferred old-fashioned paper in those days – enlivened the life of a *Today* presenter no end. I did my best to answer those sent to me directly, but it was sometimes difficult to strike the right balance, because the listeners were so divided among themselves.

During the controversy over Israel's use of white phosphorus shells during the Gaza conflict of 2008–9, I interviewed an Israeli government spokesman in a manner that left one listener enraged. He sent me a copy of the blast he had directed at my editor: 'I was astonished this morning to hear Ed Stourton's aggressive questioning of an Israeli official on this and other matters without any apparent attempt at balance and objectivity. This interview smacked of policy rather than accuracy and fairness.' That same day I found this missive in my pigeonhole: 'Dear Mr Stourton, I just wanted to say that your interview this morning with the gentleman from Israel about the alleged use of white phosphorus was, quite simply, to my mind, brilliant ... The interview should be carefully preserved and made compulsory listening for all radio presenters ... as a model of how the job should be done.'

One of Rod's other passions – alongside the pleasure he took in playing the class game – was avant-garde writers, ideally those with the added glamour of decadence. Will Self became a regular on the programme, and our editor was especially thrilled by the works of the French novelist Michel Houellebecq. As a so-called 'miserabilist', Houellebecq shared some of Rod's penchants, including aggressively off-putting clothing and descriptions of disgusting sex, and had a relentlessly bleak, nihilistic vision of the modern world that clearly struck a chord in the Liddle sensibility.

When *Les particules élémentaires* was published in English (under the title *Atomized*), Houellebecq was booked for a prime-time slot on a Saturday morning. The book was widely interpreted as a brutal condemnation of the emptiness and promiscuity of culture in the 1960s, and also a very personal attack on the author's own mother. When I bade him good morning, live at 8.20, I was looking forward to a rewarding encounter. Monsieur Houellebecq had even been good enough to come into Studio 1A at Television Centre, and face-to-face interviews always work best.

It very quickly became apparent that, great wordsmith though he might have been in his native language, he did not, in the normal sense of the phrase, speak English. I am sure he could have ordered from most British menus, and he gave every sign of understanding what I asked him, but he never quite succeeded in getting the grammar and vocabulary together in a way that would allow him to frame a coherent sentence.

Having once or twice risked live appearances on French television, I had great sympathy. But five minutes is a lot of airtime to fill with someone who cannot speak the language your audience understands. I took refuge in ever more prolix questions, piling on the sub-clauses and offering our guest – who remained perfectly cheerful and not one whit abashed – the opportunity to say a simple *oui* or *non*. We finally ground to a halt with my very tentative attempts to be challenging in the *Today* tradition.

Me: You've done it cleverly, but essentially this is just a tabloid newspaper trick.

MH: Mmm . . . maybe, yes.

Me: You've talked about the sex, and people will talk about the sex because there's an awful lot of it in this book. You could argue that it is simply pornographic.

MH: Oh, yes, it is pornographic sometimes, yes.

That was it.

We went early to sport.

The Houellebecq debacle makes a cheerful sort of war story: no one got hurt, and the great French author (I now read all his books as soon as they are published) seemed to feel it had all gone rather well. He did not even pass comment on the very un-French quality of the croissants offered alongside the limp toast on the Green Room trolley.

The N-word incident did not feel funny at all.

General Patrick Cordingley is an extremely nice man. He commanded the Desert Rats during the first Gulf War, and after his retirement in 2000 he became something of a regular on *Today* as an authoritative commentator on military matters. During the national debate about the British Army's role in southern Iraq following the 2003 invasion, he came on one morning to discuss whether the Iraqi Army and police were sufficiently well-prepared to take responsibility for their country's security. The army, he assured me, were well on their way, but he feared the police would be 'the n— in the woodpile'.

Describing the incident not long afterwards I wrote that

> I completely believe the theory that a drowning man sees his whole life flash before his eyes before he goes, because at a live broadcasting moment like that the world really does slow down. My pause probably sounded like a nanosecond to the listeners, but to me it felt as if the memories of all the bad moments in a quarter of a century of broadcasting experience were flashing back and forth across my synapses as I desperately tried to formulate an appropriate response.

In that nanosecond I decided to pretend it had not happened. I knew the general a little, and I was quite sure he was not a racist. Most of our audience would, I hazarded, assume that he had made a slip characteristic of his age and class, and would object to me drawing attention to his mistake. And I concluded that picking him up would turn an unfortunate incident into something much bigger and worse. When I next burst out of the studio – gasping for breath like a landed fish – my editor reassured me with the not entirely comforting view that 'There is no right response to something like that.'

Was my judgement right, then? I do not know. But I am quite

sure that it would be wrong today because public perceptions about racism and language have changed significantly in the intervening years. If a general was to commit the same word crime now, I would certainly haul him (or, since 2015, her) up. Split-second judgements on the way taste and standards change are a necessary part of the live presenter's skill set.

On programmes broadcast later in the day you can wind down from moments of high-wire tension like that over a convivial drink and laughter with the rest of the team. Not so, for obvious reasons, on *Today*: there was a time when the menu provided on the breakfast trolley included a bottle of Scotch, but those days are, happily, long gone.

The programme did, however, offer a more cerebral form of post-broadcast recovery: the office was always awash with books. Publishers sent in absolutely everything that might have a chance of making an item, and part of the fun of presenting the programme lay in stretching the intellectual legs a little in the final half-hour, which usually included more literary and ideas-based debate.

Given the time pressure in the early morning, we could only dip into the volumes that sometimes appeared on top of those briefing notes, and I fell into the habit of taking one to read in the back of the car while I was being driven home. After a while this became just as much of a vice as drinking whisky for breakfast: I have a terrible weakness for filling the shelves, and around halfway through my *Today* years we had to move house to accommodate the books.

I celebrated my fiftieth birthday while I was on *Today*. John, Jim and Sue were all older. The production team, by contrast, were mostly much younger men and women at an early stage of their careers. This was partly because the working pattern required of producers and editors, which included frequent all-night shifts, was physically punishing. The one event that brought old and young together was the annual skiing trip, always organized by Jim Naughtie, who approached the task with the enthusiasm and sense of adventure that marked his journalism.

It always began with a Friday flight to the chosen Alpine destination, a big and bibulous dinner that evening, followed by two days of bashing the slopes and a Monday-morning return to Blighty. That it led to several long-term relationships between team members was a mark of its success.

On one trip the male/female balance of numbers was badly awry, and I found myself allocated a room in the women's chalet. A young broadcast assistant informed me that this was because I had been judged to be 'non-predatory'. This was, of course, one of the kindest compliments I have ever been paid, but it did make me feel a little like that fantasy High Court judge of the *Guardian*.

17 · SEND IN THE BUTLER WITH THE BRANDY AND THE REVOLVER

Presenting *Today* fools you into thinking you matter. You get asked to chair charities and review books, the party invites pour in and everyone wants you to speak at their annual dinners.

I most enjoyed being put on the French ambassador's list of journalists worth cultivating. His seduction technique was a regular breakfast appointment at his elegant residence overlooking Kensington Gardens: the grub was, of course, always beautifully served, and the scrambled eggs were cooked to perfection.

The favoured few generally included one other broadcaster plus half a dozen columnists and senior correspondents from the more serious papers, and as we enjoyed our sumptuous *petit déjeuner*, Gérard Errera briefed the French 'line' on the international story of the day. His Excellency was the model of a serpentine diplomat, spoke perfect English with a comedy French accent and was extremely witty.

One morning during the diplomatic crisis that preceded the 2003 invasion of Iraq, with Paris and Washington in a stand-off at the United Nations over military action, he greeted us with an especially grave demeanour. 'We have been concerned for some time that the White House is refusing to serve French wine, and apparently Freedom Fries have replaced French Fries on the president's menu,' he told us, 'but now we know things are really serious. We have intelligence that George Bush has stopped reading Proust.'

Because most of my reporting career was spent covering foreign news, I had lived largely outside the 'Westminster Bubble', which it is now so fashionable to deride (the MPs who condemn it most vocally are usually the ones who most enjoy its gossip and plotting), but I had been given the odd glimpse of how things worked in this fabled hothouse.

During the 1992 general election I was taken off my diplomatic beat to cover John Major and, just before the campaign began, we spent a day filming with the prime minister and his wife at their constituency home in Huntingdonshire. It was partly a bonding exercise for the team – elections create a temporary but intense intimacy between the hunters and the hunted, and we would be spending almost every waking hour glued to the PM's person for the duration. Major, who had much more personal charm than he was given credit for, ordered an Indian takeaway for lunch.

As we enjoyed our poppadoms with the prime ministerial couple, I noticed that they had a substantial collection of off-air recordings on a shelf under the television set. Closer inspection revealed that most of them were my own reports on some of the official trips he had made abroad. I had, of course, swotted up on him for this assignment, but the idea that he would swot up on me had never occurred.

The neatly written labels told me that one of the tapes included my report on a charity cricket match Mr Major had played during the Commonwealth heads of government meeting in Zimbabwe the previous year; the prime minister had a slight limp thanks to a bad knee, and in my commentary, I suggested that he was deter-mined to bat with enough skill to show that he 'was not a lame duck prime minister'. It seemed quite a clever line at the time, but remembering this while sitting at the Major kitchen table turned me quite cold with embarrassment.

Almost all relations between journalists and politicians are fraught with ethical dilemma. Specialist reporters have to cultivate their contacts – it is the way to secure stories – and that naturally encourages a temptation to curry favour in their reporting. For presenters on a programme like *Today*, the danger lies in the clubbiness that comes with membership (or at least the illusion of membership) of a magic circle at the heart of the nation's affairs. It is, of course, flattering to be treated as a friend by senior cabinet ministers.

I learnt the dangers of friendship after a country-house weekend with a Tory grandee. It was during Iain Duncan Smith's time as the party's leader, and our host was one of the growing number of MPs who were losing patience with their miserable polling numbers and the uninspiring performances of 'the quiet man' – a nickname Duncan Smith gave himself to excuse his lack of impact – at party conferences. 'The time has come,' our host declared, over a very good vintage port late on Saturday night, 'to send in the butler with the brandy and the revolver.'

The following week said host was fingered in the papers as part of a plot to unseat Duncan Smith. Central Office sent him to *Today* to kill the story and profess undying loyalty, which he duly did. I was the interviewer, but what could I say? 'You lying toad. Only days ago I heard you in your cups myself. And you were calling for a swift political quietus' seemed a rotten thank-you for what had been a very enjoyable weekend.

My colleagues dealt with this dilemma in different ways. John Humphrys was austere, and seldom saw politicians outside the studio. James Naughtie loved the parties and the chat, and was always superbly well informed on who was in and who was out. Kevin Marsh, who succeeded Rod Liddle as editor, was positively puritanical, pledging himself to end any friendships that might compromise his independence. I decided on a course somewhere in the middle, resisting new political friendships but refusing to abandon those with a long past.

Today and the political world were so closely intertwined that the febrile quality of Westminster life infected the programme. I found that to keep my moral compass steady in my encounters with politicians I needed complete confidence that my own position was safe: you can risk dangerous, challenging questions to ministers only if you are secure in the support of your bosses.

Like most BBC presenters of the day I was employed as a freelance rather than a member of staff. But I had grown used to this uncertain way of life, and I thought I could rely on my antennae for office politics: they were reasonably well tuned, not least because I had been through a couple of nasty near-misses during my telly career.

By the winter of 2008, after nearly a decade on *Today*, my place there felt very settled, and I was completely unprepared for a call one evening requiring me to report to a senior manager the following day. I explained that I would be on a train to Harrogate, where I had agreed to give a lunchtime speech about my latest book, but the peremptory nature of the instruction rang alarm bells. I emailed the boss in question with an apology and explanation of why I could not appear in his office. Nothing came back, and the feeling that something bad was up nagged at me all the way from King's Cross.

North Yorkshire has long felt like home turf. I first set foot in the county in 1970, when I arrived on the train at York to begin my time at Ampleforth, and my parents bought their first house there just as I was leaving the school a few years later. I always enjoy going back, and I arrived in Harrogate a little early so that I could have a meeting with my bank manager to discuss the financing of a house we were considering in France. The literary lunch at the Majestic Hotel went well: the audience seemed to like what I had to say in *It's a PC World, what it means to live in a world gone politically correct*. It felt like the life I had worked hard for.

But when I switched on my phone after the Q and A, I found a message from the journalist Cole Moreton, who had interviewed me about the book the previous week, and was planning a profile piece for that Sunday's edition of the *Independent*. There was, he explained, a nib in the *Mail* suggesting that I was to be replaced on *Today* by Justin Webb, then the BBC's North America editor. Was it true? he asked. A call to the programme's editor, Ceri Thomas, established that it was.

This was obviously quite big news for me. The BBC's account of how I came to hear it in this astonishingly cack-handed manner was included in a letter, which was later drafted to answer the hundreds of complaints the Corporation received: 'We are very sorry, of course, that Ed should have heard this news in the way that he did, and we have offered him our apologies for the way the announcement was handled. We had arrangements in place to meet Ed less than twenty-four hours later to discuss our plans but, regrettably, someone involved in the process chose to leak the news to the *Daily Mail*.'

I did not see this letter at the time, and can quote it now only thanks to one of my parents' Yorkshire neighbours, who serendipitously came across her copy among some old papers while I was writing this book. The word 'rubbish' had been written in the margin, and she was right. 'Arrangements' were not in place in the controlled manner the smooth tone suggests. The next few days saw the BBC fire-fighting an entirely avoidable PR disaster.

The BBC was quite within its rights to dump me from the programme. You could even argue that I was not really 'sacked' at all, since they were simply proposing that they would not renew my annual contract. But the way I learnt about my defenestration gave me a huge tactical advantage. There is obviously a danger of losing one's objectivity in such circumstances, but it seemed pretty clear to me that I had, by any normal professional standards, been shabbily treated.

I am not a natural rebel, but when my delayed meeting with the senior manager finally took place, it cleared up any doubts I had about raising Cain. During the discussion about the way my departure would be managed he suggested to me that it would be in my own interest to add a supportive quote to the press release announcing that I was to be replaced by Justin. 'Your future employers', he explained to me (God knows who they might have been), would expect to see evidence of such loyal behaviour.

By this time I had worked for the BBC for nearly twenty years, and for the previous decade the Corporation had been paying me (quite handsomely) to spot bullshit being peddled by politicians. Why, I wondered, did my manager expect me to turn off my bullshit detectors when he was doing the peddling? It was a moment of perfect clarity, and oddly liberating. For all those years I had been inside the BBC tent, dedicated to its ethic and no doubt also absorbing the group-think that permeates any big institution. Suddenly everything flipped: I was an outsider, and I could see all too clearly where the institutional ethic stopped and the group-think began.

It was the realization that I was being taken for a complete mug that really made me dig my heels in. My manager was startled when I refused to shake his hand. He had clearly expected me to salute smartly, say, 'Aye, aye, sir,' and walk the plank like a decent fellow. I think everyone was startled – I certainly was – by the way my fate became, as Max Hastings put it in a column in the *Mail*, the kind of story that 'brings the dogs from their kennels, the slumbering from their beds and the dead from their graves'.

The first indication that anyone minded about what had happened came in the form of a telephone call from a sympathetic producer on *Today* who had been watching the programme's inbox over the weekend. The messages of support for me were pouring in, she said, and many of the emailers took a most unflattering view of the way the BBC had handled things

Next my children – Ivo, Eleanor, Tom and Rosy – very loyally started a Facebook campaign on my behalf, and it quickly attracted supporters. The *Daily Telegraph* piled in too, with an online petition for my reinstatement, and there were several thousand signatures within days.

Most surreally, two MPs, Jeremy Hunt and Keith Vaz, put down an early-day motion in the Commons. EDM 293 proposed that 'This House deplores the sacking of Edward Stourton as a presenter of the *Today* programme' and called for me to be reinstated. One of the sponsors became health secretary and a contender for the Tory leadership, the other, whom I had known at university, later had to resign in distressing circumstances, so they were an odd pairing. I suspected the hidden hand of my old Cambridge friend Andrew Mitchell. Ninety MPs signed the motion.

Some of this was mischief-making – there are plenty of MPs and journalists for whom BBC-baiting is a more than acceptable form of blood sport. And the climate for beating up Auntie was propitious, because the episode came hard on the heels of what became known as 'Manuelgate', the much more serious scandal involving the actor Andrew Sachs, widely regarded as a national treasure because of his role as Manuel the Spanish waiter in *Fawlty Towers*.

The comedian Russell Brand and the talk-show host Jonathan Ross left a series of lewd messages on Sachs's answerphone, many of them relating to Brand's brief relationship with Sachs's granddaughter ('He fucked your granddaughter,' Ross shouted at the phone), and all this was broadcast on Ross's radio show. As a result of the ensuing public ruckus, Ross was suspended from all his BBC programmes for twelve weeks. The contrast between his suspension for what almost everyone agreed was an especially egregious lapse of taste and my own termination without having done anything wrong proved irresistible, and the Mandrake column in the *Telegraph* exploited it especially well, securing a charming quote about me from Sachs himself.

The letters that piled high in my pigeonhole were personally heartening, and a reminder that friendships endure even in the febrile world of journalism. One of the nicest came from Phil Moger, the chief sub film on the *5.45* news right back in my trainee days at ITN. The programme had long since died, but Phil kept the spirit of the show alive: 'I won't mess about: I'll give it to you in *5.45* terms . . . absolutely bloody appalling!!!!!', he began, still faithful to his conviction that every story needs a strong top line.

But most of the correspondence came from people I had never met, and reading the letters back, I realize that they were not really about me at all. They were about a community and its values.

I first got a real sense of what Radio 4 means to its family by doing some holiday-cover shifts for Jonathan Dimbleby on *Any Questions*. After the show there was always a brief drinks reception for the audience. These events felt very 'local', partly because we usually broadcast from schools, parish churches, village halls and the like, and the punters, who had all applied for tickets, were generally hardcore Radio 4 fans.

After a few of these outings a very obvious but hugely important fact began to dawn on me, one I still believe to be true. Most members of the Radio 4 family of listeners believe the network belongs to them and not to us. Almost everyone I met over a glass of *Any Questions* wine was completely uninhibited with their views on programmes and individual broadcasters – and they were often very trenchant. And if they wanted to critique – or praise – one of my own performances, they picked up on what I had said on-air as if we were simply continuing a conversation.

Radio encourages this unusually close relationship between audience and broadcaster. The communications guru Marshall McLuhan (famous for dictums like 'the medium is the message' and phrases like 'the global village') coined the distinction between 'hot' and 'cold' media. Telly is definitely cold: it erects a barrier between those who appear and those who watch, and both groups recognize that they inhabit different worlds. Radio, by contrast, is hot, as hot as hot can be: you listen in your bath or even on the loo, and the people who talk to you regularly become part of your circle of friends. When I presented television news programmes I used to be stopped in the street from time to time with complaints about my choice of tie or suit. While I was on *Today* the complaints were about a particular line of questioning or, probably more often, a lapse in grammatical propriety.

After a decade of early-morning appearances, I was part of the Radio 4 family, and there was nothing the BBC or I could do about that: the audience who had heard me for so long regarded me in that way. Beyond that, many of them also saw the manner of my defenestration as a violation of some of the values that bound the family together. The letters I received were full of references to the qualities that make the network so distinctive – things like lively debate, courtesy and intellectual rigour. Whether or not I could really claim to represent such things was, in a way, irrelevant.

The sharp critics I met at *Any Questions* drinks parties and the kind, invariably cultured letter-writers who sent me their sympathy turned the way I thought about my work on its head. I understood that they, and not the managers who gave me (or refused me) contracts, were my real bosses.

All this occurred before social media really got going, but for a few days I did feel I was being borne aloft on what we might now call a Trumpian Twitter storm. In fact, it was quite the opposite. I was supported because I stood for the values of an institution, not because I was an inspired independent 'influencer'. Good tweets are born of strong emotions and decided opinions; my broadcasting was based on scepticism and curiosity rather than conviction.

I do understand the journalistic advantages of following Twitter, but even now I refuse to tweet: I simply cannot see why anyone would be interested in my views unless I have had time to weigh them carefully and write about them in a considered way.

The word 'posh' came up a lot in the commentary about my sacking. I have been assured that none of the BBC managers involved in the debate about my future used it, and I am sure that is true. I did, however, pick up a lead suggesting there had been an earlier plot to prise me off *Today* to make way for a presenter on the more demotic Radio 5 Live, known colloquially at the time as Radio Bloke. There was also a strange story in the *Mail on Sunday*, clearly based on a BBC briefing, pointing out that I had on one occasion refused to play conkers in the studio. This grave cultural crime was cited as evidence of snootiness.

So perhaps those class and educational neuroses, those social and cultural cross-currents I first encountered as a trainee at ITN, really were still eddying around the corridors of Television Centre and New Broadcasting House. Perhaps, indeed, the news editor of the *Newcastle Journal* was right all those years ago: there is no escaping the curse of a cosmopolitan background.

The most enjoyable indication that the BBC found the whole episode difficult to handle was a brief contribution to the letters page of the *Telegraph*.

Sir – Iain Dale [then a *Telegraph* columnist] gave *Today*'s
address for readers to express their view on Ed Stourton's

departure. I emailed, because I am delighted he is going. I find his dull monotonous voice hard to take, and I immediately switch off when he is on. To my surprise, I received a response saying that many others like me had written to say how sorry they were about his departure and that my regrets would be passed on to Mr Stourton.

You can take on your employer in the court of public opinion for only so long. Around about the time this letter appeared, the BBC offered me enough future work – including some on *Today* – to make it worth my while staying on. The perks that go with *Today* dropped away pretty quickly – the Christmas cards from 'Gordon and Sarah' and 'David and Sam' stopped pronto, as did those satisfyingly stiff invitation cards to the American ambassador's summer party – but I am still broadcasting on Radio 4 more than a decade later.

There is a quotation attributed to St Augustine – master of the aphorism as well as a great confessor – which I commend to anyone who goes through a similar experience: 'Feeling resentment is like drinking poison and hoping the other person will die.' Once the future was settled, I let matters lie. Worrying over the wound would only keep it open.

If anyone asked, my stock reply was that I felt like the victim in a reverse version of *Murder on the Orient Express.* In Agatha Christie's classic everyone on the train finally admits to having stabbed the dead man because they all, for individual reasons, hated him. In my case no one seemed willing to admit to wielding the knife; Poirot had a body, but there was apparently no perpetrator. Even more puzzlingly, everyone, if the BBC's public statements were to be believed, loved me.

But when I began to write this book I decided to dig around a bit. Quite how useful that was I am not entirely sure. All of this took place a good while ago, but the laws of libel must still be observed, and sources protected. I also doubt that, unless you belong to the very small subset of readers who were actually involved in what happened, you are likely to be gripped by a detailed account of which BBC 'suit' said what to whom.

But I did turn up one intriguing insight: one of the ideas kicked around behind the scenes was to make me the BBC's religion editor by way of compensation for losing the *Today* berth. The job did not exist then, and the first person to hold it was Martin Bashir, the *Panorama* reporter who later resigned under a mighty cloud over that Diana interview. What a lot of trouble the BBC could have saved themselves!

Being fired from *Today* gave me a higher profile than any other event of my career. I still listen now, and every morning there is at least one interview that I know – not think, *know* – I would have done better. You do not spend ten years there without acquiring a measure of monsterishness.

A MATTER OF FAITH

18 · CANONICAL DELICTS

Presenting lunchtime news has taught me that there is a real skill to writing official reports. They are often released sometime around noon, giving the team on programmes like *The World at One* (where I found a part-time home after leaving *Today*) an hour to fillet out the key findings. Sometimes they run to hundreds of pages, and the meat is buried in footnotes and appendices, so that 'first draft of history' to which journalism lays claim misses the real story.

Not so with the 2018 report on Ampleforth and Downside (an equally prominent Benedictine boarding school outside Bath) for the Independent Inquiry into Child Sex Abuse (IICSA). Whoever wrote that was a master of the art, and no one could miss the story it told. It is sweeping in its verdict; the tone balances dispassionate respect for the evidence with barely suppressed rage; and the detail is brutal.

The headline finding hits you in paragraph three, a gift to any deadline-pressed producer or sub-editor:

> It is difficult to describe the appalling sexual abuse inflicted over decades on children aged as young as seven at Ampleforth School, and eleven at Downside School. Ten individuals, mostly monks, connected to these two institutions have been convicted or cautioned in relation to offences involving sexual activity with a large number of children, or offences concerning pornography. The true scale of the abuse however is likely to be considerably higher.

And then comes some of that brutal detail. One abuse victim described how a monk 'made him remove his clothes in the

227

confessional of the chapel, then beat his bare bottom. Another incident took place in a bathroom when he was forced to strip naked and to place his hands and feet on each side of a bathtub, so he was straddling the bath, with his genitals hanging down. He was then beaten on his bare bottom, an event he found "absolutely terrifying".' During these beatings, the paragraph concludes, the monk would masturbate.

And all of that before you reach the end of page one of the Executive Summary.

Not long after the report's publication, my wife and I drove out to the country for an evening's tennis. Both the other men of the party were old school friends, one a knighted public servant, the other, our host, a financial master of the universe. As the late summer shadows lengthened over his lawns (his drive was so long it seemed to stretch over several time zones), he entertained us to dinner with good wine, and the conversation turned to our shared past.

All three of us had been shocked by the story the IICSA report told, and agreed that it simply did not square with our own experience of our *alma mater*. And then, during a pause in the conversation, the knighted public servant remarked, 'Mind you, Father X did try to snog me . . . and made a declaration of love. I told him to push off and not to be so ridiculous.' In five decades of friendship, he had not mentioned this before. He is a close friend, and has never shown any sign of being traumatized by his school days. He confirmed to me that he had remained on good terms with Father X and, long after leaving the school, entertained him at his home with his wife and children. The oddness of this, we agreed, merited investigation.

Conversations with other old boys and contemporaries revealed that the IICSA report had, in a similarly unsettling way, set all of us on a course of re-exploring our own past, wondering whether our Ampleforth years had really been quite as happy and carefree as most of us remembered them.

Members of a monastery describe themselves as a 'community' – the word appears repeatedly in the sixth-century Rule of St Benedict, which still underpins the way they live, and it means something slightly different from its general use today. Strictly speaking it refers to 'the brethren', but it is a useful term because it can be stretched to describe the wider web of relationships that an institution like Ampleforth forges.

That embraces current and former pupils, parents, lay teachers and staff, many of those who live in the adjacent villages, working on the monastic farms and in the orchards or simply coming to mass on Sundays, parishioners in the churches run by the abbey across the north of England, pupils and dons at St Benet's, the hall of residence the monks established at Oxford, and even the monastic foundations planted in Chile and Zimbabwe with the support of Ampleforth monks.

The network is animated by the idea that monasteries provide a spiritual resource, and that because they exist apart from the world they can replenish the spirits of those of us who live in it. Ampleforth – like most Benedictine monasteries – offers 'retreats', stays during which people can live at the abbey for a few days while reflecting on their lives, and these visitors are also often drawn into this web of relationships. By living according to their traditions, the monks offer constancy with values that have endured for centuries, and at its best a monastery can be a pool of serenity, protected from the currents of a fast-changing world.

In the days following the IICSA report its impact spread right across this wider community. It was not so much a pebble that sent out ripples, it was more like a rock crashing in from nowhere,

229

throwing up angry gouts and sprays. And one of those hit especially hard by the waves was my father.

His example is a good illustration of how enduring and sustaining Ampleforth's community has often been. He arrived at the school in the autumn of 1945, at the age of sixteen, after a wartime adolescence that today we would certainly describe – despite what was in many ways a privileged upbringing – as traumatic, although of course no one used that kind of language then.

In 1940 his police-officer father was posted to the port city of Aden, on the approach to the Red Sea, which was strategically important and considered too dangerous for the family. To be as close to him as possible my father, his siblings (an elder sister and younger brother) and my grandmother decamped to South Africa. The two boys were sent to a boarding school run by the notorious Christian Brothers order, which my father later described as 'barbaric, each day starting at six o'clock with Brother Hurley walking through the vast dormitory carrying a *sjambok* [a lash made of rhino hide] to strike any late riser'.

The following year my grandfather managed a period of 'leave', which the family spent trekking and riding in the Drakensberg Mountains, and when it was over my grandmother decided to risk accompanying my grandfather back to Aden for a while. The children were split up and billeted on various cousins near Durban on the Indian Ocean.

They never saw their mother again: her ship was torpedoed as it approached land on her return journey. The three children spent the rest of the war with the kind but not especially close cousins (seeing their father once, during another brief leave in 1943), and in the spring of 1945 they were put on a ship to Liverpool without any idea of who or what they would find at the other end.

By the time they were eventually reunited as a family, after five years' living apart, my grandfather had remarried. The children met their new stepmother – my father recalled this detail in a memoir he wrote for his own family – in the middle of a Sussex tennis party given by the maiden aunts who had looked after them when they got back from South Africa.

So, my father cannot have been a very settled or confident teenager when he took the train to York for the first time in the autumn of that year. In his memoir he wrote that 'The whole Benedictine concept and management of the school were so totally foreign to me as to be wholly disorientating . . . so disorientating was it that I drafted a letter to your grandpa asking him to remove me from this unfathomable place, but happily I never sent this.' He lived in fear of being beaten as he had been by the Christian Brothers. Within a year my grandfather was posted to Uganda, and the family was separated again.

The monks became, in a way, a substitute, scooping my father up and, with what he calls their 'precious Benedictine values', launching him into adulthood. His gratitude to Ampleforth was enduring, and in 1975, when he began to think about life after his globe-trotting career, he and my mother bought a house in a village on the edge of the Yorkshire Dales, about forty minutes' drive from the abbey.

In the decades that followed, and even after downsizing to a cottage nearby, they kept up a regular two-way traffic with the monastery, often driving to mass there on high days and holidays, and going to concerts in the abbey church, while monks in search of a good lunch beat a regular path to their door. And when my parents celebrated their fiftieth wedding anniversary with a party at our home in London, one of the older monks – whom I have known since he gave retreats at my prep school back in the 1960s – said mass in our drawing room.

So when I spoke to my father in the aftermath of the IICSA report's publication, he was, unsurprisingly, distraught. For decades Ampleforth had been central to his sense of self. 'Now,' he told me, 'I feel ashamed to say where I went to school.'

I had my own reasons for some soul-searching too.

When the first stories about abuse at Ampleforth began to surface in the press – in the early 2000s – I had a call from Dom Dominic Milroy, who had taught me French (inspiringly) during my school days, and later became headmaster. I had always got on well with him, and he said he wanted some advice, suggesting we meet in a discreet restaurant near King's Cross before he hopped on his train back north.

Over lunch he asked whether I had any ideas about how the fallout from the abuse stories could be managed and, more worryingly, explained his concern that some of his fellow monks did not fully appreciate just how damaging they were.

The episode brought into tight focus the contradictions between the values I had learnt growing up and those I had developed as an adult. I was working on the *Today* programme at the time, and we had run several prominent reports on abuse, including revelations of the way Cardinal Cormac Murphy O'Connor, then Archbishop of Westminster, had been complicit in covering up priestly crimes earlier in his career. In the journalistic culture of the day, priests and monks were generally regarded as guilty unless proven otherwise, and the bright, young – and very secular-minded – producers I worked with were absolutely unforgiving in their judgements.

I shared their view that the idea of 'managing' stories about abuse was itself a problem – that abuse is not a PR issue, but a catastrophic moral failure and a serious crime. And I suggested to Father Dominic that if Ampleforth really wanted to show the world it had got to grips with this reality, the monastery should let in a documentary team to record the way the monks handled an offender living among them. Father Dominic was rather taken with this idea – he had always liked bold thinking – but he doubted the monks would buy it. We parted on our usual good terms and I put Ampleforth's travails out of my mind.

But in 2005 I had a call at home from an embarrassed BBC press officer. 'I don't know quite how to ask this,' he said, but 'one of the papers wants to know whether you were ever interfered with by a monk.' I reacted with indignation – the journalist making enquiries had in fact muddled me with someone else – and for a long time I told the story as an amusing anecdote to illustrate how monks get stereotyped. The way the suggestion was framed sounded quite unreal, a leering tale from the world of smutty seaside postcards. More than a decade later, the IICSA headlines brought home that that world was all too real, and that there was nothing remotely funny about it.

And I began to wonder whether I myself had a case to answer. The report covered the 1960s until the present day, so it included all my time at Ampleforth. As head of school for a full year during this grim saga, surely I would have – and certainly should have – known something of what was happening? Was I guilty of negligence, even of collusion in the conspiracy of silence that allowed the abuse to continue for so long?

I had long recognized that my skills as a detective during my time as head boy left much to be desired, although I had always thought of my crime-fighting failures as youthful escapades to be laughed about with old friends.

The winter of 1975 saw a scandal that became known in Ampleforth lore as 'the taking and driving of monastic Land Rovers'. Someone (or several someones) took to jump-starting these vehicles in the middle of the night and driving them wildly all over the sports pitches down in the valley, always abandoning the wheel before a posse from the school buildings – usually led by me – could catch them.

I posted my school monitors on patrol at strategic points around the monastic garages, and on a chill Yorkshire night I even spotted one of the villains. I chased him through the Monks' Wood, crashing over the graves of long-dead holy men as I pursued the fleeing figure in camouflage and balaclava. But he got away, and I never cracked the case, discovering the identity of the ring leader only years later – by which time he had become a respected judge renowned for his tough sentences.

But if the IICSA report was to be believed, no detective work should have been needed to spot the flagrant abuse that was going on: 'Many perpetrators did not hide their sexual interests from the children,' it stated. 'At Ampleforth, this included communal activities both outdoors and indoors where there was fondling of children, mutual masturbation and group masturbation. Participation was encouraged and sometimes demanded. The blatant openness of these activities demonstrates there was a culture of acceptance of abusive behaviour.'

I have learnt that memory can be fallible and even partisan, but group masturbation, whether indoors or outdoors, is something I really do not recall. A skim-read of the report gave me some reassurance: during my years at the school, the really serious crimes were being committed at Gilling Castle, Ampleforth's prep school, three miles away across the valley. I did not know the abusing monks involved, and I had never visited Gilling. I was in the clear – and the case, sorry saga though it might have been, could, in my own mind at least, be closed.

Except that it could not be, not really. Events kept nudging it open again – just as they have done with the abuse scandals in the wider Church. It is some thirty years since priestly abuse became a real focus for media attention. Popes, bishops and priests keep saying sorry and vowing that it must never happen again, and then another dump of devastating evidence comes crashing down. Like the Church as a whole, Ampleforth found it very difficult to shake off the sins of its past.

A year after the IICSA report, inspectors from the schools regulator OFSTED descended on the school for an unannounced visit and found that Ampleforth was still not meeting child-protection standards. The head, who had recently been appointed precisely because of her experience in safeguarding, resigned almost immediately – which meant that the school had four head teachers in just over a year, a crisis in leadership by any standards.

At the same time the monastery was caught in the coils of a bizarre conflict with its own abbot – over abuse allegations. Dom Cuthbert Madden was one of the few monks to come out of the IICSA report relatively well, but in 2016 he was himself accused of a historic sex crime. He denied the charges, stepping aside while the matter was investigated, and neither North Yorkshire police nor the Catholic Safeguarding Adviser Service found against him. But the wider English Benedictine congregation, of which Ampleforth is a part, refused to allow him to return to the abbey.

Father Cuthbert took his case to the High Court in London and to the Vatican, which eventually ruled that while he had 'not committed any canonical delict nor been convicted of any civil crime' he should not be allowed to return to the abbey. It seemed a weirdly inconclusive resolution to the whole affair, which did great reputational damage – monks are not supposed to row with one another, especially in such a public way. And the words 'Ampleforth' and 'abuse' continued to appear in close proximity in news reports.

And then, in the autumn of 2020, amid all the trauma and

dislocation of the Covid pandemic, a truly mighty blow fell upon the school. After another surprise inspection by OFSTED, the education secretary, Gavin Williamson, issued a 'restriction order', banning Ampleforth from taking any new pupils – a ban that would, if it remained in force, kill the place altogether. The OFSTED findings were vague – a point quickly seized upon by the school, which appealed against the education secretary's decision – but the old sins were at the heart of them. 'Leaders have not taken precise enough account of the long-standing historical failures at Ampleforth in their current practice,' the report declared.

'How can they STILL be getting it wrong?' emailed one old school friend. Most of the contemporaries I spoke to reacted in the same exasperated way, and I shared their frustration. It was now a decade and a half since that lunch with Father Dominic: it seemed inconceivable that after all the monastery had gone through the monks still did not, in that ugly but in this case apposite expression, 'get it'.

And, of course, I again began to get calls from fellow journalists looking for dirt.

I steeled myself for another read, a real study rather than a quick skim, of the IICSA report. And this time I found a date that made me realize I could not quite write all this out of my own story.

It relates to a monk called Father Piers Grant-Ferris, who was the son of a distinguished Tory MP and wartime fighter pilot. Sir Robert Grant-Ferris was nicknamed 'the Voice of the Vatican' by his colleagues in Parliament, and ennobled as Lord Harvington when he left the Commons. I never met Father Piers, but he had the kind of upper-crust, dashing profile that was characteristic of the more charismatic Ampleforth monks. He had been an officer in the Irish Guards before he joined the monastery, and had a reputation as a fiercely athletic and daring mountaineer.

To protect the anonymity of its witnesses (and indeed some of the monks who had been accused but not convicted), the abuse report 'ciphered' their names. This paragraph introduces one of the most painful of all the stories IICSA told.

> **48.** In 1975, the then Abbot Basil Hume received a complaint from the parents of a pupil, RC-A152, that Fr Piers had inappropriately touched their son. The abbot, together with Fr Justin Caldwell and Fr Patrick Barry (then headmasters of Gilling Castle and Ampleforth College respectively), launched an internal investigation.

Here, at the heart of things, were two of the monks I had most admired, and they were conducting their investigation into Father Piers at just the time I came to know them best – when I was having those joshing chats with Father Basil about high-jump techniques and sitting through those awkward head monitor's sessions with Father Patrick about the morale of the school.

Basil Hume and his tribunal did not accept RC-A152's allegation that Father Piers was guilty of 'inappropriate touching', but their investigation turned up something from another boy that was more difficult to deal with: 'RC-A170 stated that Fr Piers had repeatedly fondled his genitals while he was sleeping at night in his dormitory and taken his temperature rectally.' The report continues, in its painfully precise way, 'Fr Piers admitted going to RC-A170's dormitory at night but said he merely wanted to teach him how to pull back his foreskin when urinating to avoid dribbling. He denied any sexual gratification.'

Because of that admission Basil Hume concluded – 'reluctantly', according to the IICSA report – that Father Piers could no longer be allowed to work with children, and moved him to a parish near Leeds. The police were not informed of the allegations against him, and over the next twenty-five years he worked in six parishes across North Yorkshire, Lancashire and Cumbria.

It was not until 2005 that the past really caught up with him, and it did so with a vengeance. He was convicted of twenty counts of indecent assault against fifteen former Gilling Castle pupils from 1965 to 1975. He was sentenced to two years in gaol and placed on the Sex Offenders Register for ten years. The accumulated evidence of his long history of abuse, recorded in the IICSA report, is simply sickening: it supplied some of the eye-catching details the IICSA team included in their Executive Summary.

After being sentenced in early 2006, Father Piers wrote to his former parishioners in Workington to thank them for their support, and he asked them not to contact him in prison because he did not want his fellow inmates to 'become envious of my apparent popularity'. The letter concluded with these astonishing sentences: 'While keeping a place for each other in our minds and hearts, may I ask you to pray for my victims and all those whose lives we touch. I think it is good to do this because our quality of life depends on the way we relate to other people ...' The letter contains no other mention of those on whom he had inflicted such pain, misery and enduring trauma.

Piers Grant-Ferris died a few years after his release from gaol. Looking at the key dates in his case, I now realize it was his trial that prompted the awkward phone conversation with a BBC press officer – a call I took so lightly at the time.

After wading through this horrible story I could not help asking myself how we should judge the role of Basil Hume, a Church leader who probably commanded wider public esteem than any other of his era. His monkish manner inspired people to call him 'holy' without it seeming trite, and his Englishness made Catholics seem less odd in British society. His twenty-three years as Archbishop of Westminster spanned the terms of three archbishops of

Canterbury and he often outclassed them in his ability to capture the national mood.

Was all the good he did cancelled by that terrible lapse in judgement (as we would, at a minimum, call it today) back in 1975? The question matters to me because after leaving Ampleforth I often met him for personal and professional reasons, and my admiration for him continued to grow.

I conducted what I think was his final interview. In April 1999 there was a nail-bomb attack on a gay pub in Soho, the Admiral Duncan, which killed three people and injured some seventy others. Defying both the advanced cancer that would soon kill him and the censorious views of conservative Catholics, Cardinal Hume came onto the *Today* programme and, in a voice shaken by his illness, condemned the attack in as public and uncompromising a way as possible. When he died that summer the BBC televised his funeral live – usually popes are the only Catholic leaders who rate that kind of treatment – and I led the commentary team.

Questions about his judgement so many years ago are probably unanswerable: we cannot know with any certainty how he reached his decision, or really understand the instincts that guided him: the assumptions he grew up with were certainly very different from today's.

But his appearance in the IICSA report underscores an uncomfortable fact: I did not know the monks accused of actual abuse (at least, not those whose names appear *en clair* rather than in cipher) but I did know those who were complicit in covering things up, and they were all monks I would once have said embodied the 'precious Benedictine values' my father and I admired. A close reading of the IICSA report has driven me to a painful conclusion: the worm at the bottom of this bucket is that the abuse story at Ampleforth had a distinctive Benedictine character.

19 · LOVING THEM IN THEIR COMPULSION

One of the IICSA report's most striking quotations is taken from a document written by Dom Timothy Wright, who was a teacher when I was at school (not an especially admired one) and served as Ampleforth's abbot from 1997 until 2005. 'If paedophilia is a form of compulsive illness then the degree of responsibility for their [paedophiles'] actions is to some extent diminished . . .' he stated. 'God continues to love them in their compulsion. They are not cast out of the Church.'

It is another of those statements that brings the contrast between the world of my upbringing and the world I live in today into stark relief. Any Catholic will tell you that Father Timothy's concept of God's love – all-embracing and all-forgiving – is standard Church teaching, part of the radical core of Christianity. But if you read those words out in, say, the BBC newsroom, you would provoke uproar. To any secular mind they sound like a nasty piece of sophistry, shifting the guilt away from offenders, and they include absolutely no acknowledgement that the harm done to victims should be part of the moral equation.

Father Timothy's view of the 'compulsive' quality of paedophilia was, it seems, elastic. He also wrote,

> It is likely that there are many who by prayer and self-discipline have been able to control their emotions and have never offended. Others again who have offended once and following treatment have been able to lead to work well in the community [sic]. In the light of this, it is both wrong and unjust to treat them in the same

way, assuming that those who admit to a single offence are concealing further offences.

So, monks who resisted their compulsion towards sex with children deserved mitigation in the light of their moral fortitude, while those who failed to resist bore little moral blame.

Father Timothy's logic had disastrous practical consequences. 2001 saw the publication of the Nolan Report, the first serious attempt by the Catholic Church in England and Wales to develop a real policy to deal with abuse. Lord Nolan, a former Appeal Court judge (and, as it happened, an Ampleforth Old Boy), stated unambiguously that all abuse allegations, whether current or historic, should be reported to the statutory authorities, and made it clear that this applied also to all disclosures of abuse by perpetrators.

Father Timothy told his prior (the second most senior monk in the abbey) that he regarded many of the documents about child protection, which began to arrive, as 'utterly ridiculous', and his own notes on the subject show him resorting to bizarre hair-splitting to get round the Nolan recommendations (which were immediately adopted as policy by the leadership of the Catholic Church in England and Wales).

He tried to draw a distinction between a 'disclosure' and an 'admission': 'If a religious [a member of a religious order] was to own up to abuse to his superior, he should be advised to make only an admission,' he wrote. 'In that way there is no obligation to report the matter.'

A 'disclosure', however – and the difference between the two is far from clear in his musings – is not protected in the same way. 'It is recognized that a disclosure carries no confidentiality,' the memo continues. 'The subject [the monk] needs to know that before informing the superior . . . individuals should be advised that it is better to remain silent than make any comment which might be used against them . . .'

This was very close to the idea of 'equivocation' or 'moral reservation', which gave Catholics – Jesuits in particular – such a bad name during the Reformation. It held that when there was a conflict between justice and veracity, justice should prevail, so it was permissible to 'equivocate' – or, as we might more simply say today, to be economical with the truth.

During the persecution of Catholics in the sixteenth and seventeenth centuries that was an arguable position: telling a fib to protect a priest from the kind of grisly martyrdom experienced by the men who gave their names to my prep-school dormitories is surely a defensible proposition. Doing so to protect a paedophile priest is not.

Father Timothy's logic was, however, driven by his understanding of the duty of care an abbot owes to the monks who form his community. 'For the ongoing health of community relations it is important that trust and confidentiality are maintained,' he writes, and 'that the brethren do not see their superior as both "father in God" and "police informer" at the same time.'

Father Timothy was from a real 'Ampleforth family'. He was educated at the school and, like two of his brothers, he went straight from school to monastery, studying at St Benet's, Ampleforth's foundation in Oxford, for his degree, then returning to what was now his monastic home. Almost all of his life had been lived according to the principles and prescriptions in the Rule of St Benedict.

Chapter 27, with the title 'The abbot's care for the excommunicated', lays down that 'The abbot should show the utmost care and concern for those brothers who have done wrong', and 'He should exercise great care and extreme sensitivity, making every effort not to lose any of the sheep entrusted to him. He must bear in mind that he has undertaken care of weak souls, not a tyranny over those who are strong.' However wrong-headed Father Timothy's thinking may have been, you can see where it came from.

Father Timothy's attempts to justify his approach to abuse reveal a sad irony: the worst of Ampleforth's response – the cover-ups, the resistance to outside interference, the way the monastic authorities always seemed to care more about their criminals than their victims – was rooted in a distortion of those very values that in other ways made the place so special. The pool of serenity the abbey offered and the cesspit revealed in the abuse inquiry shared the same source.

Perhaps we boys instinctively understood this connection, even if we did not articulate it. Perhaps we tolerated, even suppressed from our consciousness, the worst because we were so giddy with the best of an Ampleforth education. That might explain my knighted friend's continued affection for a monk who tried to kiss him – and I confess that, this lapse aside, I always thought of Father X as a kind and decent man.

The greatest harm done by abuse at Ampleforth was, of course, borne by its victims – and until the truth was told, many of them had had to carry that burden on their own. Another harm – almost negligible by comparison, but a harm nonetheless – touches those of us who were not ourselves abused: our past has been poisoned.

Looking back at the way I described my time at Ampleforth earlier I can see many things that are open to a darker interpretation. The cheerful monkish disregard for civil law and that record of beatings on the Monitors' Room wall, which we all thought belonged to a long-distant past, suggest that violence and cover-up were much closer to the surface of our lives than I remember.

Going back to my school-days diaries, I find passages that hint at the kind of sexual culture revealed in the IICSA report. I described being profoundly upset by a conversation among a group of sixth-formers who were boasting about which younger boys they had 'had on toast', and which of the school's maids were 'good for a shag'. One of my near contemporaries was the actor Rupert Everett, and I recorded that he was the victim of a 'debagging', noting that 'Miss Rupert Everett' was found guilty of 'making a vivacious nuisance' – a phrase that surely says more about me and the debaggers than it does about him.

I also reported a random statement from my housemaster that 'they were performing oral masturbation in there, sucking-off, they call it', though there is no explanation of who 'they' were or where this was happening. And it seems I took part in a conference of house monitors on 'the question of vice in St Hugh's' (my own house). 'We have almost every conceivable vice: drugs, homosexuality, auto-sexuality . . .' I wrote '. . . corruption, voyeurism, sadism, even the hint of adultery and perhaps the odd Oedipus.' This was – with retrospective apology for the casual homophobia – surely simply a teenage rant. Or was it? It is queasy-making to find the sands of your past shifting under you like this.

My parents kept their links with the abbey despite the jolt the IICSA revelations gave to my father. The two-way traffic between their home and the monastery continued, and they remained close to some of the older monks who were not touched by the abuse scandal – although towards the end of my father's life they made the journey from the Dales to the North Yorkshire moors less often.

Their route is full of reminders of the way England's character and culture were formed by monasteries.

As you drive down the A1 you pass signs to Fountains Abbey, the monumental complex of ruins outside Ripon that was once home to one of the most powerful institutions in the north of England. In their four centuries on the banks of the river Skell, the

Cistercian monks here amassed huge wealth, and when Henry VIII's commissioners arrived to seize their property for the Crown in 1539 they found ornaments and vestments worth £700 – some £200,000 in today's money – nearly two thousand horned cattle, over a thousand sheep and nearly a hundred horses. It is one of the best-preserved monastic ruins anywhere, and what remains evokes a famous description of Cluny Abbey in France: 'a world in itself, given wholly to the worship of God in a setting of incomparable splendour and untouched by secular intrigue'.

If you take the low road from Thirsk you encounter the stark skeleton of Byland's abbey church and cloister a few miles short of Ampleforth village. The high road, climbing onto the moors through the wonderfully named Sutton-under-Whitestonecliffe and up the precipitous slope of Sutton Bank, takes you close to another set of Cistercian ruins at Rievaulx.

Together these three monasteries were known as the 'luminaries of the north', and Rievaulx, set imposingly on the slope of a hill beside the river Ure, is perhaps the most luminous of all of them. It has enjoyed a curious return to fame as the home of St Ailred, a twelfth-century abbot who, on the basis of his writings about friendship and the evidence advanced by some historians, has become an icon for some twenty-first-century groups of gay Christians.

An altar table found at Byland was moved to Ampleforth and now sits in the abbey church. During my time at the school the cricket team made an annual outing to play on a pitch in the shadow of Rievaulx's ruins, surely one of the most romantic cricketing settings anywhere. And the monks organized pilgrimages for the boys to a Marian shrine at Mount Grace, another monastic ruin a little further north.

These connections were quite deliberate: Ampleforth saw itself as part of the same story as these ancient foundations, and its self-confidence at the zenith of its success carried a message about the enduring power of the monastic ideal. Hundreds of years after Henry VIII's history-changing campaign of dissolution the monks were back. Here they ran a great British institution, vigorous, popular, rich and influential.

But the Ampleforth you find today when you drop down from the moors and turn into the abbey grounds and the valley below is a very different place. Ampleforth's ambition is still to be 'a place given wholly to the worship of God in a setting of incomparable splendour', but it is no longer untouched by 'secular intrigue', and the secular authorities have turned it into a place of locked doors and electronic keypads.

The only way the school could be kept open was a divorce from the monastery. In formal terms the two institutions are now run by separate charitable trusts, and very few monks teach the boys and girls. Those monks – the majority – who are not involved with the school are barred from entering its premises because monks have shown they are not to be trusted. And because the school and monastic buildings were designed to integrate the two communities they house, the business of keeping them apart is obtrusive. The easy intercourse that made Ampleforth a single community when I was there has gone.

And with it has gone the claim Ampleforth made in that old school prospectus I found in my father's files. No longer could it boast that it 'traces its origins to St Edward the Confessor', that 'the present school inherits through Westminster and Dieulouard an ancient English tradition', or that 'the ideal of Christian education in the liberal arts, which had been fostered and preserved by the monasteries, still inspires its work'. Gavin Williamson's ban on new pupils was eventually lifted, and at the time of writing Ampleforth is flourishing. But it is no longer a monastic school – certainly not in the way it was during my time there.

The presence of the monks was once considered Ampleforth's greatest asset, something that set it apart; today it is the school's greatest handicap, and there is talk of the monastery moving out of its existing home altogether – perhaps decamping, in a grim irony, to Gilling Castle, the source of so many of the community's woes.

And the damage has been done not by the kind of commissars sent in by Thomas Cromwell all those centuries ago, or by Harold Wilson's socialist zealots, so feared in my time by Father Patrick. It has been done by the monks themselves.

20 · PERHAPS BECAUSE I AM
JUST CONSERVATIVE

'We are all drowning in filth,' George Orwell confided to his diary in April 1942, overcome with disgust at the propaganda that came across his desk during his wartime service at the BBC. Presenting Radio 4's *Sunday* programme felt a bit like that in the early years of the last decade.

The programme's brief is the 'religious and ethical news of the week', and it is one of the very few outlets in mainstream broadcasting – or print journalism, come to that – which properly reflects the impact religion has on current affairs. It was just my luck to take on the main presenting role in the middle of one of the sorriest stretches of the whole sorry saga of abuse within the Catholic Church. Every week seemed to produce more revolting evidence, and, though I hugely enjoyed the programme (and still do), the Catholic bit of me began to dread my shifts.

A thorough Catholic education of the kind that Ampleforth provided had taught me to distinguish between 'the office and the man' (and in the Catholic Church an office-holder almost always is a man). Thus the fact that many popes and cardinals in late medieval and Renaissance Italy lived disreputable lives, fathering bastards and corruptly amassing fortunes, does not of itself mean that the offices of pope and cardinal are bad.

But this crisis went way beyond that glib logic. Being confronted, on an almost routine basis, by the scale of abuse, the depth of the pain it inflicted and by the Church's shameful failure to deal with all this honestly or competently of course made me question the credibility of the institution and its claims. Any other reaction would have been less than human. It was a miserable time to be a Catholic, and in the end the pope himself (Benedict XVI) gave up and resigned.

Working on *Sunday*, which became my main broadcasting home when I left *Today*, corroded my Catholicism in other, unexpected, ways.

It would be nice to think that religious leaders at least aspire to loftier ambitions than their political counterparts. In fact, regular contact with them in the form of interviews (and this is not a Catholic-specific observation, but one that applies to religious leaders more generally) persuaded me that they are often every bit as 'political' (even if not party political), and sometimes as venal, in the way they think and operate.

But the most difficult personal challenge presented by *Sunday* was a practical one. The programme was then broadcast from the BBC's Manchester studios in Oxford Road, so I spent most of my weekends travelling, and Sunday mornings, when the majority of good practising Catholics go to mass, usually found me on a Virgin train, cursing yet another rerouting via Rugby thanks to some of those 'weekend works on the line', which always seem to overrun. Instead of the hour of quiet reflection and communion with fellow Catholics that weekly mass offers, I watched the clock stealing my life, and tried to console myself with a sandwich bought from Pret A Manger at Manchester Piccadilly station.

Weekly mass attendance is one of those obligations that gives Catholicism a bad press as a rigidly rules-based religion, and I confess I have been, to put it politely, uneven in my observance over the decades. But because *Today* always gave me a day off on Sundays, I had fallen into a routine, going to mass either in Westminster Cathedral (for music and solemnity), which is just across the river from our home, or, even closer, at Corpus Christi on Brixton Hill. I was a remarried divorcee by this stage, and the inspirational parish priest, Father Tom Heneghan, was especially welcoming to those in difficult relationships with the Church.

Mass on Sundays became a comfortable habit, not an obligation. The suspension of services in churches during the Covid pandemic proved extremely painful to regular churchgoers, and their reaction provided a reminder that most of them regard it as a blessing and not a chore. It is ironic that my Covid-moment of regularly missing mass came early as a consequence of working on a programme dedicated to religious issues. I now present *Sunday* from London, but my early days there underscored that Catholicism is as much a way of life as a state of mind.

Reporting religion was never one of my ambitions: I fell into it as a result of my ambition to be noticed. When John Paul II came to Britain in 1982 he was at the height of the rock-star reputation he enjoyed in the early years of his pontificate. It was the first ever visit here by a reigning pope, and ITN planned to mark it with a series of live special programmes, which would dominate the ITV schedules for the six days of his nine-city tour. It was a huge logistical undertaking, and a brave test of the new television technology known as electronic newsgathering.

The one weakness in ITN's armour lay in the fact that almost no one knew anything about Catholicism, which was, in British society more generally as well as the office, still widely regarded as slightly weird and cultish, alien and un-British. Brandishing my Ampleforth credentials, I took on the task of preparing briefing notes for the reporting and presenting team, explaining everything from papal infallibility to transubstantiation. They went down well, although one Catholic friend remarked wryly that if I really had explained the mystery of transubstantiation, I had achieved something no theologian had ever managed.

Every little edge makes a difference when you are starting out as a reporter, and I found I could corner the market in religious stories. John Paul proved very good for trade – it is easy now to forget the extraordinary dynamism of his early days in office, and his trips to Poland had already proved that a pope could change politics. I got religious stories on the air surprisingly often.

Watching the waves the Polish pope made as he so restlessly criss-crossed the globe also persuaded me of an argument that has now become something of a hobby horse.

For the vast bulk of humanity, religion is a far more powerful source of motivation than politics. This is not a value judgement, and I always fight shy when asked to draw broad conclusions about whether the impact of religion is benign or malign. And it certainly has no bearing whatsoever on the question of whether any particular religion is true or false. It is simply an observation, and, if you turn it over for a moment or two, a very obvious one.

But we northern Europeans live in a strangely (judged by the standards of most of the world) secular corner, and secularism is even more marked among journalists and opinion-formers than it is in the population as a whole. As a result, we routinely misinterpret, and sometimes simply miss altogether, a hugely important dimension that ought to inform our reporting. It is an especially damaging lacuna in our profession: people turn to us for information and judgement that is full as well as accurate.

I have already confessed to some deeply embarrassing bits and pieces in my old papers and files; I have enjoyed finding the odd – much rarer – item that made me smile. In 1983 I persuaded the *Channel 4 News* foreign desk to despatch me to the tiny Bosnian mountain village of Medjugorje, where, it was reported, a group of six children were having regular visions of the Virgin Mary.

Today the site attracts tens of thousands of pilgrims and is bountifully endowed with hotels and shops selling bottled holy water, but in those days simply reaching this wild and remote place was quite an adventure. We filmed the children during their ecstasy – mouthing silently in a trance, and then letting out a collective cry of 'She is gone' as, they explained, the Madonna departed. The pictures caused something of a stir when we broadcast them.

Bosnia was still part of the old Yugoslavia then, and Tito, the country's founder and father, had recently died. In my memo selling the story I played up its political ramifications. 'The greatest fear of the Yugoslav government is that the unity of the country will be destroyed by a resurgence of religious nationalism,' I told the foreign desk. 'All the national divisions within Yugoslavia are strengthened by the religious divisions between Catholic Croats, Orthodox Serbs, Islamic Albanians etc. . . . Bosnia is the centre of religious friction – large numbers of Orthodox Serbs were massacred by Fascist Catholics there during the Second World War, and it has a majority Muslim population. So the appearance of the Virgin is very sensitive. She talks about peace a lot, but she speaks in Croat and appears to Croat children.'

That obviously fell well short of a prediction that I would next be in Bosnia a decade later in the midst of an especially horrible sectarian war, but, reading it back now, I cannot help feeling just a little proud of my twenty-five-year-old self. And I do not think I would have clocked this dimension of the story if I had been less sensitive to the power of religion.

It was my reporting in the Middle East that really turned this into a hobby horse, and it has become one I ride whenever I am asked to give a talk or write a piece about religious broadcasting. I often cite the way Western analysts – those working for governments as well as newspapers and broadcasters – were so completely blindsided by the success of the radical group Hamas in the 2006 legislative elections in the Palestinian Authority. Yasser Arafat's Fatah movement and the Palestinian Liberation Organization it dominated, the long-standing champions of Palestinian rights, were secular, and offered a home to Palestinian Christians as well as Muslims. No one expected that when ordinary Palestinians were given a chance to cast a vote, they would hand a majority not to Fatah, but to an avowedly religious movement – but they did, and the electoral process was generally held to have passed muster as free and fair.

The Hamas charter notoriously states that 'The land of Palestine has been an Islamic land throughout the generations, and until the Day of Resurrection, no one can renounce part of it . . . Hamas is a distinct Palestinian Movement which owes its loyalty to Allah, derives from Islam its way of life, and strives to raise the banner of Allah over every inch of Palestine.' The Western way of interpreting that is political: it is a denial of Israel's right to exist, and Hamas is therefore condemned by Western governments as a terrorist organization.

But that was only half of the story: the Hamas of that era took its religious duties seriously, developing a successful programme of religiously based social welfare, and in contrast to many of those then running the Palestinian Authority, its officials were not corrupt. That is why it was popular with the voters. The conflict between Israel and the Palestinians was always big news in those days, and the American Colony Hotel in Jerusalem could boast more journalists per bar stool than almost anywhere else in the world. But we all got the story wrong because we watched it through the kind of secular lenses we wore to interpret events at home.

I am writing this during the turmoil created by the United States' 2021 withdrawal from Afghanistan, and the way the Western world's leaders have been caught asleep at the wheel by the return of the austerely fundamentalist Taliban (the name comes from *talib*, the Pashto for a student educated at a traditional Islamic school) seems like a similar, but even more catastrophic, misreading of the power of religion.

The secular character of journalism was also reflected in a consensus that it was in the very worst possible taste to discuss one's personal beliefs, especially in public. My first book was about the way the Catholic Church worked in the world, and during a discussion at a literary festival the interviewer asked me about my personal faith. She approached the question as if she was raising some appalling form of sexual deviance. Good form dictated I remain silent on such matters, and by and large I did. Looking back at the few public remarks I made about Catholicism when I was young (and young-ish), that was probably just as well.

In the mid-1990s the Catholic Church attracted several high-profile converts who left the Church of England when it began ordaining women priests. Most of them argued that it was not the ordination of women *per se* they objected to, rather that the C of E had, in their view, erected an impassable barrier to the eventual unity of a single universal Church. Basil Hume capitalized on the sense of crisis among Anglican traditionalists by cutting a deal with the Vatican to suspend the discipline of celibacy. Married Anglican vicars who 'poped' were allowed to continue in the exercise of their priestly vocation.

All of this led to heady talk of an end to the so-called Elizabethan settlement, the process by which the first Queen Elizabeth cemented the establishment of the Church of England. Even Cardinal Hume, usually so sure-footed in his public comments, allowed himself to be tempted into a reference to 'the conversion of England, for which we have prayed all these years' during an interview with the Catholic weekly the *Tablet*.

I wrote a counter-intuitive piece in the *Telegraph* praising the 'clannishness' of the English Church, and arguing that this prospect in fact presented a serious challenge to the powerful sense of identity English Catholics had developed. 'A feeling of being in some way different has come to play a central part in the way English Catholics think about themselves,' I declared. 'I still catch myself sniffing around for my co-religionists, and if Catholics, even the lapsed, find themselves together, they tend to fall into conversation about their peculiar institution. It is both the strength and the weakness of the Roman Catholic tradition in England, and adjustment to life without it may be traumatic.'

At around the same time, Hodder & Stoughton brought out a book of interviews with Catholic worthies ranging from Delia Smith to the TV nun Sister Wendy Beckett. My contribution to *Why I Am a Catholic** had a brassy arrogance of tone that now sets my teeth on edge. I set my face firmly against divorce – 'The Catholic objection to divorce is a helpful underpinning of family life,' I find myself saying.

And I dismissed the idea of women priests as an unachievable fantasy: 'I have . . . difficulty with women priests, perhaps because I am just conservative. Probably I have been intellectually lazy about it for the simple reason that it doesn't seem to be an immediate prospect.' The intellectual laziness was, I now think, a consequence of being a cradle Catholic: having been born into the club, I did not have to spend too much time and energy fretting about the rules.

Two developments stirred me out of this complacent tribalism, one professional, the other personal.

The BBC still had generous budgets in the 1990s, and the invitation to front a four-part BBC Two series on the modern Catholic Church was irresistible. We had the money to film pretty much everywhere we wanted to – Brazil, El Salvador, India, Poland, Sri

---

*   Published 1995, edited by Rowanne Pasco.

Lanka, the United States, Zambia and, of course, Rome. My encounter with the wider Church radically changed how I saw my faith.

To my surprise, it turned out that Catholic leaders across most of the world worried about things other than sex, which had become something of an obsession in the European Church. In Latin America, Catholicism was intimately tied up with the search for social justice. In Africa, good nuns and priests wrestled with the Church's ban on condoms and the reality of the AIDS crisis. In India, the Catholic teaching that every human being is loved by God provided a rallying point against the idea that people can be declared 'untouchable'. These sweeping life-and-death issues dwarfed the tribal preoccupations of the Catholic world in which I had grown up.

All of that was exhilarating. The personal change in my life was more disorienting. I went through a divorce and remarried – despite my cheerful acceptance of the Church's teaching on this issue just a few years earlier – and thus effectively expelled myself from the club I had taken for granted all my life.

The idea that the Church 'bans' remarried divorcees from communion is not quite right: the ban is something you impose on yourself by accepting a condition of life regarded as inherently sinful. And the impact is very public. Most Catholics now take communion every time they go to mass. Remaining seated in the pews when the rest of the congregation queued to receive the host became a routine reminder that I had placed myself outside the Catholic family.

The experience brought home to me a paradox that lies at the heart of Catholicism: it is both exclusive and universal, a closed club with its own rules that is at the same time open to all humankind.

That tension goes right back to Christianity's earliest days. The idea of a universal Church, which would have been completely alien to most people two thousand years ago, was born in the extraordinary religious imagination of St Paul, and it is reflected in some of the most attractive passages in his letters. 'There is neither Jew nor Greek, slave nor free, male nor female,' he famously told the Galatians, 'for you are all one in Christ Jesus.' And he wrote to the Corinthians in similar terms: 'For we were all baptized by one Spirit so as to form one body – whether Jews or Gentiles, slave or free – and we were all given the one Spirit to drink.'

And yet he can also brandish the rules with an almost Pitt-Clubbish zeal for exclusivity. Those same Corinthians – they were notorious for their loose morals, and 'to Corinth' was rude slang for having sex – were also instructed that they should not 'associate with anyone who bears the name of brother or sister who is sexually immoral or greedy, or is an idolator, reviler, drunkard or robber. Do not eat with such a one . . . Drive out the wicked person from among you.'

The tension is also reflected in one of the best advertising slogans of all time, one that the Church has been using to drive traffic since the third century AD: *extra ecclesiam nulla salus* – there is no salvation outside the Church. If this is true, it is obviously a very powerful incentive for becoming a Catholic, since the alternative (for those who believe in an after-life) is eternal damnation. On the other hand, it is quite a claim for any human institution to make, and it is difficult to square with the idea that God loves all of us. Theologians have been debating the real meaning of the statement for centuries, and although you do not often hear it now, it was a hot topic of debate right up until the Second Vatican Council in the 1960s.

All this suddenly became rather personal, and the comfortable certainties I had been brought up with melted away. Even priests I spoke to could not give me clear answers. One suggested I try to have my first marriage annulled, which seemed ridiculous to me after twenty years and three much-loved children. Another, a wise old monk from Ampleforth, called me over after mass one day and told me to take communion anyway because 'we all need it'.

Ten years after the publication of *Why I Am a Catholic*, that collection of interviews with Catholic worthies, Hodder & Stoughton revisited the idea under the slightly more tentative title *Why I Am Still a Catholic** (my emphasis). This time I described my faith as 'a work in progress'.

---

*   Published 2005, edited by Peter Stanford.

21 · TEARS AND LAMENTABLE CRIES

John Stourton had just turned twenty when, early in 1573, he tried
to escape to France. His Catholic tutor, who was banged up in Marshalsea at the time – Marshalsea was the main prison for obstinate
Catholics during Queen Elizabeth I's reign – advised him to 'steal
away beyond the sea' so that he could practise his religion without
fear of persecution.

But the plan was frustrated by Elizabeth's formidable intelligence network. He was caught at Dover, thanks to – in the words of
an early account – 'some means or secret intelligence', and arrested,
'the Queen being then very jealous of her subjects, especially per-
sons of honour, going out of England, lest they might, with the
King of Spain, combine against her'.

What happened next provides an insight into the sheer cleverness of Elizabethan statecraft. Instead of being sent to do porridge
with his seditious tutor in Marshalsea, John was put under a benign
form of house arrest in Lambeth Palace, where the Archbishop of
Canterbury, Matthew Parker, set about converting him.

Parker reported that at first he found John 'very stiff, insomuch
as he could not hear of the disabling of his religion, and of the rea-
sonableness of ours', and he failed to persuade young Stourton to
'come to the daily prayers, in the chapel with the household'. But
the archbishop was a great scholar – one of Anglicanism's founding
theological fathers – and over the months his arguments seem to
have prevailed. In November 1573 he wrote to William Cecil, Elizabeth's closest adviser, with the news that John Stourton was
'conforming', as it was known: '. . . I can testify of his [John's]

coming into my chapel with the rest of my household, and that he giveth ear to the lessons there read, and heareth such sermons as are made there.'

Armed with a religious pass mark from the Archbishop of Canterbury, John Stourton was able to enjoy life at the heart of the Elizabethan establishment. He took his seat in the House of Lords in 1575 (having promised his fellow privy councillors that he would not repeat his attempts to abscond abroad) and in 1580 acquired a wife related to those Cecils who were so close to Elizabeth.

In the summer of 1588, when Elizabeth faced the Spanish Armada and the threat of Catholic invasion, John rallied to the Crown, like any loyal English lord, sending 'six lances and fourteen light horses of his own household servants' to help fight the invaders, and offering himself 'to attend on her Majesty's sacred person'. The family fortunes had taken a bit of a battering during his father's time (the previous Lord Stourton was a notorious murderer, but that is another story) and John added how sorry he was that 'his ability yielded not a far greater number' of soldiers.

But throughout all this, John Stourton was playing a double game: conforming with Anglicanism in public, but praying as a Catholic in private. He kept two priests on standby at Stourton House in Wiltshire (on the site of what is now the wonderful National Trust garden of Stourhead) so that he could be sure of scrambling back into the embrace of the Catholic Church before he died.

By some terrible trick of fate, both priests were absent when he fell mortally ill in his mid-thirties, and the archives of the English Jesuits record that before he died 'God in His great mercy infused into the Baron's heart so lively a sense of the horror of his sin and so deep a contrition, that, not satisfied with begging pardon of God and promising within his own mind amendment and satisfaction, he called together his wife, stewards and all the family, and with floods of tears acknowledged before them his crime and the scandal he had given.'

Father John Cornelius, a Jesuit priest who would later be martyred, said a requiem mass for John's soul, and reported a terrifying vision while he was at the altar: 'Before him was presented a forest of immense size in which all was fire and flame, and in the midst he perceived the soul of the deceased Lord, who with tears and lamentable cries accused himself of the evil life he had led for several years especially whilst at court, and his dissimulation in frequenting the Protestant Church, though still a Catholic, to the scandal and grievous hurt of the souls of his relations.'

John Stourton was one of those nineteen barons John Prescott brandished at me with such indignation in the *Today* studio, and I found out about his tortured tale thanks to a clever idea from my colleagues in the BBC's Religion and Ethics Department.

Martin Luther nailed his ninety-five theses to the church door in Wittenberg in October 1517, so 2017 was held to be the five-hundredth anniversary of the Reformation. It was a natural focus for programmes on Radio 4 – which thrives on anniversaries – but making appealing radio out of a great religious upheaval half a millennium ago is quite a challenge.

One of our producers brilliantly suggested some discreet borrowing from the BBC One series *Who Do You Think You Are?* which had been launched the previous decade and proved a hit. The format was driven by a celebrity investigating his or her family tree, discovering some startling and revealing piece of ancestral information in the process. Why not tell the Reformation story through the eyes of three people whose ancestors were directly caught up in it? Radio 4 bought the idea and commissioned three programmes. I am not sure the three of us selected to take part quite qualified as celebrities, but I got the Catholic gig.

John's story was refreshing because it was so completely human. During my Catholic education, the Reformation was generally told more as propaganda than as history. Our prep-school dormitories were named for martyrs so that we would admire and remember their courage and steadfastness. The grisly manner of their death also served as a constant reminder of the wickedness and cruelty of the Protestant regime that punished them.

Yet here was a tale in which the Protestants seemed to have behaved both cleverly and in a civilized manner, while the Catholic at the centre of the narrative showed himself to be anything but heroic. Not for the first time I was reminded that, while bad history makes things simple and fires strong emotions, good history reveals complexity and ambiguity.

The Catholic records of what happened to John are themselves coloured by propaganda; Father Cornelius's vision was reported during a papal campaign to intensify pressure on English Catholics, and giving them a good fright about what they might face if they caved in and conformed was no doubt helpful. But John's desire to have his cake and eat it seems completely natural, and just occasionally a real person wrestling with his weaknesses peeps through the sixteenth-century sources.

So, unravelling John's story made for a most enjoyable programme – for me, at least, and I hope the listeners: if broadcasters are excited by the material they unearth when putting together a programme, that enthusiasm usually comes through. But I failed the production team dismally at what should have been the climax of the recording.

The *Who Do You Think You Are?* format depends heavily on a Big Reveal, which prompts a strong emotional reaction in the celebrity subject. Jeremy Paxman in tears at Bradford town hall when death certificates revealed that his paternal great-grandparents both died of TB and, in his great-grandmother's case, 'exhaustion' is a good example.

I was told only that my Big Reveal would take place in the Palace of Westminster. After a good lunch in Smith Square, the producer and I tottered across to the Victoria Tower with the distinguished Cambridge historian Eamon Duffy. A lift took us up to a muniment room overlooking the Thames, where we found an impressive parchment scroll laid out on a green baize cloth.

This, Professor Duffy informed us, was the judgement on Mary, Queen of Scots, accused of treason by her cousin Elizabeth, and – there was much theatrical rustling of parchment pages as a prelude to this moment – there, on the very document that condemned Mary to her death, was the signature of Lord Stourton. John Stourton was one of twenty-four peers sent to Fotheringhay Castle in Northamptonshire to sit in judgement at Mary's trial, and here was clear evidence of his complicity in her execution.

This was certainly shocking news about a Catholic of the day: many of them nurtured hopes that Mary, a Catholic herself, would restore the English Crown to the true faith. And I did find it interesting, because it cast a very different light on the family narrative of heroic Stourton resistance to wicked Tudor tyranny.

But could I squeeze out a tear or two, or even a gasp of shock? I could not. All this happened several hundred years ago, and it would have been ridiculous to feel a sense of personal connection to John's act of betrayal, monstrous though it was. We know from accounts of his death that he lamented this sin over all others, but I could hardly share in his sense of guilt. The producer, who had banked on an emotional scene, held the microphone close and watched me like a hawk for signs of existential distress. He was disappointed.

The incident finally put the kibosh on the atavism that had

always been so central to my understanding of what it means to be an English Catholic. If you visit the English College in Rome, where priests were trained during the decades of persecution, you are likely to be shown a vast oil painting, called the Martyrs' Picture, around which the students would gather to celebrate with a triumphant *Te Deum* whenever they heard news that one of their number had been executed back in England. The Reformation was, for them, a deadly serious business. To indulge such emotions in the twenty-first century suddenly seemed frivolous. Tribalism, I concluded, is a rotten way of deciding what you believe.

And yet ... and yet ... I defy any Catholic who witnesses a papal conclave not to feel at least a twitch of tribal pride. I have covered two, and confess myself bewitched by the whole carry-on.

The first proved unexpectedly hazardous. On 2 April 2005 I flew to Rome with a *Today* programme team, and rumours that Pope John Paul II had died while we were in the air reached us at the baggage carousel. We abandoned our luggage and grabbed the first taxi we could find. The driver had a television on his dashboard, and we made the mistake of telling him that we wanted to reach St Peter's as quickly as possible. While travelling at a hair-raising speed down the *autostrada*, he kept his eyes fixed on the live transmission from the Vatican, turning round regularly to give us updates in his broken English.

In fact John Paul held on until later that evening, and news of his death reached us as we were finishing dinner in a restaurant just off the Piazza Navona. We walked back across the Tiber – it was a balmy spring evening – and found St Peter's Square entirely illuminated by candles, a vast, silent sea of pilgrims praying, many of them on their knees as they gazed up at the windows of the papal apartments. That space, embraced by the arms of Bernini's colonnade and dominated by the Basilica of St Peter's, is perhaps the greatest stage in the world, both intensely intimate and impossibly grand. Nowhere else – not the White House or Downing Street – offers anything like such a powerful setting for the transfer of power.

And then there is the richness of the process of choosing a new pope: the tradition of locking up the Church's leaders until they make up their minds ('conclave' simply means 'with a key' in Latin), the combination of extreme secrecy and the addiction to gossip that is such a prominent feature of Vatican life, the rickety old stove where the ballots are burnt to send smoke to a waiting world, the theory – no doubt ridiculous to non-believers, but it still has currency among Catholics – that the Holy Spirit guides Their Eminences during their deliberations. All that and good Roman lunches too: covering a conclave is, in purely journalistic terms, very good fun.

And, of course, the College of Cardinals – which can perhaps claim the title of the world's smallest but most sophisticated electorate – springs surprises. I was back in St Peter's when the white smoke puffed out in March 2013, following Pope Benedict's resignation. When the name of Jorge Bergoglio rang out from the balcony of St Peter's I whipped out my microphone in search of reaction, happily chancing on a group of Americans in the crowd: 'I have no idea who he is,' one declared, 'but I know he'll be a great pope.' He was right – at least I think he was. Pope Francis very soon took the dread out of my Sunday-morning broadcasting.

I had a good personal reason to be cheered by the new man in the Vatican: one of Francis's first priorities was the condition of divorced and remarried Catholics like me. This is not the place to rehearse the way that battle unfolded – it took several years and two synods – but the outcome was instructive. Francis did open the way to allowing us – at least some of us – to take communion again, but because the reform was so controversial, he smuggled the change into a footnote to *The Joy of Love*, the document he published at the end of it all. It was an oddly tentative solution in a Church that has traditionally relied so heavily on the idea that it has a monopoly on the truth.

The Francis footnote included a characteristic flourish: communion, he wrote, 'is not a prize for the perfect, but a powerful medicine and nourishment for the weak' – rather the point that that kindly Ampleforth monk was making when he told me that 'we all need it'. The change and the debates that led to it – some of them were very bitter – marked a broader move to a different kind of Church leadership.

The secular press soon had Francis down as a 'liberal' pope, and for a while he acquired the status of a left-wing icon: there were stories of students tearing down their Che Guevara posters and putting up Francis's face instead, and Elton John declared that he should be canonized, without even waiting for him to die. But he is in many ways a rather traditional Catholic, and conventional political terms do not quite work when you are trying to explain what he is about. I came to think of him in a slightly different way after being asked to work on his obituary (you will not, I imagine, be surprised to hear that Radio 4 prepares and keeps a good stock of these ready to roll; I very much hope this one will not be broadcast for a long time to come).

One of our guests, a radical American nun, defined the Francis approach like this: 'Reality or stories of real people are more important than your ideas or your theories . . . you can argue for ever about a theory, but when you meet a person, then that changes it, changes how we come at it . . . I don't think you can call it liberal, progressive or conservative. I call it a pastoral human approach to this embodiment of the gospel.' To put it another way, Francis is really the Reporter Pope. He has not abandoned the Church's traditions and teaching, but he has listened to the stories told in the lives of ordinary Catholics, and they have changed him. It is exactly the experience I have tried – in a much more modest way – to describe in this book.

He has also – and almost every Catholic I know gives three cheers for this – brought some of the fun back into the faith, banishing those gloomy ghosts that haunted us all so dankly during the last years presided over by his predecessor. Another contributor to our obituary programme, the Francis biographer Paul Vallely, summed up the change with a punchy quote we used right at the end of the programme: 'No one can now say that the only way to be a Catholic is to be dour and rules-based. Another kind of Catholicism is possible, Pope Francis said. And those who've lived through his papacy won't forget that. He demonstrated not just a different way of being a pope. He showed the world a different way of being a Catholic. And he said to people of all faiths and none that, in our troubled times, the gospel is actually good news. If it's embraced with mercy and humility and joy, it can be something that makes the world a better place.' What a relief it is to be able to make even a half-convincing case for that.

The return of cheerful Catholicism mattered especially to me because I was putting together the pope's obituary around the time I was thinking about my own for the reasons I explained at the beginning of this book.

Having an incurable cancer should, logically, make me reflect on the Church's promise of resurrection and eternal life – and, of course, the threat of damnation – but it has not done that at all: I find I think no more about such things than I did when I was healthy, and I have never been much given to agonized contemplation of eternity (unlike my troubled ancestor John). And I realize now – anyone who takes their faith seriously is bound to keep learning new things about it – that my attachment to Catholicism owes much more to a sense that it is a good guide to this life than to any conviction that it is a passport to the next.

That might be read to suggest I use the Church's teachings in some systematic way, but that is not what I mean at all. It is a much more haphazard business, more an accumulation of moments when the idea of a world redeemed by a God who became human simply seems to make more sense than anything else.

They come unexpectedly, often prompted by unlikely connections. While walking the dogs in Battersea Park one luminous autumn day, my wife and I bumped into a Catholic acquaintance who remarked that it was a 'Manley Hopkins morning'. As it happened, we had recently read one of that Jesuit poet's most famous sonnets.

After a dreamy al-fresco lunch watching the red kites and buzzards that often circle above our house in France, Gerard Manley Hopkins's description of a raptor seemed more inspired than ever.

I caught this morning morning's minion, king-
dom of daylight's dauphin, dapple-dawn-drawn Falcon, in his riding
Of the rolling level underneath him steady air, and striding
High there, how he rung upon the rein of a wimpling wing
In his ecstasy! then off, off forth on swing,
As a skate's heel sweeps smooth on a bow-bend: the hurl and gliding
Rebuffed the big wind. My heart in hiding
Stirred for a bird,—the achieve of, the mastery of the thing!

Father Gerard dedicated 'The Windhover' to 'Christ our Lord' and, like many of his poems, it evokes the beauty of the natural world as evidence for a divinity. My Battersea Park acquaintance, of course, had no idea about our French bird-watching, but his reference to Manley Hopkins was a kind of code. He is of a similar age and educational background; I immediately understood the Catholic worldview he was alluding to – there was some of that old tribal clubbishness at play in our exchange.

The beauty of the morning, the memory of those birds flying so miraculously high above our French home and the power of the poetry, lingering in the mind like the finish on a fine wine, conspired – for that passing moment – to nudge me towards the conviction that, as another Manley Hopkins poem puts it, 'The World is charged with the grandeur of God'.

And at moments like that it is simply easier to acquiesce.

WRITING

22 · *UN CIEL VOILÉ*

John Stourton's abortive attempt to escape across the Channel was part of a pattern. The penal laws imposed against Catholics during the sixteenth and seventeenth centuries – with bans on everything from voting and holding public office to importing religious items from Rome – made life in England wearisome, especially during periods when the legislation was enforced with vigour. It was commonplace for Catholics who felt their homeland no longer represented their values to seek solace in French exile.

The most significant exodus followed the Glorious Revolution of 1688, when James II, driven from his throne because of his faith, fled to France. So many Catholic nobles followed him that he was able to establish his own court at St Germain-en-Laye, just outside Paris, where Louis XIV generously loaned him a palace. Court life was lived just as it had been back at home, with all the flummery of chamberlains, equerries, orders of precedence and royal ritual.

The episode has long intrigued me because most of those who followed James to France would have assumed that their exile was temporary, and the enterprise was sustained imaginatively by what we can now see was a fantasy – one in which the Catholic king returned to give England a Catholic future. Reality came brutally to these Jacobites, first with the defeat of James's invasion of Ireland at the Battle of the Boyne in 1690, then, more finally, with the Battle of La Hogue, a clash off the coast of Normandy two years later, which ended Louis XIV's hopes of invading England and restoring a Catholic monarchy.

What can it have been like coming to terms with the realization that you had gambled yourself so definitively onto the wrong side of history? James's followers had bet every chip they had on a different outcome. And there were thousands of exiled Irish soldiers – known as the Wild Geese – swilling around Paris along with the English aristos. It felt fertile territory for a novel, and I resolved to try. The decision was driven partly, if I'm honest, by competition with my elder son: Ivo published two novels immediately after leaving university, and he seemed able to magic characters into life quite effortlessly.

I had a protagonist readily to hand, because there was a real Edward Stourton who followed James into exile. All we really know about him is that he married the daughter of one of James's equerries, and that his brother was captain of the guard at court. He funded his exile by selling ever larger tracts of Wiltshire land, and his miserable end was a fitting reflection of Jacobite hopes: he 'died in Paris, intestate and without issue, in 1720', according to a family history. 'The exact date of his death is unknown, as are also the place of his burial, the date of the death of his wife, and the place of her burial.'

I spent some happy hours in my writing shed filling this blank canvas with a plot, weaving this unfortunate into the real history of his time. I even tried to cheer him up with a love affair with the wonderful seventeenth-century letter-writer Madame de Sévigné.

But the novel-writing experiment was a disaster: I found that I had been nailed down to the journeyman's task of truth-telling for far too long to make things up. Confronted by – say – a hunting scene, I would spend several cheerful days researching seventeenth-century falconry and animal husbandry . . . then freeze completely when I had to make my characters do and say things. I could not convincingly get them onto a horse, let alone bring them autonomously alive.

The dream of a French escape, however, remained. France is a passion my wife and I share, and from the earliest days of our marriage – a second one for both of us, and we were in our forties – we escaped regularly in search of a likely location for a part-time French future. In a rolling programme of long weekends, we overdosed on the châteaux of the Loire Valley, walked the noble stones of La Rochelle and ate *fruits de mer* on the fashionable Île de Ré. We explored the meandering rivers of the Venise Verte in the Vendée and the warren of streets around Marseille's Vieux Port. We took our time over the search, partly because it was fun and partly because we knew it would be years before we could afford to buy anything.

The list of criteria we eventually drew up seemed impossible to reconcile. Fiona insisted that we should buy below what she called 'the cicada line' – far enough south to enjoy the sound of their stridulation on warm evenings. I wanted to be in striking distance of mountains: I had long since escaped the mania that once drove me obsessively up and down the ski slopes day after long cold day, but I still quite fancied a morning's red runs followed by lunch in the sun. We agreed on being close enough to an airport to make long weekends a realistic possibility – and, critically, whatever we bought had to be cheap.

Ariège is one of those secrets the French keep to themselves. It is about as far south as it is possible to go without leaving the country altogether, running into the Pyrenees and right down to the border with Spain and Andorra. But it is within easy distance of Toulouse airport, and it is, to anyone familiar with the lunacies of the London property market, almost comically cheap. The mountain climate can make for uncertain summers, but winter sunshine more than compensates for the occasional soaked week in August; we have often enjoyed Christmas turkeys (supplied by the poultry farmer up the lane) in blazing sunshine.

We rejected several houses because they were perched so pre-cipitously on hill or mountainsides, and chose ours because it has enough flat land for a garden – a rare quality in the sculpted land-scape of the Massif du Plantaurel. It is built on a spine of land that rises along the centre of a wide valley, so the views from both sides are dramatic. With outbuildings, an orchard and meadowland, which falls away on both sides of the hill, it cost less than half the price of a one-bedroom flat in Tooting.

The heart of the property is a solid stone farmhouse, with walls close to a metre thick: in the summer they make it a cool haven from the southern sun; in the winter they soak up and keep the warmth of our open fire. This original rectangle once provided space for farm animals below and a single, open-plan area for family life above – there is an outside staircase to what was once the front door.

But it has grown organically and sometimes eccentrically: the farming family who used to live here turned a stable at the back into bedrooms, but when we moved in the upper one could only be reached via a balcony. A door on the first-floor landing opened onto a two-storey barn, and, by creating a cathedral-ceilinged bedroom in what had been a loft full of agricultural machinery, we pushed the living area out a little further. The big space downstairs, which once provided shelter for cows and sheep, is now a kitchen and sit-ting room.

Even with the improvements we have made – the sanitation arrangements we inherited consisted of a pipe dug into the nearest field – it remains determinedly modest. We have sometimes looked longingly at those vast, dreamy *manoirs*, *gentilhommières* and *châteaux* that you find in the property pages of the weekend *Financial Times*, but whenever I meet someone who has succumbed to that particular temptation they are either complaining about the cost of restoring the moat or selling up, defeated by the stress of it all. We, rather smugly, can lock the front door and forget about the place, confident that the farmer's wife, who passes every day on her way to the village, will alert us if anything goes wrong.

Initially this venture into the international property market had more to do with reading than with writing. It is an exaggeration to say that we bought the house to provide more shelf-space, but only a mild one: our London home is simply bursting with books. Fiona and I both had substantial libraries when we got married, and all our children have, to a greater or lesser degree, been touched by bibliomania.

Ivo collects first editions of late-twentieth-century fiction, Eleanor worked in bookshops before settling into her career as a charity fundraiser, and Rosy talks about the scent of old books as if she's discussing a bath oil. Only Tom, my younger son, makes do with scruffy paperbacks, but his business is film and television, and he spends more time writing than any of us. Any attempt to slim down the shelves would prompt a mutiny in this literary next generation.

It very quickly became apparent, however, that, while our new French home indeed had the capacity to absorb more shelving (all the paperbacks came out in the back of the car almost immediately), it also offered new temptations.

We usually do our weekly shop in the Saturday market at Saint-Girons, the nearest town of any size. It lies at the confluence of three rivers – the Salat, the Lèze and the Baup – and on clear days the water sparkles alongside the market square, roaring over a weir opposite the solid bulk of the town's eponymous church (it is said to contain some relics of the saint himself, a fifth-century Vandal convert murdered by the Visigoths).

A few stalls are obligatory stops: the cheese man, who can be guaranteed to provide mountain cheeses at their creamiest best – they last just a few days before turning hard or, in the summer heat,

277

overripe – a fishmonger for oysters, in the appropriate months (essential at Christmas), and, at the heart of the market sprawl, earthy seasonal veg. Tomatoes and carrots '*à l'ancien*' are particular favourites: they range through a startling spectrum of colours, from the familiar orange and red to the purple of a Roman toga.

Our market routine always culminates in a beer from the Basque country, served in the sort of deep chalice you might find on an altar, at Le Bouchon in the Place des Poilus – which roughly translates as 'The Cork in Tommy Square'. Even in deep winter the tables outside are packed with people: you come to be social, not just to buy things.

But the irresistible seduction that really trumps my natural aversion to shopping is the treasure trove to be found in what was once the Grand Café de l'Union, just across from the terrace outside Le Bouchon. Saint-Girons, which is a gateway town to the Couserans mountain region, enjoyed a brief belle-époque celebrity as a fashionable holiday destination, and the café, with its frescoed ceiling, generous windows and the sculptural flourishes on its façade, bears the unmistakable hallmarks of that era. Its days as the haunt of haughty waiters and their beau-monde clientele are long since gone. It is now the most enticing second-hand bookshop you can imagine.

Our department, Ariège, is hippie territory – local lore has it that supporters of the 1968 *évènements* in Paris took refuge down here and never went home – so a good number of shelves are devoted to the properties of crystals, alternative medicine and meditation techniques. There is a rich section on local history and life, and lots of those floppy but physically satisfying paperbacks which – with their rough-edged pages – are such a distinctive feature of French bookshops. But the greatest prizes are to be found in the shelves of antique and precious books just to the right of the main entrance.

Whenever I am let off the shopping leash, I indulge my addiction here. I quite quickly found nice editions of books I had learnt to love at school – Racine's *Britannicus*, some Balzac novels – and I was soon drawn into habits that lead to libraries getting out of hand. I found, for example, a very handsome edition of the poems of François Villon . . . only to discover that his fifteenth-century French was well beyond my abilities. I had to get hold of an English translation to help me through it, adding two books to the shelves instead of one. The historian Antonia Fraser once confided in me – after an interview for a BBC programme – that she believes books copulate and reproduce on the shelves whenever you leave the room.

So, as a solution to our book crisis the house has proved a failure. But as a sanctuary to write in, it has been a notable success.

This is partly for obvious advantages having to do with quiet and an absence of distraction: the stillness of the place – and it is stillness as opposed to silence, because on some days the lulling tinkle of cowbells drifts across the valley almost continuously – is of a different order from even the most tranquil London garden. But there is also a deeper and more unexpected reason.

I began my writing career in television, moved to radio, and now spend more and more of my time on books – I sometimes wonder whether I shall soon move on to illuminating parchment or carving hieroglyphics. The backwards trajectory through those mediums has propelled me inexorably towards those olden days that dominated my childhood. I started serious book-writing late – my first came out just after my fortieth birthday – and most of what I have produced since then (unsuccessful sallies into fiction notwithstanding) could be broadly classed as history. Our part of France has, in an easy-going way, the trick of making history seem alive – without it feeling like a burden.

Our local paper, *La Dépêche*, for example, organizes its weather forecasts by saints' days: today is the feast of St Theodore and the prospect is an 'over-cast sky followed by clouds which will become more dominant' this morning, while this afternoon the weather will 'get worse, with the showers intensifying'. A few French literary flourishes – that overcast sky is described as *voilé*, or 'veiled' – somehow make this rather grim *météo* easier to face.

No one seems to have any idea who these saints were or what they did, but the weather really matters in these Pyrenean foothills, so the forecasts are often the first place we all turn to on buying the paper; daily contact with this litany of often strange and euphonious names echoes a connection with tradition that is widely felt here.

During a gardening chat with one of our neighbours – we were both bedding things down for winter – she informed me that on St Catherine's Day, 25 November, anything you plant, whether a rose cutting or a stick of vine, will take root and flourish. She and her husband have never shown any special signs of piety, far less mysticism, but the information was delivered with complete conviction and absolute sincerity.

The past is honoured, and nothing is ever thrown away: bits of rubble and carving from the monastery that once dominated our *commune* have been recycled into village houses built many decades after the monastery was destroyed during France's Wars of Religion. Like our neighbours, we have salvaged old milk churns and pieces of agricultural machinery to serve as garden ornaments. Fortnum's biscuit tins we have given as Christmas presents are proudly preserved on *étagères* around the hamlet.

When we had the façade of our house stripped back to its original honey-coloured stone, I asked the *façadier* how old the building might be. He thought for a moment or two and replied, with great reverence, '*Ancien.*' Old is good, the details of exactly *how* old do not matter too much.

This relaxed sense of connection with the past creates a benign climate for history-writing, and encourages a more generous interpretation of the meaning of history itself. The best history is made from multiple sources, and I have had to learn to be less dogmatic about what is true.

When putting together a programme for television or radio, I have always been a timeline Fascist: both media – television especially – are best suited to straight story-telling because we consume them in a linear way. We watch and listen to programmes as we live, with one thing following another. That narrative method works when you are sure of the facts.

When I worked as a television news reporter, I believed that if someone sat in front of my camera and gave me an account of an event they had witnessed, what they said was likely to be an objective and accurate account of what had happened. In news journalism, when people are usually remembering very recent events, that is a reasonably reliable assumption – although, of course, if the event was in some way controversial you have to make allowances for that.

But when I began working in current affairs and long-form journalism, I realized that memory can be an altogether more complex and capricious agent.

My 1990s BBC series on the history of the modern Catholic Church began with the Second Vatican Council, the great gathering of bishops in Rome that ran from 1962 to 1965. Our main witnesses had all been senior figures – bishops and cardinals – at the Council, so by the time they gave us interviews thirty years later most were a very great age. Some of them – the nonagenarian Cardinal König of Vienna stands out in my mind – were brilliant men, and they gave us vivid accounts of what had happened. But when I set their stories against the written histories and contemporary press coverage, I sometimes found that the two did not quite match.

A decade later, I produced a radio series and a book about Second World War escapers. Some of those I interviewed – again, most of them were, for obvious reasons, elderly people – had told their stories many times before, and I found that the way they told them to me was sometimes subtly different from their earlier versions. Just occasionally they would describe things I knew – because of the record of the way the war unfolded – could not have happened.

My doubts about the reliability of memory were confirmed by the first book I wrote in which everyone was dead – a history of the BBC during the Second World War. I based it partly on what I found in the paper record in the BBC's huge written archive at Caversham, and partly on memoirs by some of the key figures involved. I found that even some of the memoir accounts, which were written quite soon after the events they described, were at odds with the hard facts I established from the archive. That is not to say the memoirs had no value – far from it, they helped to recreate atmosphere, and often shed revealing light on some of my characters – but they were not always, strictly speaking, accurate. While writing this book I have done my best to check my memory against dates and diary entries, and have often found it played me false.

Of course we all forget things, the more so as we get older and feebler in our minds, but I am now persuaded that misremembering is a positive act. Sometimes we remember in a way that flatters us, and there is always a temptation to tell our stories so that they reflect well on us. We all also – especially journalists – like to polish a story so that it makes a bright, shiny anecdote. But some of my most vivid memories are of painful or humiliating moments, so I do not think we misremember things simply to suit ourselves. Memory can, I now realize, be a ruthless editor, and oddly independent, cutting out some chunks of our lives and rewriting others for reasons we do not consciously understand. The way we remember is part of who we are, and it changes as we change.

Books are better at capturing that subtle interplay, and the uncertainties and ambiguities it creates. They can be digested in a slightly different way from television and radio programmes. Even if you are gripped and read one straight through – on a long journey, say – you might go back and reread passages you have not fully understood, or want to reflect on further. You can put books aside for long periods and pick them up again when you want to, read several at once, skip bits that do not interest you, flip through the photos or allow your attention to be diverted for a while by a footnote. That flexibility for the reader creates freedom for the writer.

Sometimes my face or voice pops up unexpectedly in the middle of a television or radio documentary about the past, and when it happens I meet myself as a stranger. No doubt whatever story I was reporting or discussing seemed vital at the time, but my mental filing cabinet is so stuffed with big stories that many of them are buried at the bottom of a drawer. Books, in contrast, stay alive for longer than broadcast programmes, even in an age when so much radio and telly is captured online. And live events, like literary festivals, can take you right back to the journey you made when you were researching and writing, and give you insights you missed at the time.

They can also bring unexpected treats. At a festival in Wiltshire,* as I was signing copies of my book about Second World War escapers, I was approached by a county lady with a voice as loud as her tweed. 'I am so glad you've got George's story in here,' she declared. Knowing that the George in question was dead, I asked politely whether she had known him. 'Known him!' she boomed.

---

* Jane Pleydell-Bouverie's Chalke Valley History Festival.

'We were lovers for his last fifteen years, before he died at ninety-five, and it was worth every moment.' What a wonderful way to be remembered, and how I wished I could have included it in my book!

As a journalist I have always sought to simplify, driving the facts towards a hard conclusion. At this stage of my backwards journey through different media I find I am being led in the opposite direction. Writing history makes me challenge conclusions, ask new questions, and look for new and different stories. Learning to love uncertainty – in place of all those easy assumptions I embraced when I set out – is, it turns out, a great gift of a life lived with words.

ACKNOWLEDGEMENTS

When I began this project I imagined that I would be my own best editor; it is, after all, the story of my life. How very wrong I was. Without the creative and thoughtful commentary offered by Susanna Wadeson, my editor at Transworld, the book would never have made it into print; she showed me how to give shape to the story. It took time, and Gordon Wise, my agent at Curtis Brown, remained encouraging throughout. I am profoundly grateful to them both.

Katherine Cowdrey and Shakira Teelwah, both members of Susanna's team at Transworld, read the manuscript closely and provided sharp insights. Hazel Orme, the copy editor, was, as ever, rigorous and sensitive in equal measure. And Vivien Thompson, the production editor, hunted down the last few howlers and managed the final stages of turning the manuscript into a book with calm authority. I am also grateful to Richard Shailer for the imaginative cover design.

Friends who read sections of the manuscript and offered helpful advice include Nicholas Coleridge, Martin Jennings, Charles Moore, Nicholas Mostyn, and James Stourton. Beyond them I owe thanks to all the friends who have helped to make this a cheerful story – whether or not they feature in the book.

My wife Fiona was the first reader of everything, so in reality I had the guidance of not one, but two super-editors.

INDEX